REQUIEM for the EGO

REQUIEM for the EGO

Freud and the Origins of Postmodernism

ALFRED I. TAUBER

STANFORD UNIVERSITY PRESS

Stanford, California

Stanford University Press
Stanford, California

Printed in the United States of America
on acid-free, archival-quality paper

Library of Congress Cataloging-in-Publication Data

Tauber, Alfred I., author.
 Requiem for the ego : Freud and the origins of postmodernism /
Alfred I. Tauber.
  pages cm
 Includes bibliographical references and index.
 ISBN 978-0-8047-8744-4 (cloth : alk. paper)
 ISBN 978-0-8047-8829-8 (pbk. : alk. paper)
  1. Freud, Sigmund, 1856–1939—Philosophy. 2. Ego
(Psychology)—Philosophy. 3. Psychoanalysis and philosophy. I.
Title.
BF109.F74T388 2013
150.19'52092—dc23

                                        2013005911

ISBN 978-0-8047-8830-4 (electronic)

IN MEMORY OF BRUCE LEWIS

A consciousness of one's own self and a consciousness of other things, are in truth given to us immediately, and the two are given in such a fundamentally different way that no other difference compares with this. About *himself* everyone knows directly, about everything else only very indirectly. This is the fact and the problem.

— ARTHUR SCHOPENHAUER,
The World as Will and Representation

On the horizon of any human science there is the project of bringing man's consciousness back to its real conditions, of restoring it to the contents and forms that brought it into being, and elude us within it; this is why the problem of unconsciousness—its possibility, status, mode of existence, the means of knowing it and bringing it to light—is not simply a problem within the human sciences which they can be thought of as encountering by chance in their steps; it is a problem that is ultimately coextensive with their very existence.

— MICHEL FOUCAULT,
The Order of Things

Contents

Preface

There is nothing in theory, and certainly nothing in experience, to support the extraordinary judgment that it is the truth about himself that is the easiest for a person to know.

—HARRY FRANKFURT, *On Bullshit*

Requiem for the Ego is a curious book, a mystery story yet to find its conclusion. The ego's demise has been reported, and despite bountiful evidence, the case cannot be closed. The fact of an attempted "egocide" (Rogozinski 2010, p. 5) seems clear enough. The actors of this drama are well known, and their declared motives and philosophical positions have been diligently rehearsed. Thus, the question is not who or why but rather *what* has been achieved and what lost?

The story begins with Descartes, whose cogito resides at the foundation of modernism. This Cartesian ego perceives and *represents* to itself the world and inner mental states from its own singular perspective. Freud adopted this subject-object divide in developing his own theory of the mind, and with that move, he joined the quandary of the ego functioning as both a subject and as an object of itself. The analytic endeavor endows the analysand with the capacity to reflect, interpret, and thereby ultimately achieve some degree of understanding about unconscious desire. This is the ego of Kant, whose autonomy, even in the Freudian context, sustains the effort to *know* and, more, to know the *truth*, by steadfastly holding on to the potential (and the integrity) of its critical faculties. However, this construction is fraught with difficulties, because the object of interpretation, the subject herself, must be presented (as a *representation*) to an undefinable conscious homunculus whose reflexive regression comes to no end.

When the psyche becomes an *object*, then the subject-object divide opens an unbridgeable "space" between the knowing self and its "other." This construction leaves the philosophical structure of the ego intact (at least from the modernist perspective), but at the same time the obscurity of the psyche leads to a deep skepticism. Who is this intimate other who shadows my consciousness and leaves "me" to ponder my own identity? The cogito thus loses the certainty of the Cartesian self as its individual insularity has been compromised. Indeed, the psychoanalytic ego has been conceived with contradictory characteristics: Facing an irredeemable obscurity within its own psyche, the subject still claims autonomy and self-knowledge. The identity problem is hardly confined to the psychoanalytic scenario but extends throughout Western self-consciousness. We are all Freudians in the sense that man "no longer knows what he is; but simultaneously also *knows that* he does not have the answer" (Scheler 1958, p. 65). In short, the mind's irresolvable division leads to alienation, where the ego's self-knowledge becomes a *problem*.

Freud's own ambivalence about the ego he entrusted to enact his therapy—endowed with analytic rationality—proved prescient as philosophical assaults against modernism, and the ego more particularly, gained momentum. He ironically contributed to the efforts that would dislodge notions of autonomy by positing a knowing agency that has proven unstable and subject to the very forces from which it seeks to distance itself. Consequently, even though Freud offered a portrait of agency with interpretive capacities and various degrees of autonomy, he also described the subject as fragile and vulnerable to its own inner psychic forces. I have previously described this multilayered depiction of personal identity in the context of measuring Freud's humanism against his science ideal, where he appears as neither a systematic philosopher nor the positivist scientist he hoped to be but rather as a moralist (Tauber 2009a, 2009b, 2010) and social reformer (Tauber 2012a). Committed to Enlightenment ideals, he believed in the power of reason, the autonomy of the individual, and the potential for assuming ultimate responsibility for human being. Balancing a well-acknowledged pessimism, he still offered a way of understanding the psyche, which he put to work as a psychotherapy. In that effort he sided with a fragile optimism, working to redeem his patients from their suffering. That venture rested on a humanistic understanding of agency that would suffer grievous assault. After all, as the last great metaphysician of modernity, Freud posed the cardinal question of our era: Will the humanism he hoped to protect be saved? This drama— Freud's defense of human autonomy (albeit severely compromised by unconscious forces inimical to its apparent ideals) versus those who would dismantle this notion of agency altogether—takes place on a large stage.

While Freud held a rear-guard action to save the cogito, his early philosophical inquisitors—principally Theodor Adorno, Martin Heidegger, and Ludwig Wittgenstein—saw no feasible defense and gave no quarter in their deconstruction of the modernist ego. The subject observing the world and herself dispassionately was, in their view, a conceit, and more, such a conception of subjectivity supported those oppressive forces that constricted human potential. Freudianism thus became a target of a wide-ranging philosophical revolt against a discarded epistemology, and with that revision, subjectivity would be reconfigured in tandem. *Requiem for the Ego* describes how Freud's description of the ego united the key revisionists of the Enlightenment understanding of agency as they crossed the historical "inflection point" marking modernity's slide into postmodernity. From radically different orientations, Adorno, Heidegger, and Wittgenstein attempted to disassemble the very foundations of the Freudian ego, not so much as a discredit of psychoanalysis but rather as part of the larger project of overturning the Cartesian-Kantian representational philosophy of mind. Each of Freud's antagonists concurred that the metaphysics of a knowing ego observing its inner psyche cannot be sustained as a basis for understanding personal identity. This theme, which unifies otherwise disparate philosophies, exposes the Achilles' heel of the psychoanalytic project and provides a fecund means by which to understand Freud's theory and, more broadly, the key conceptual sources of postmodernism.

The array of issues ushered in by the critiques of subjectivity considered here extends beyond the particular elements of the revolt against Freud's modernist conception of the ego. These include debates about "civilization and its discontents"; the character of the social and the challenge of moral relativism; the nature and role of reason; the understanding of consciousness and unconsciousness; the basis of the normative; the imbroglio of free will; and the quandaries posed by the absence of epistemological foundations. These discussions, which have marked the modernity-postmodernity controversies in various venues, seem far from over, and we still seek a perspective from which such diverse issues might be organized. Here, we nominate the philosophical attacks on the Freudian ego as offering such a vantage point.

The cultural outcome of this chapter of intellectual history remains unclear. The standing of personal autonomy, self-knowledge, and rational deliberation underlying psychoanalysis has not been settled. Some, content with historical reflections, would have us pay our respects at the tomb of the Freudian ego, ponder how it expired, and consider what ghost has risen from that sarcophagus. Freud holds their analytic interest as contributing to the transition of modernism into its late twentieth-century guise. Others maintain that the ego's requiem still awaits its final composition as they

hold to a vision of the subject that will not abide its putative deconstruction. While acknowledging that the fate of psychoanalysis is
part of a profound shift of philosophical and cultural valences, they
tenaciously grip an older vision of personal identity, where the ego,
bruised and battered, remains standing. Much is at stake, and we
do well to consider the argument carefully.

Boscawen, New Hampshire
November 1, 2012

Acknowledgments

This book began with my completion of *Freud, the Reluctant Philosopher* (Princeton, 2010), when, although satisfied that I had accurately portrayed Freud as a humanist, I still wanted to better understand his significance for our own era. If Freud had continued relevance, then perhaps the import of his work should be reevaluated in terms of social theory and current understandings of selfhood. That issue led to two seminars I taught during 2011: a graduate course at Tel Aviv University's Cohn Institute of the History and Philosophy of Science and Ideas, where we examined the history of utopia within the psychoanalytic discourse; and a seminar offered through the Van Leer Jerusalem Institute that attracted senior scholars and psychoanalysts, where the contrast between Freud and Lacan became our principal concern. To Ruth Golan, Saul Haimovich, Roee Hirshfeld, Aim Deuelle Luski, Andre Schonberg, Yossef Schwartz, and Rivka Warshawsky, a special thanks for deepening my knowledge of Lacan and the post-Freudian movements swirling around him. In various ways, the road leading to Lacan and beyond him organized the composition of *Requiem for the Ego*.

Subordinated to other matters, the social theory project faded as a focus and the challenge of delineating the philosophical fate of Freudianism in terms of an epistemological argument became paramount. The broad constellation of issues overlaps philosophy of mind, philosophy of language, and at the heart of psychoanalysis, the problem of both identifying and authenticating personal identity. How one represents oneself as "oneself" hinges on the epistemological mode of self-representation, which governs our understanding of self-consciousness, subjectivity, and ultimately, identity. And here, the various threads of twentieth-century philosophy that interest me coalesced around Freud's project. As the initial intuitions took form, further discussions with Richard Adler, Steven Ascheim, Henri Atlan, Aaron Ben-Ze'ev, Leonid Brodsky, Jeremy Fogel, Gideon Freudenthal, David Kazhdan, Bennie Morris, Jennifer Radden, Jurgen Reeder, Walter Reich, Ken Richman, Harvey Scher, Jay Steinberg, and Josh Weinstein sharpened my thoughts, and to these friends I extend my gratitude for their critical comments and informed suggestions. I also appreciate that the various venues in which I delivered aspects of this study profited from audience responses and commentators, so I thank those who invited me to speak about this project: Steve Kepnes (Colgate University), Jennifer Radden (Cambridge Philosophy-Psychology Group), Ted Kenny (Association for Psychoanalytic Medicine), David Goodman (Psychology and the Other Conference, Boston, October 2011), Lydie Fialova (University of Edinburgh), Yoram Hazony (Shalem Center, Jerusalem, Psycho-ontology Conference, December 2011), Gilberto Corbellini (University of Rome), Niall Connolly (Trinity College, Dublin), Simon Feldman (Connecticut College), and Yossi Schwartz (Tel Aviv University). And as always, to my wife, Paula Fredriksen, whose patience and good sense helped sustain the effort of composing this work, I extend my heartfelt appreciation.

Specific acknowledgments are due to three scholars: When I was teaching Freud for the first time to undergraduates in the mid-1990s, Patricia Kitcher's *Freud's Dream* (1992) proved invaluable. She clearly outlined how Freud's anthropology, neuropsychology, and biological orientations influenced the development of his theory. Showing the epistemological status of the sciences upon which he relied not only illuminated the conceptual borders of his work but also indicated a more general lesson about the dependence of the human sciences on the larger cultural context in which they function. *Requiem for the Ego* endeavors to complete Kitcher's own interpretive study by showing that the outmoded scientific models Freud employed find a parallel expression in philosophy, when an analogous destabilization (and ultimate rejection) occurs as a result of eclipsed epistemologies.

Marcia Cavell's *The Psychoanalytic Mind* (1993) and Valerie Greenberg's *Freud and His Aphasia Book* (1997) claim my second immediate intellectual debt. These works carefully examined the representational character of Freud's philosophy of mind and thereby provided a philosophical framework by which to build an analysis of psychoanalysis based upon later approaches. By extending these studies to key twentieth-century post-Freudian philosophical critiques, I have taken the opportunity to more fully explore the basic conceptual impasse Freud faced with his model of the mind.

Third, the defense of reason, an attempt to "save" rationality expounded by Menachem Fisch in *The View from Within* (Fisch and Benbaji 2011), in many respects has pushed my own response to modernity's challenge presented here. Fisch argues for what might be called "the strong program" of reason's authority by asserting arguments for the ability of an individual knower to effectively distance herself from the normative framework in which she functions in order to be self-critical and innovative. He thus asserts a Kantian orientation in attempting to define the conditions by which reason operates to effectively inquire upon itself. I am challenged by Fisch's thesis and dispute his conclusions (Tauber 2012b), and consequently, *Requiem for the Ego* has been written, in part, in answer to my friend's provocation.

Finally, this book is dedicated to Bruce Lewis, the teacher of my youth, who, perhaps more than any other individual, taught me how to think critically. May his memory be a blessing.

Introduction

It is the most serious difficulty of the history of civilization that a great intellectual process must be broken up into single, and often into what seem arbitrary categories, in order to be in any way intelligible.

—JACOB BURCKHARDT,
The Civilization of the Renaissance in Italy

Freudianism most easily associates with psychotherapy, but more profoundly its precepts have percolated throughout cultural understandings of human agency, the status of self-knowledge, the representative roles of reason, and the influence of emotions in governing human behavior. Indeed, the fundamental notion of an *ego* has unalterably been recalibrated in light of Freud's provocations. During his lifetime, philosophers too took note of these developments, and notably, no other living figure commanded the philosophical attention of all of the major philosophers of the interwar period—Adorno, Heidegger, and Wittgenstein. And well they might. Given the uncertainties he evoked, Freud reinvigorated the perennial philosophical issue of how rationality—self-conscious, deliberate reason—serves as the dominant *normative* faculty in dialogue with the passions. Fundamental as this issue might be, our philosophical protagonists probed at deeper conceptual levels: Who is the subject, and what is *the mind*? At that juncture, Freud entered into philosophical discourse by asserting that "[t]he ego stands for reason" (1933, p. 76) and thus presenting the last influential iteration of a Cartesian-Kantian–inspired ego and the representational mind that lies at its foundations.

Freud's career spanned an unusually vibrant and creative chapter of modern philosophy. By 1900, in parallel with Freud's creation of psychoanalysis, philosophy was in the throes of a major convulsion as various thrusts against idealism gained momentum. Nietzsche attempted to cut philosophy loose from its Enlightenment traditions in his attack on Socrates and his celebration of Dionysus, an effort that helped frame a zeitgeist where reason lost its hegemony to a neoromantic emotivism. In contrast, finding a basis for reestablishing Kant's general agenda of grounding reason and human autonomy organized variations of the neo-Kantian movement, which from our vantage can best be regarded as a defense of Enlightenment ideals. Freud easily joins this camp (Tauber 2010, pp. 105–15), although his claims about how the unconscious distorts human reasoning would do much damage to the modernist tenets he sought to defend. And superimposed on these deliberations, a debate about "psychologism" organized an argument about whether logic and mathematics were independent of psychology and thus universally true (i.e., independent of human consciousness).

Within the context of this intellectual maelstrom, *Requiem for the Ego* offers another interpretation of the ego's standing and reason's fate in a very particular context: (1) how Freud conceived the role of rationality in psychoanalysis, which employed a representational model of the mind; (2) how Adorno and Heidegger (the principal philosophical dissenters to the Kantian conception of Reason upon which psycho*analysis* rested) critiqued his *philosophically* constructed theory; and (3) how the philosophical trajectory of their respective positions as elaborated by Jacques Lacan and Gilles Deleuze, on the one hand, and Jürgen Habermas, on the other hand, ended in radically different formulations of the subject and reason. The narrative concludes with recounting an attack on the very notion of introspection that dispensed with the conceptual apparatus of agency altogether, namely, the "private language" argument expounded by Wittgenstein. This exposition thus delineates the conceptual structure of Freud's enterprise and its putative collapse under the assaults of philosophical opponents with whom he never interacted. Disinclined to engage philosophy in any form, Freud nevertheless provoked their attack, because he had so clearly elaborated a version of the ego they sought to destroy. Indeed, this last incarnation of the Cartesian cogito oriented their criticism.

Freud (perhaps inadvertently) revamped the Enlightenment project while working within its basic structure: Moral responsibility lay in the rational consciousness of an ego, which represented the world to itself. Each component of that understanding—the ego, representationalism, rationality/normativity, and consciousness versus unconsciousness—became a target for those who sought to disassemble the foundations that supported each of his theory's tenets. Their program attempted nothing less than a revamping of the modernist understanding of the mind and personal identity. In general, these rebuttals were based on a reassessment of predicate thinking, which served to unify philosophers with otherwise divergent interests.

In summary, *Requiem for the Ego* describes how post-Freudian philosophizing redefined "the ego" with wide-ranging ramifications in the postmodern setting. Freud thus participated, without direct professional interests, in the central developments of his era as a reluctant philosopher, for beyond the critiques of psychoanalysis per se, he helped set the agenda that would reconsider the very basis of selfhood in the postmodern era: the status of reason, the character of the self, and the underlying philosophy of mind, which structured the ever-present beguiling philosophical issues Freud faced as a psychoanalyst. That discussion ranged well beyond the couch as part of a much larger intellectual debate, so while Freud was deaf to much of the controversy swirling around him, his theory had a wide-ranging influence on those whose philosophical concerns had to take account of his teachings.

I

The psychoanalytic characterization of the ego stretches along a continuum that at one end instantiates an autonomous interpretive agent whose rationality confers authority over inner drives and desires. The other pole finds such an agent with no such authority and, indeed, ignorant of those unconscious despotic forces. The modernist agent possesses the Cartesian ability to survey objects of its own intention, which in the case of Freudian psychoanalysis is the intimate other, the unconscious. From that analysis, the ego putatively obtains various degrees of freedom from the despotic arationality of libidinal drives. Here, the Enlightenment ideal finds its full expression, and when placing Freud in this setting, we clearly see that he struggled to find an interpretive analytic for his new psychiatry for personal liberation. Committed to the ideals of reason's power, the perfection of humankind, and from the vantage of a physician, the therapeutic promise of analysis, Freud embraced a utopian ideal moderated by a powerful ambivalence (Freud 1910b; Eckstein and Caruth 1965; Strenger 1989; Werbart 2007; Tauber 2012a).

At the other end of the spectrum, acknowledging the limits of consciousness, the inability to "reason" with the unconscious, and the creation of psychic reality from the throes of desire, Freud portrayed the human subject much as Plato had—like a jockey atop a steed that would have its own way (Freud 1923a, p. 25). The basic design of the psychoanalytic mind presents a reality organized by intentional desire (conscious and unconscious), mediated by a complex normative rationality coupled to emotional drives. The line between fantasy and reality is no longer something like the difference between a mental event and a real event in some simple Cartesian sense, and reason plays only one part among other contributing faculties to create the mental world in which one lives. So while Freud insists on maintaining the Cartesian divide, where the ego's faculty of reason and self-consciousness is set in an autonomous realm, that division could not be sustained. And this fractured line reappears in different contexts throughout Freud's construction of the psychoanalytic ego: He entrusted the ego's rationality to serve as a bulwark against unconscious desire; however, he also adamantly rejected the equation of mind with consciousness, more specifically, the ego's hold on reality. He thus would dislodge "the arrogance of consciousness" (Freud 1910a, p. 39) and assert how "it is essential to abandon the overvaluation of the property of being conscious before it becomes possible to form any correct view of the origin of what is mental" (Freud 1900, p. 612). Simply, the unconscious "is the true psychic reality" (ibid., p. 613), and psychoanalysis is the means of revealing its true character. So, for Freud, the unconscious, whether considered as an entity or as a locale of subconscious mental activity, serves as the bedrock of the psyche and the continuous source of the mental. Note that "mental" at this primordial level reaches back in phylogeny to include instincts, drives, and emotional states that ascend and metamorphose into consciousness and more developed forms of rationality. The ego then becomes the evolutionary product of the unconscious mind and retains its linkage to that heritage, while reaching for its autonomy.

Psychoanalysis retells in a new vernacular the struggle of reason with the passions and thus joins a long and distinguished career in philosophy. Most immediately, Freud participated in an intellectual trajectory that began with Kierkegaard's leap into absurdity and continued with Nietzsche's celebration of Dionysus, which in the most extreme postmodern diatribe would attempt to dismantle the hegemony of reason altogether (e.g., Sloterdijk 1988; Woolgar 1988a, 1988b). The bid to dispatch reason from its august perch in Kant's transcendental philosophy reflects a historical decline of confidence in both moral and epistemological certainty, and while Freud rested his hopes for humankind in the authority of reason, his depiction of the psyche further damaged the standing of rationality. The psychoanalytic demonstration of rationalization, repression, and unconscious intentions, which apparently followed no logical constraints, must be seen as a key chapter in that intellectual history.

These two contrasting conceptions of the ego lie at the base of Freud's metaphysics. The deterministic unconscious, whose demands will not be denied by "the proud superstructure of the mind" (Freud 1919, p. 260), of course, is the central tenet of Freudianism, and wherever in his writings he discusses free will, Freud admonishes readers who assert their belief in such freedom as harboring a deep illusion (Tauber 2009a, 2010, pp. 139–45). Yet the essential feature of psychoanalysis rests upon a central paradox— we are determined, yet free, that is, in the Spinozan sense of *knowing* the extent of our imprisonment. And within this paradox lies an unresolved tension. On the one hand, Freud empowered psychoanalysis with the interpretive, rational task of deciphering the unconscious, and on the other hand, he held a skeptical view of consciousness and, more particularly, the rationality employed to present oneself to oneself. Despite the power of the psychic drives, Freud held on to the authority of reason as the tool of his epistemology, and in the end, he confirmed the promise of reason as the foundation of his own social theory, which both held a utopian promise and despaired of reason's capacity to control the self-destructive elements of the psyche. The struggle, then, between the faculty of reason and the emotions remains an abiding, unresolved conflict within psychoanalytic theory itself. And a second layer of conceptual conflicts pits reason's restrictions against the restoration afforded by analysis, or at least potentially so. Despite this multilayered ambivalence, Freud powerfully evoked the question of identity—"thinking the mystery *that I am*" (Rogozinski 2010, p. 1)—and thereby recognized that the ego's query concerning its own nature defines moral agency. In the end, psychoanalysis reduces to the Socratic dictum "the unexamined life is not worth living," by which an entire ethics has been restated.

Although these tensions remain unresolved within psychoanalytic theory, the balance of criticism pushed against the rational capacity of the ego, and thus Freud's own guarded view of self-knowing, became part of a larger intellectual story. Freud's decipherment of the arational aspects of human behavior contributed to the radical evaluation of reason as a faculty of knowing and did much to undermine the confidence in the very Enlightenment ideals he espoused. The post-Freudian criticism considered here, in dislodging the Cartesian ego with its presumptive autonomy, resolutely denied access to that domain where reason cannot traverse. As we will discuss, the spiral of the ego's deconstruction leaves little room for Freudian rationality. Yet defenders of modernism would probe reason's character more deeply (e.g., Habermas 1987) to ask, What, in fact, are the limitations of reason's representation? What is inaccessible and why? As Jurgen Reeder laconically observes, "If the limit to reason is as inevitable as the structure of knowledge does seem to imply, psychoanalysis must put its knowing to a test and investigate what it is that we do not—and cannot—know" (2002, p. 20). This mystery leaves us with both a deep insecurity and a sustained desire to know (Egginton 2007).

II

The basis of reason's functioning as an autonomous faculty rests on a metaphysical posture of the ego as a subject separate from the world. This Cartesian cogito orders experience and surveys nature, and itself, with the authority of a mind distinct from the object of its scrutiny, and it does so through representations of the world it encounters. Freud adopted this "folk" model of the mind and thus fell into a philosophical maelstrom. In the wake of Kant, transcendental idealism profoundly impacted twentieth-century philosophy to stretch across many schools and subdivisions of Continental and Anglo-American-Austrian spheres (Rockmore 2006). One might well concur that "the passage to self-representation is the passage to modernity" and all it portends (Colebrook 2005, p. 1). From the perspective considered here, Kant's version of representationalism remained central to those diverse efforts to understand how language hooks onto the world. Put succinctly,

> [T]o know is to represent accurately what is outside the mind; so to understand the possibility and nature of knowledge is to understand the way in which the mind is able to construct such representations. Philosophy's central concern is to be a general theory of representation, a theory which will divide culture up into areas which represent reality well, those which represent it less well, and those which do not represent it at all (despite their pretense of doing so). (Rorty 1979, p. 3)

The key weakness of Freud's representational view of the mind, the central problem addressed by all of the analyses considered here, is accounting for how representations link the world to the knowing subject. And these critiques concluded that the *gap* between knower (the conscious ego) and the object of scrutiny (the unconscious)—the gap psychoanalytic representations must bridge—cannot be overcome. The implications of this conclusion have far-reaching effects, which stretch along a vast social continuum from those who would model the mind to those who adjudicate human motivation and responsibility.

The representational mind is understood as an interpretive system, where perceptions and other mental states are products of unconscious inferences, computations, and similar reasoning processes characterizing abstract thinking. Accordingly, sensory data stimulate a cognitive process, which invokes unconscious inferential analysis, synthesis, and interpretation and ends with storage or application of this mental product for use in guiding behavior. From Descartes to Locke to Kant, and to Freud, the fundamental characteristic of their shared "cognitivist" program is a reasoning, intellectual system built upon a causal theory of perception: Objects are perceived as sensory data, which then follow a trajectory that ends in a mental percept that corresponds to that object. Freud fully accepted this mental architecture and applied it to mental states: "All the categories which we employ to describe conscious mental acts, such as ideas, purposes, resolutions, and so on, can be applied to them [unconscious latent states]" (1915b, p. 168). In other words, he made the unconscious discernible in the same terms used to describe conscious states. And with that move, his theory was drawn into a rigorous philosophical controversy about meaning, reference, and representation.

The protagonists of the three philosophical movements with which we are concerned—Adorno, Heidegger, and Wittgenstein—despite their radically different philosophies, each responded directly to Freud's theory at its very foundations, namely, its representational model of the mind: Each would deny the authority of the Freudian ego to construct psychic life from its own conscious perspective and with a particular kind of objectification that exemplified the scientific posture psychoanalysis assumed. To know the human psyche, according to our philosophical protagonists, requires a different strategy.

Beyond the interesting fact that no other figure of the era commanded their collective philosophical interest, we must ask, Why did Freud's theory become a target of the key philosophers of the interwar period? What themes that dominated philosophical discourse resonated with Freud's own project, and how did his work get swept into the currents that ran from his own modernism to what followed? Given that Freud's theory has been characterized as outmoded anthropology, neuroscience, and biology (Kitcher 1992), why not consider the widely rejected philosophy that grounds psychoanalysis as well? Through such an exercise, we will assess the significance of the Freudian formulation of the ego in the postmodern era.

Here, a canvas drawn with broad strokes shows how Adorno, Heidegger, and Wittgenstein each contributed to a determined assault on the Kantian edifice, which housed psychoanalytic theory. By dismissing out of hand the very notion of an autonomous ego that might apply its objective stare to its own mental life, they revealed an emperor with no clothes. Their target, representationalism, thus became a discarded product of a rejected subject-object epistemology and the metaphysics derived from it. For whether we invoke Heidegger's Dasein, Wittgenstein's critique of private language, or Adorno's non-identity thinking, the predicate thinking Freud employed is abandoned and alternative epistemologies followed. In large measure, the fate of psychoanalysis in our own era reflects that larger philosophical debate about reference, most specifically to inner mental states, and more generally, the very notion of a subject set against the world as object, a world that might also include one's own subjectivity.

The rejection of Freudianism along these lines becomes just another example of a widespread critique, which assumed distinctive formats. For Adorno, instead of the scientific schema of identification and control, a reconception of reason dispenses with identity (representational) thinking for a more expansive rationality. He, like Nietzsche, developed an aesthetic-based approach to emancipate thought. Along similar lines (and for similar reasons) Heidegger's description of science as providing a restrictive "picture of the world" (1977a) predicated on the Cartesian subject would be replaced by Dasein's engagement with Being. Instead of scrutinizing the world as a separate cogito, Dasein would be embedded (Heidegger 1962, 1976). Note that Adorno, in seeking to revise the "dialectic of the Enlightenment," still holds on to a conception of *agency* and thus opposes Heidegger at the heart of the formulation of Dasein. So Adorno, who offered a reformation, as opposed to a rejection of the modernist subject, serves as the balancing voice to Heidegger in the philosophical choir. Whereas Dasein authenticates "truth" on the basis of its authenticity (based upon a "disclosedness" that characterizes openness to the world, to others, and to one's self), Adorno chose "emphatic experience" of an ego (experiential experience that provides access to the nonconceptual) (Zuidervaart 2008). *Dialectic of Enlightenment* (Horkheimer and Adorno 1993) was hardly extreme when compared to the works that followed, for while Adorno had set the initial path, poststructuralists created more radical formulations of reasoned discourse and the rational mind as they attempted to dispense with representationalism altogether. Those efforts were no less than groping for a new metaphysics, for in overturning representationalism, what would be the replacement and what consequences for epistemology and ethics would arise as a result? The dominant postmodern themes considered here originate with Heidegger, who deeply influenced Lacan's reformulation of Freudianism. Upon that platform, the revision of agency attains its full maturity in the works of French culture critics in the 1970s, who may have shared Adorno's Marxist orientation but more directly drew their conceptions of the ego from Heidegger's antihumanism.

Assaulting the humanist position under the postmodernist dual banner of celebrating the sensuous and demoting reason begins with Lacan's slogan "return to Freud." Those who wrote searchingly on the problematic of desire (e.g., Barthes [1978]; Kristeva [1987]; Foucault [1986]; Deleuze and Guattari [1977]) were deeply influenced by Lacan's controversial argument that desire has its own legitimacy. In contrast to Freud's vision grounded in Enlightenment ideals, the Parisian train conducted by Lacan dismissed the strength of reason and the autonomy of the individual, and in displacing the ego from the center of psychoanalytic theory, Lacan offered a theoretical framework for those who would construct their own social theories on a psychoanalytic scaffolding. This reconfiguration composed a social vision of subjects living in a psychological matrix quite different from the one Freud described. Following Lacan, Jean-François Lyotard, Deleuze, and Félix Guattari attacked the hegemony of reason to celebrate a libidinal psychology and to pursue a politics of desire. By challenging the Freudian conception of the psyche, Man would fall and a new subjectivity would arise, or at least thought these Frenchmen.

In the Wittgensteinian critique, we find the third leg of the stool upon which the deconstruction of selfhood sits. For Wittgenstein, there is nothing "beyond" and certainly no order or explanation that might be posited as accounting for what humans know. He argued that instead of seeking "hidden reality" that gives order to the world, philosophy should discern how language functions to *present* the world. He thus discarded metaphysics and limited philosophy to the task of deriving clarity by an examination of language itself, which must suffice to present reality to us. His solution, to the extent he offered one, rested on his later development of a pragmatic use of language. This venture discarded both Enlightenment and romantic meta-agendas: For the scientist/modernist, "the point of language is to represent a hidden reality which lies outside us, [whereas the romantic] . . . thinks its purpose is to express a hidden reality which lies within us" (Rorty 1989b, p. 19). Freud, of course, followed an older metaphysics. He attempted to bridge both the inner and outer realms through a newly conceived "language"—a system that would represent inner mental states. This entire effort would be rejected out of hand.

In sum, Freud, as portrayed by his philosophical inquisitors, was the paramount metaphysician who sought the hidden mystery of a metaphysical construct, the unconscious. So, to accept the positions advanced by Heidegger or Wittgenstein is to dismiss the psychoanalytic corpus altogether, because of the theory's inability to fulfill the criteria of *knowledge.* And for that matter, all the philosophy grounding Freud's theory is similarly discarded as misdirected and incoherent. The implications for the Freudian ego cannot be overestimated inasmuch as the repercussions of the "antiphilosophy" resignations leave agency without a philosophical foundation. Such an assessment does not mean that the antimetaphysicians have vanquished their opponents and that we truly are at "the end of philosophy" (Thomas-Fogiel 2011), for in many respects none of our philosophical protagonists could achieve their radical ambitions. But the question of philosophy's demise is not our immediate concern; we need not provide a final verdict on such efforts as we affirm that their respective critiques offered important insights about the margins of thought and more specifically, the philosophical status of representationalism.

III

Do representations come to constitute reality or reflect it? Whether viewed from the perspective of Adorno, Heidegger, or Wittgenstein, reality consists of more than what can be represented; language stifles the expansive potential of experience by confinement to its representations. So Freud, in examining the unconscious as a representational system (i.e., understood in terms of consciousness), falls into the vortex of this criticism. His mistake (as regarded by the critiques considered here) cannot be construed as imprudent or ill informed, for the picture theory of the world, in which reality is viewed in the "Cartesian Theater" (Dennett 1991a), has commonsensical and assumed validity. Indeed, internal representational states forming the basis of human cognition are so deeply ingrained that some believe the abandonment of this paradigm would be "beyond comparison, the greatest intellectual catastrophe in the history of our species" (Fodor 1987, p. xii).[1] Despite such commitments, basic weaknesses (if not flaws)—both experimental and philosophical—have increasingly commanded attention because the fundamental assumption of the cognitive paradigm, that sensory perception parallels conscious thinking, has proven problematic.

The tremors that began to shake the cognitivist edifice may be traced back to Freud's mature period when the question of *meaning* took center stage in philosophical discourse. Traditionally, meaning in public language was thought to derive from the ideas or mental images that words are used to express. Such representational properties of this *idea theory* might simply be a basic (inexplicable) property of the mind (Descartes), a resemblance between ideas and things (Locke), or a synthetic function of a complex transcendental "understanding" (Kant). This semantic theory of meaning began to unravel when, during the fin de siècle, Franz Brentano and Edmund

Husserl successfully shifted the problem of meaning to the problem of *intentionality* (Tauber 2010, pp. 45–46, 234–35). The controversy that ensued revolved around whether meaning (and truth) reduced to psychological states of speakers, a debate that led to later phenomenological accounts and the pragmatic, instrumental orientation of cognitive meaning originating with Wittgenstein.

In the analytic philosophy tradition, later criticism focused on the characterization of the mind as a computational system operating on languagelike representations. This orientation reflects naturalistic commitments and thus draws from cognitive science, neurology, and psychology, where the cognitivist paradigm has reigned supreme (Chase and Reynolds 2010, pp. 202–10.). However, the manipulation of computer-based models of symbolic representation has highlighted that the elements of the machine program are treated solely in syntactical operations without any reference to interpretation of them. In other words, the representations cannot establish reference outside their own network and thus form a web consisting solely of elements constituting the system. More generally, representationalism supposes that ideas represent something else without having access to this idea except through another idea. How then does the mind escape its own representations to acquire content beyond the representations themselves? The verdict: "Reference, on which the entire representational edifice stands, lies outside the explanatory scope of the representational framework" (Shanon 1993, p. 94).

Heidegger also set the mainstream of Continental schools on a steadfast antirepresentational track by making the philosophy of mind inseparable from ontology and epistemology. This philosophical posture actually draws from a complex tradition of reaction against Kantianism, originating with Hegel (and other romantics [Helfer 1996]), progressing to Nietzsche and then forward to the postmodernisms of Jacques Derrida, Gilles Deleuze, and Richard Rorty, whose arguments have percolated throughout literary studies and social theory as identifying a "crisis" of thought (Chase and

Reynolds 2010, pp. 210–15). Whether formulated in terms of Adorno's "non-identity thinking" or Deleuze's "différence," representational thinking, according to such views, fails to capture experience in any of knowledge's domains—social, literary, political, aesthetic, and even scientific. Thus, from this general perspective, the critique of representationalism centers on the indispensability of conceptual analysis of belief, desire, and so forth in order to understand the "'magical connection' between putative vehicles of representation and what they stand for . . . [i.e.,] to explain how reference is possible" (Marbach 1993, p. 9; see also Jackson 2003). The post hoc rationalized imposition of a template of "identity" posing as "representational" putatively omits, disfigures, restricts, and misrepresents that which it seeks to capture. Simply, representations are the product of a thirdhand view of the mind's negotiation with the world and therefore misconceive firsthand experience.

Freud remained entrenched in the semantic tradition, which in the psychoanalytic context plays out in a drama between the reasoning (rational) ego and the representation of its "other"—the unconscious. He described the unconscious by assigning representations (language, symbols, and secondary epiphenomena) to the drive's attachment to *ideas* (Freud 1915a). Since ideas postulated or inferred unconscious drives, Freud required a language in which those ideas were given meaning within a narrative of psychic trauma. Thus, dream images assumed symbolic meaning as derived from both a larger symbolic universe (the words of psychoanalytic language) and the emotional constellation in which the dream is interpreted (the interpretive context). These ideas become the métier of psycho-*analysis*, that is, these representations serve as purveyors of the drives' associated ideas, which have been repressed and when deciphered point to an intrapsychic other. (Note that the idea is repressed, not the drive per se, whose expression through desire continues its own quest in defiance of repressive effects.) Accordingly, the psychoanalytic unconscious is a product of the representational mind, one with a particular philosophical orientation: As the other of the conscious mind, and most evidently as deciphered by psychoanalytic interpretation, the unconscious mirrors the semantic structure of consciousness, which, according to the verdict chronicled here, is a testament to the disjunction (and distortion) imposed by the Cartesian metaphysics of selfhood.

This construction proved unstable. In Freud's last formulation he described the mental as a continuum, which begins with self-consciousness and extends into a shadowy area of preconscious thought and then to the unconscious domain (1923a). The deep unconscious remains untapped and therefore utterly anonymous, while a second portion may serve as a reservoir of preconscious thought. In either case, this other, residing at the depths of the psyche, cannot be directly known, leaving both the ego and its other with nebulous borders of identity. As the other assumes ill-defined contours, so does the ego.[2] And thus beyond the problem of defining one's otherness, a reciprocal confusion of the ego's own identity results, for when asking, Who is this "other," whom "I" cannot discern yet must acknowledge?, the Hegelian construct, whereby the self is defined in relation to the other, falls into disarray. Here the immediacy of the Cartesian assertion that "I am; I exist" becomes a declaration that belies the murkiness of self-identity. By establishing the epistemological ambiguity of the ego, Freud perhaps inadvertently supported the "egocide" refutations (Rogozinski 2010, p. 5), which abide no essentialisms and certainly no conceptual foundations for any such being. Our philosophical protagonists staked their territory in this "no-man's land."

The Adorno-Heidegger-Wittgenstein offensive only continued a deconstruction of the Cartesian legacy that was already at full throttle by the mid-eighteenth century. Thus, this philosophical confrontation has a long history: Stalwart defenders of the Enlightenment have ventured onto the field of battle with at least an implicit acceptance of a knowing, self-reflective ego. The struggle for the human soul, the psyche, is contested on the basis of this authority. The defenders would revise reason and employ rational faculties to create successful sublimations, much along the lines originally presented by Freud himself (Tauber 2012a). However, no ready response appears to the philosophical critique of the subject; certainly no schemas convincingly trump the current intellectual fashions, which would disenfranchise the individual and her subjectivity. Thus, the challenge to save an older humanism rests at the base of this controversy over the ego.

Both lines of criticism converge on Freudian psychology as committing the typical "modern" error of assuming a subject-object epistemological structure as the basis of all knowledge. The Cartesian-Kantian subject dissociates from the world, and itself, to obtain a view from nowhere by objectifying and representing the world and the self to itself. Indeed, the subject must adopt such a posture to achieve the autonomy required for such knowledge and the truth claimed by objectivity. But why might one assume that inner mental states can be represented by the same methods as phenomena in the external world? As we will discuss in detail, Freud's philosophical inquisitors argued that his science was inadequate because the unconscious, as theorized, was a metaphysical construct that remains undecipherable as a scientific object. Simply, mental states as objects could not be represented. Both cognitive psychological evidence, which has shown that duplication of the conscious mental realm in the unconscious is unwarranted (Shanon 1993; Ben-Ze'ev 1993, pp. 103ff.), and the philosophical argument seem compelling: "If the mental image . . . could not itself be tested for correctness, how could it [be] confirm[ed]?" (Wittgenstein 1968, § 265, p. 94e). Accordingly, the regress of determining the veridical character of the representation is like someone who bought "several copies of the morning paper to assure himself that what it said was true" (ibid.).

In sum, to apply the same subject-object relationship to psychic life that is employed to represent nature, according to the various critiques discussed here, leaves a bitter conclusion: Freudian "alchemy" cannot produce *analytic* gold because inner mental states do not possess the same objective status as do objects in the natural world. The subject-object epistemology designed for scientific undertakings is not suitable for defining subjective mental events and experiences, for the emotional private life Freud sought to describe lies beyond the reach of positivist understanding. Indeed, if the philosophical issue hinges on how "to conceive of a pre-linguistic relationship to objects" (i.e., as representation [Tugendhat 1982]) has proven a most formidable task for an epistemology of nature, for mental states such a strategy seems intractable.

So, when the deeper reaches of the self become the object of the analysand's inquiry, one faces the apparent "paradox of subjectivity: being a subject for the world and at the same time being an object in the world" (Husserl 1970, p. 178). However, the claims—being a subject and an object—are not symmetrical. The epistemology so effective in characterizing the external world has only an assumed jurisdiction in the inner mental life. Human experience demands different kinds of knowing, and to argue for some singular method or universal epistemological structure belies, and ultimately distorts, the complexities of how humans live in their psychological, social, and natural worlds. Ignoring this seemingly obvious observation has led to much controversy, exemplified by the contentious history swirling around Freud's theory.

IV

In several respects, this book is a sequel to *Freud, the Reluctant Philosopher*, which concluded with a vague suggestion:

Contemporary philosophy has largely left Freud's metaphysical inquiry for other pursuits. Accordingly, the sequel to my study might be *Freud and the Reluctant Philosophers*, which would explore why those disinclined to probe the questions that drove Freud's own humane venture conceived his project as misconceived, and how, at the same time (appearing averse), they have pursued Freud's general agenda in different ways. For now, the suggestion will have to suffice. (Tauber 2010, p. 226)

Here, I have endeavored to respond to my own vexation by placing Freud in the philosophical context of the generation that led twentieth-century philosophy to a repudiation of the metaphysical infrastructure of psychoanalysis. The reluctant philosophers to whom I referred are those who would seek an escape from the epistemology that grounded Freud's own thought. Their reluctance was, in fact, an utter rejection of the Kantianism Freud himself followed: a variant of the Cartesian-subject-object representation of the world and ourselves to ourselves.[3] In that move, the foundation of postmodernism, already set by Nietzsche, found its firm underpinnings.

If we put aside the analytic discussions, for poststructuralists, the "scar of representation" (Colebrook 2005) has become the focus of rigorous efforts to redeem knowledge and experience from what these critics regard as a kind of epistemological and political imprisonment or, more modestly, veil of obstruction. Within the contours of this discussion, several basic "solutions" have been offered:

1. Nietzsche's dismissal of Western metaphysics and replacement of reason with the "will to power" attacked modernism at its core. He foreshadowed later postmodern critiques (e.g., Heidegger, Georges Bataille, Deleuze, Michel Foucault, Jacques Derrida), each of which reconfigured moral agency as they deconstructed the Cartesian ego. Heidegger, most prominently, offered the exemplar of going beyond Reason through Dasein's receptivity to Being, where the autonomous, insular self's confrontation with the world is replaced by an authentic Dasein, who is ontologically rooted in the world. Such a view of agency escapes the strictures of a representational subject-object dichotomy of inner and outer realities. Indeed, as an expression of the phenomenological orientation adapted from Husserl, representationalism had been discarded in exchange for the construction that would express (or capture) direct experience.

2. An opposing "modernist" group, led by Adorno and others, has valiantly attempted to hold back the postmodern tides originating with Nietzsche and Heidegger by arguing for the power and moral sanctity of self-reflection and reason through a critique designed to preserve Enlightenment ideals. Pragmatically oriented "communicative rationality" claims that objectivity and rational discourse are achieved by the reasoned exchange of rational agents (Habermas 1984, 1987, 1990; Rawls 1971). They opposed those who have delivered reason "over to the dynamics of withdrawal and retreat, of expulsion and proscription, with such impotence that narrow-minded subjectivity can never, by its own powers of anamnesis and analysis, reach what escapes it or holds itself at a remove from it. Self-reflection is sealed off from the other of reason" (Habermas 1987, p. 103).

3. A third movement originates with Wittgenstein, who discharged the metaphysics of a Cartesian ego with its accompanying understanding of reason, and more particularly, "to bring words back from their metaphysical to their everyday use" (1968, § 116, p. 48e). The utter rejection of representing subjective experience is best associated with the early Wittgenstein of the *Tractatus*, where he famously asserted (referring to ethics, aesthetics, spirituality, and metaphysics writ large), "Whereof one cannot speak, thereof one must be silent" (1981, p. 160). Accordingly, he did not deny the *reality* of ethics, aesthetics, and religious experience, but he rejected philosophical solutions to addressing questions posed in these realms as serving an outmoded metaphysics. Of more pertinence for this study is the pragmatic philosophy he later developed, whereby language is conceived without appeal to inner mental states. That move had broad repercussions for rejecting representationalism and largely defined Wittgenstein's dismissal of "private language" and the philosophical foundations upon which such a psychology was based.

4. Of less lasting influence, Henri Bergson's concept of *duration* (*durée*) explicitly addressed the problem of representing a process that can be understood only in its entirety, for example, a melody, and centers on the inadequacy of a representational model to depict the ceaseless change of phenomena and experience in time. This attempt to describe "the intuition of duration" (Bergson letter, 1915, quoted by Lacey

1989, p. 36) shares the same general agenda with other philosophical attempts to capture consciousness framed by the same quandary of experience *in* time (e.g., Husserlian phenomenology). Accordingly, "there are no things, there are only actions" (Bergson 1907 [*Creative Evolution*], quoted by Lacey 1989, p. 95).[4]

5. Pragmatism also contributes its own version of antirepresentational philosophy. For example, William James opined that "nothing *happens* in the realm of *concepts*" and only perception, not conception (representation), can give insight into moving life (James 1909 [*A Pluralistic Universe*], quoted by Lacey 1989, p. 159). John Dewey, following the same course, asserted that "mind is primarily a verb" (1980, p. 263) and thus the Cartesian split of mind and body, following from the predicate structure of Western language, distorted the reality of consciousness.[5] "The chief service of pragmatism, as regards epistemology," he wrote a friend in 1905, "will be . . . to give the *coup de grace to representationalism*" (quoted by Menand 2001, p. 361; emphasis in original), whose program has been best exemplified recently by Rorty (1979).

Although the contributions of Nietzsche, Husserl, Bergson, James, and Dewey are salient to the critique of representationalism generally, as already discussed, we will focus on those who directly confronted Freudian psychoanalysis and made its philosophy of mind a target of their respective assessments. Their collective effort, while divergent in the particulars of their methods and thematic concerns, sought to recast epistemology, expand experience, recast moral agency, and thus radically reformulate notions of personal autonomy. From their mosaic of ideas, alliances have been made and new traditions established. What was at risk? Simply, nothing less than the future of philosophy, and Freudianism was caught in that trial.

The indictment against Freud's project highlighted his characterization of the ego, which he had assumed would serve as the rational agent of insight and moral responsibility. If we put aside Freud's own struggle to assess the claims of reason's authority, the verdict of these judges condemns the self-conscious rationality with which Freud built psychoanalysis; simply, we are left with, at most, a residual concept of a self conceived as a rational cogito.[6] Certainly rationality resides securely in its own domain; indeed, how could a philosopher disparage the analytic tool of her trade! So the issue nagging the postmodern critique is not whether reason might be dethroned as an instrument of human intercourse and industry but rather how we might better understand the limits of reason and recognize its role in self-understanding. The question underlying psycho-*analysis* has always been the role of interpretation and its just expectations in self-knowing. However, that question has been radically restated and reframed by post-Freudian philosophical analyses.

In conclusion, this book addresses those who have a general interest in contemporary philosophy and seek a wide-ranging perspective on the issues swirling around agency and subjectivity as framed by Freudianism. Specifically, we are concerned with the stubborn problem of representing mental states that arose from the philosophy in which Freud set psychoanalysis. As that conception was disassembled by the critiques considered here, a theme clearly emerges, which captures much of twentieth-century philosophy by crossing into several domains. These matters hardly can be retained within the particular borders of the epistemological discussion, for the reconfiguration of Freud's philosophy of mind demands a revision of moral agency upon which he built his entire enterprise. Contesting the very notion of an autonomous rational agent also shifts the moral possibilities attached to such a subject. After all, the standing of the ego following Freud depends not so much on his epistemological description but more profoundly on how the self sits within the moral structure of Western metaphysics that provides the framework in which he described psychic agency. So at this juncture—after Adorno, after Heidegger, after Wittgenstein, after Lacan and Deleuze—we must ponder how their various notions of the ego now present post-Freudian ethics. With the disassembly of the modernist ego and the lost authority of a rational-based self-knowledge, an ethics grounded in autonomy and self-responsibility seems fanciful. From this perspective, the struggle over Freudian psychoanalysis becomes a moral incision centered on a humanist understanding of humankind. So if one asks, Of what relevance are the various philosophical voices singing the requiem of the ego?, the answer offered here revolves around the characterization of moral agency.

The resurrection of an independent ego is a daunting test for humanists, for if the epistemology upon which psychoanalysis is based has been so radically revised by later philosophical critiques, we may well ask, What of Freud's modernist project persists? The irony, of course, is that in some fundamental way, we have never been modern (Latour 1993). Indeed, the conundrum of setting a knowing, self-responsible ego against a passion-driven, arational psychic force characterizes prominent philosophical debates from Descartes's *Rules* to Freud's *Interpretation of Dreams*. In further destabilizing the ego, psychoanalysis joins that historical trajectory, which, following the psychoanalytic formulation, has pushed Cartesian doubt to even deeper depths of beguilement and skepticism. Accordingly, the question with which the Freudian Age began no longer concerns *how* are we to *know* unconscious mental life but rather whether the question grounded in an *analytic* interpretation remains coherent as posed. Freud, despite his own reluctance to philosophize, drove his respondents to the very foundations of Western metaphysics as they engaged him. That story easily claims standing as one of the most exciting intellectual chapters of our time, for not only are we intrigued with the conceptual challenges and ponder the social implications of this argument but the ethics that must arise from our understanding of personhood shadow the dispute, and in the end, we must respond.

1   The Psychoanalytic Ego

In the final analysis, in its transcendent constructions and its best phenomenological texts, Freudianism holds deep within it what our era most lacks. That is undoubtedly the reason—despite its theoretical uncertainties, contradictions, even absurdities—for its strange success. Psychoanalysis therefore does not belong to the body of the sciences of man to which it is now attached and from which it will here be carefully dissociated. It is rather, the antithesis of those sciences.

—MICHEL HENRY, *The Genealogy of Psychoanalysis*

Freud conceived a conscious (rational) ego, beyond its outward engagement with the world at large, as an inward-peering agent examining a mysterious unconscious. Thus, the mental consists of an aggregate of conscious and unconscious faculties, of which the latter dominates, at least in regard to establishing intentionality. Consciousness, the medium by which the ego intuits the unconscious and "knows" itself, serves as a monitoring system of choice and action—both conscious and unconscious.[1] As such, the *self-conscious I* (that which is designated the seat of consciousness) observes (evaluates, assesses) the unconscious *other*, which in exercising its own behavior is judged (again, in the Freudian therapeutic context of neurosis) as failing rational rules as it follows an agenda unbounded by time or logic. Reason then becomes the ego's faculty that would control the unconscious, but within this construct a fault line appears, and it grows as Freud further developed his theory: Because no neat division between an ego-consciousness and an unruly and hidden unconscious exists in Freud's mature theory (Freud 1923a; Tauber 2013), identity becomes a question. To the extent that an other is sought, an ego must relate to some primordial *thing*—perhaps an intimate other, but nevertheless not the self-conscious *me* yet *mine*. This problematic "presence" poses the fundamental Freudian question: "Who, then, is this other to whom I am more attached than to myself, since, at the heart of the assent to my identity, it is still he who agitates me?" (Lacan 2001, p. 130; 2006, p. 436). To address that question, Freud sought to decipher the doppelgänger accompanying the conscious self with a philosophy of mind, which fulfilled his commitment to a therapeutic *science*. That strategy imposed restrictions that he could not predict, or at least he chose to ignore. Unpacking Freud's philosophy of mind illuminates the conceptual infrastructure of his theory and the tensions within it, of which the most prominent is the problem of representing the unconscious in language alien to its own Logos.

I

To create the odd mosaic of psychoanalytic theory and practice, Freud extrapolated from fundamental tenets of physical science to construct the cardinal precept of mental activity: An uninterrupted stream of cause and effect governs all mental functions.[2] While consciousness exhibits apparent gaps in its sequence of events, Freud speculated that unconscious causation accounted for these gaps, which was revealed once repression yielded to analytic interpretation.[3] However, since the unconscious mind as he interpreted its manifestations did not correspond to the laws of logic and natural order found in physical phenomena, how might those mental events be understood in terms of the normative structure seemingly beheld in the world at large?[4] In other words, Freud's theory required that the logic he discerned in rational thought (so applicable to observed natural phenomena) also be applied to study unconscious thought. In many ways this was a naïve assumption.[5]

The philosophical genesis of Freud's psychoanalytic theory originates with Kant's representational conception of mind.[6] As argued elsewhere (Tauber 2009a, 2010), Freud was in several important respects a Kantian, albeit a particular kind of neo-Kantian. In some sense this allegiance is unexpected, given Freud's naturalism and his positivist aspirations, but consistency is not at issue; an accurate philosophical description is. To place Freud within this Kantian universe reveals important insights into both the particulars of Freudianism and, directly pertinent to our theme, the later philosophical criticism directed against Kant's epistemology that swept Freudianism along its torrential path.

According to Kant, the human mental structure organizes knowledge of the world, and for that matter our own thought, by its innate cognitive character. He posited the necessary a priori requirements for human cognition, which included space, time, causality, number, and so forth, as transcendental characteristics (necessary conditions) of the mind, which configure reality through such mental categories. Thus, the *noumenon*, the thing-in-itself, could not be known as such, that is, unmediated by mental processing. And because Kant's antirealist epistemology asserts that the thing-in-itself cannot be known in a first-order way, reality is constructed (Tauber 2009c) with certain architectonics established by a point of view with embedded a priori forms of reason. The entire enterprise rests on a fundamental separation of self from the world, and thus a representation or picture of the world is required to depict reality—*what* is known requires a re-presentation to a subject. Thus, the rational faculty, both autonomous and self-critical, serves as the linchpin of Kant's epistemology.

Because all mental activity is mediated as representations, there is no immediate knowledge of the world. That construction is determined not only by the innate cognitive structure of the mind as a perceptive organ but also by social (learned) forms of knowledge that are framed by linguistic constraints, cultural-historical parameters, political ideologies, and so on. Once integrated, these various modes of knowing present a particularized picture of the world and oneself in it. Freud inherited this philosophical understanding and built upon its basic postulates.

According to this Kantian formulation, even knowledge of the self is a representation (e.g., Damasio 1994; Metzinger 2003, 2009). As the subject of experience (as opposed to a Cartesian entity), the self upon its own scrutiny becomes a natural object, and, as such, it is perceived as a *phenomenon* through sensory faculties organized by the a priori categories of knowing (e.g., time, number, causality): "I represent myself to myself neither as I am nor as I appear to myself, but rather I think myself only as I do every object in general from whose kind of intuition I abstract" (Kant 1998 [B 429], p. 456). And thus the self-reflexive ego is subject to the same epistemological structure of all knowing: Because the world is not a given, the Kantian ego essentially becomes a representational function or logical power, one that also becomes a representational relation to itself (a being that possesses only a "self-relation" to itself).[7] Note that "the transition from a subject of representing to the nominalized I [the ego] is . . . made by the notion of self-reflexivity . . . [and] Kant always identifies I-ness with self-reflexivity" (Frank 1997, p. 11). So the locution "I think"—from Leibniz to Kant—holds two meanings: (1) self-reflection of consciousness, that is, self-consciousness; and (2) the representing function of something, that is, perceptual object(s).[8] And here, the nature of Freud's philosophical construction clearly appears as a representational model of mind.

Freud characterized consciousness as a "sense organ for the perception of psychical qualities" (1900, p. 615).[9] So the presentation of the unconscious to the conscious sensory faculty (albeit through complex pathways) comprised a metaphorical extension of the brain's general perceptive qualities (Natsoulas 1984, 1985, 2001), namely, all conscious items are ultimately sensations or associated with sensations, and thoughts enter consciousness by "parasitizing sensation" (D. Smith 1999b, p. 417). Simply, the unconscious would be perceived as the ego perceives the external world. However, given that the unconscious is not governed by conscious time or causality, how then would this ontologically separated domain register in the realm of representations? Freud responded to this challenge by closely following Kantian epistemological principles.

Psychoanalytic theory rests on accepting that *the unconscious cannot be directly known*, inasmuch as it follows its own "laws" of cause and temporality and thus, at least from Freud's perspective, fulfills the criteria of a *noumenon*. Freud treated it as such and referred to the *noumenal* character of the unconscious from at least 1910,[10] through the metapsychology period (1915b, p. 171; Eriksson 2012), until his last writings:

> In our science as in the others the problem is the same: behind the attributes (qualities) of the object under examination [the unconscious] which are presented directly to our perception, we have to discover something else which is more independent of the particular receptive capacity of our sense organs and which approximates more closely to what may be supposed to be the real state of affairs. *We have no hope of being able to reach the latter itself,* since it is evident that everything new that we have inferred must nevertheless be translated back into the language of our perceptions, from which it is simply impossible for us to free ourselves. But herein lies the very nature and limitation of our science. . . . *Reality will always remain "unknowable."* (Freud 1940, p.196; emphasis added)

Thus for Freud, the unconscious would be perceived, like nature, indirectly, as a representation—a phenomena recognized by the mind's organizing faculties.[11] This capacity assembles perceptions and synthesizes them through an interpretive function residing in reason. Accordingly, Freud invented a "language of our perceptions"[12] (i.e., a system of representations) to capture phenomena just as a physicist portrays natural forces.[13]

Freud, following Kant, conceived reality as a product of mind and nature, for given the constitutive role of the mind in creating any knowledge of nature, a cognitive construction of reality, employing representations, must occur.[14] Truth then is the correspondence between those representations and nature. In other words, the normative structure of the mind allows an accurate map to be drawn of reality, which for Freud includes the reality of inner mental states as well. So what Kant devised as a philosophy to study nature, Freud applied to the psyche;[15] however, whereas Kant devised a philosophy to ground science and objective truth, Freud revised notions of human reality, radically. Indeed, psychoanalysis makes a unique contribution to the notion of reality by posing it as obstacle to fantasy and wish, the object of desire (Henry 1993, p. 392; Cousins 2005). And here the psychic calculus becomes operative, one in which a Janus-like ego peering simultaneously inward and outward to satisfy its mandate, mediates reality in two senses: (1) the traditional facilitation of fulfilling psychic desire; and (2) mediation by defining that reality, which in the psychoanalytic universe is the world of possibilities—objects of desire, targets of fantasy, opportunities for gratification. Thus, the real is determined by the meeting of mind with its intentional object, or in the terms of psychoanalysis, *fantasy*. "Success," at least from this point of view, is the (maximal) fulfillment of desire in the encounter, and "failure" becomes its frustration. In either case, the real consists of the mental and its other, locked together.

Integration of unconscious states sets the ego's vision of the world, and as libidinal forces find their intentional objects, fantasy and its object meet. But that other holds no final subjective-free status, because the other is conceived and then refracted through the psychic lens directed (intended) by wish, and then the object transmutes into various derivative representations. The cathexis may be attached either to an inner ego object (narcissistic investment) or to an external object of desire: The subjective object, of course, remains resolutely nonobjectified; and the external object itself is also conceived with heavy emotive components. Consequently, a distinct line between fantasy and the real cannot be drawn, for the mind's intention, according to Freudian theory, constructs its reality through its own emotional structures and affective requirements. If fantasy dominates, the primary narcissism of the subject then must struggle in its rejection of the stimuli of the outside world, or, alternatively, desire seeks its object and reality becomes the site for its gratification. Thus, reality emerges as a negotiation between fantasy and its obstacle to become an achievement of sorts. The unconscious—whether lodged in the ego or the id (Freud 1923a)— alienates the subject from full acceptance of external reality so that ultimately the subject is the battleground over which reality and fantasy lay their respective claims.[16] In short, the world—the psychic world—is a reality organized by the mind's intentional desire, mediated by a complex normative rationality coupled to psychic drives ("emo-reason") and largely perceived subconsciously. The conscious picture of reality is thus only a superficial gloss of a deeper dynamic.

II

As discussed, Freud's basic philosophical move treats unconscious ideas as *objects* of scrutiny, albeit *mental* objects, which could be represented by the conscious mind. In other words, he assumed mental states have the same basic epistemological standing of entities and processes found in nature, and so to establish his science of the mind, he would apply the same principles established for the scientific study of nature to the unconscious mental life of humans. That crucial extrapolation rests on an implicit commitment to a representational epistemology, whereby the world is truly known because of the correspondence of our mental picture or representations of that world with the world itself. In other words, our minds mirror reality through the representations we employ (Rorty 1979). When Freud modeled the mind, albeit with novel *interpretive* methods, he confidently proceeded as if the correspondence of that representational strategy employed to study exterior nature would also hold for his studies of the psyche.[17]

Freud went to great lengths to show how the dynamics of the unconscious differs from those governing the conscious ego (i.e., the lack of intelligible notions of time and space; the seeming arationality and amorality of dreams; the inscrutable disjunctions of sequences that pass for loss of causality); nevertheless, in the key metapsychological paper "The Unconscious," he declares that despite all distortions relative to reasoned thought, unconscious dynamics would be treated in the same terms one characterizes conscious thought: "All the categories which we employ to describe conscious mental acts, such as ideas, purposes, resolutions, and so on, can be applied to them [unconscious latent states]" (1915b, p. 168). In other words, he made the unconscious discernible in the same terms used to describe consciousness and thereby claimed an objective status for mental states.[18] So despite the hermeneutical connotations of "interpretation," Freud relentlessly presented his project as a science, namely, an analysis that objectified unconscious motivations and uncovered hidden meanings. And with this commitment to positivism, Freud devised a representational language, the métier of science, to "capture" the phenomena: "Thus we shall not hesitate to treat them [unconscious latent states] as *objects* of psychological research, and to deal with them in the most intimate connection with conscious mental acts" (ibid.; emphasis added). Let us unpack these assertions.[19]

Conceiving unconsciousness in the semantic tradition firmly places the representations of unconscious drives as ways of thinking *about* them. Indeed, Freud (1915a) recognized that the drives themselves are never represented as such but appear in the psyche as ideas to which the drives attach themselves. In "The Unconscious," Freud explicitly addresses the relationship of language (representations) with the unconscious object, where he asserted that the "thing-presentation" cannot become conscious until associated with words, and this step occurs in the preconscious (not the unconscious, which knows no language as such). At the interface of conscious and unconscious mental life, this associative locale, where unconscious objects or drives become associated with language, provides the key link between the sectors of the psyche to offer the coherence required for normal mentation.[20]

This "associative" formulation dates to Freud's 1891 prepsychoanalytic writings on aphasia (Freud 1953). Framed by the neurological discourse of the time, he joined attempts to model the relationship of brain localization studies to speech, namely, how to balance the contributions made by areas with localized language competence (e.g., Broca's area) and the complex processing that must occur as sensory data ascend to higher cortical regions. Very much in the same spirit of his later hypothesis presented in the *Project for a Scientific Psychology*, where he postulated that different types of neurons fulfill different neurological functions, Freud assumed that a nerve on its way to the cerebral cortex changed its functional significance (or meaning) (1895, p. 52).[21] Making the case for a more global integration, Freud relied on some modality by which "a word sound image" associates with an "impression of word innervation" (ibid., p. 73), and he suggested that the word concept appears as a "closed" complex of images of visual and auditory perceptions that processes the object through both specialized and more general anatomic locales.[22] Then Freud makes the representational move: "In light of observations in speech disorders we have formed the view that the word *concept* (the idea of the word) is linked with its sensory part, in particular through its sound impressions, to the object *concept*" (ibid., pp. 77–78; emphasis added), which is then processed through the ascendant and integrative functions of various specialized anatomic centers.

If we put aside the controversies about language of the period (reviewed by Greenberg 1997, pp. 140ff.), Freud's position (which he cites as supported from neuropathology) later appeared in his psychoanalytic theorizing, where he posited an essential *symbolic* function of language, one independent of the sensory domain. While "verbal aphasia, in which only the associations between the single elements of the word concept [word-presentation] are disturbed," a second *asymbolic aphasia* is defined as occurring when "the association between word concept and object concept are disturbed" (Freud 1953, p. 78).[23] Freud goes on to explain that he uses *asymbolic* as a designation for the relationship between the word and the idea of the object, as opposed to the relationship of the object and its idea. In other words, the word represents the idea of the object, not the object itself. Note that Strachey "stretches" his translation to make the point more explicitly that *symbolic* captures the relation between word presentation (*Vorstellung*) and object presentation, rather than that between object and object presentation (Freud 1915b, p. 214). As Greenberg observes, "[T]he word is not a symbol of the object—which would imply a nonarbitrary or necessary connection—but rather the relationship is between the idea (*Vorstellung*) of the word and the idea of the object" (1997, p. 171).

Freud extended this basic construction to the psychoanalytic scenario for deciphering the unconscious. There, unlike external objects, the inner psychic objects are the drives. These are promiscuous and attach themselves to different ideas, and given their breadth of "meaning," they disguise their origin. Freud interpreted this shifting of attachments as the reason the drives may be misconstrued, that is, having moved from one association to another as a result of repressive effects. Psychoanalysis would place the correct (i.e., original) idea with the drive and thus, through a process of insight (led by an inferential strategy), account for the initial trauma, repression, conflict, and ultimately, anxiety. Effective therapies putatively depend on shifting the misplaced (and misconstrued) false (repressed or defensive) idea to a truer one, and thereby identify the drive (or its desire) more accurately. In sum, the entire structure of the theory rests on a particular understanding of the mind as a representational faculty, where the associated ideas serve as the currency of mental dynamics (Freud 1915a). Putatively, psychoanalysis is the science that would accurately discern those associations.

Freud held that it is the representation that is unconscious, and, through repression, the representation may be displaced from its original connection to the affect. "If we restore the true connection, we call the original affective impulse an 'unconscious' one. Yet its affect was never unconscious; all that had happened was that its *idea* had undergone repression" (Freud 1915b, pp. 177–78). The analytic work of psychoanalysis is to restore the original meaning of the representation, that is, more closely link the idea to the original affect and correct the misconstrual and thereby relieve repression and ultimately anxiety (Freud 1916, pp. 403–4, 409). So, while the affect moves from one representation to another, and the representative experience is repressed, the feeling remains (Henry 1993, p. 304). The cardinal finding of this reading drives to an ironic result: While representations and their associated ideas are repressed and thus point to an intrapsychic other, the unconscious does not exist as such (ibid., p. 315) but appears only as the artifact of its representational status.

Thus, for Freud, as for Kant, "it is not the thing itself, but a representation of it, that is being interpreted" (Rieff 1959, p. 105), that is, "the object of either conscious or unconscious mental processes is not the world itself but a *mental representation* of it, outer world or inner as the case may be" (M. Cavell 1993, p. 14). Freud claimed that through "interposition [of word-presentations] internal thought-processes are made into perceptions" (Freud 1923a, p. 23), so a private wordless thought is followed by words, "which somehow provide the lens through which the thinker perceives his thoughts" (M. Cavell 1993, p. 47). Thus, word-presentations serve as the base of the psychoanalytic understanding of the mind, where psychic experiences are re-presented with a conscious-accessible vocabulary and grammar; the objective reality of our judgments arises from a merging of conscious perceptions mediated by psychic "categories of understanding," and their synthesis in a consciousness capable of self-reflection offered psychoanalysis its basis of study. Upon this philosophical foundation Freud built his clinical theory.

With this conceptual structure Freud held to a version of knowledge steadfastly based on a subject-object structure, amenable to scientific investigation. Using representation as the epistemological mediator between the two psychic domains, psychoanalysis radically asserts its ability to accomplish just this task: Because

> we know for certain that they [unconscious processes] have abundant points of contact with conscious mental processes; with the help of a certain amount of work they can be transformed into, or replaced by, conscious mental processes, and all the categories which we employ to describe conscious mental acts, such as ideas, purposes, resolutions, and so on, can be applied to them. Indeed, we are obliged to say of some of these latent states that the only respect in which they differ from conscious ones is precisely in the absence of consciousness. Thus we shall not hesitate to treat them as objects of psychological research, and to deal with them in the most intimate connection with conscious mental acts. (Freud 1915b, p. 168)

However, the matter hardly ends here, for while confidently asserting his intent, and ability, to interpret that which emerges from the unconscious, Freud also acknowledges that the clues offered through dreams and other manifest behaviors and speech become decipherable only in the terms of consciousness. Indeed, that was the basis of his new "science of the mind." However, psychoanalysis, at least in principle, has access to the unconscious in terms of affective expression, and while Freud recognized that locus of interest, emotion as part of his cognitive theory is conspicuously absent. This omission will become a target of later criticism.

III

Because of his own philosophical and scientific commitments, Freud was guided by the ultimate desire to reduce the unconscious to a physical reality (i.e., a product of brain states), and then, in practice, he settled for a reduction to consciousness through representative modalities (via language, symbols, secondary manifestations), which he identified (defined) as epiphenomena of unconscious processes. So the drive (or instinct, *Trieb*) that characterizes the unconscious escapes the laws of consciousness and thus must be represented to consciousness as an idea by which we "know" it:

> The antithesis of conscious and unconscious is not applicable to instincts. An instinct can never become an object of consciousness—*only the idea that represents the instinct can.* Even in the unconscious, moreover, an instinct cannot be *represented* otherwise than by an idea.[24] (Freud 1915b, p. 177; emphasis added)

Freud makes the mental state an object of scrutiny as he donned the role of the scientist, because for him, knowledge existed only as positivist knowledge, and he would press the unconscious into an objective mold and thereby re-present what was presented directly, the emotions. As discussed, he accomplished that task by assigning ideas to the affects. Note that ideas are not the affections with which they associate but remain only their representation.

In some respects Freud failed to consider how the *experience* of the unconscious might fall into a domain inaccessible to certain kinds of objectification and analysis. Emotion, at least in its "native" state, functions on its own level (beneath conscious analyticity) and presents itself as affects, feelings, moods. When the emotive drifts into consciousness and becomes accessible to self-awareness and analysis, it may frame the ideation that serves as the psychoanalytic substrate of analysis, but it has no direct cognitive standing of its own. Freud offered sparse theoretical consideration concerning the character of emotional intentionality (what establishes a vector of expression) or what constitutes an emotion's distinctive relation to its object (Deigh 2010, p. 24). He thus left undeveloped a theoretical conception of emotions qua emotions, and the various formulations of the pleasure principle seeking its fulfillment were, in parallel, left obscure. A tale of obstructed energies and rising tensions hardly fulfills the requirements of a metapsychology of the affective life, which Freud described in terms of a psychobiology but ended with a psychoanalytic myth.

Having left a theory of the affections undeveloped, Freud formulated a secondary description of how consciousness perceived the unconscious. So in terms of the development of his analytics, emotions per se do not appear as part of Freud's major concerns, and as a result a conceptual impasse appears in his theory. And an ironic omission it is. After all, Freud's theory originated in his diagnosis of the psychosomatic illness of his patients—the spasm, cough, paralysis, pain afflicting his celebrated patients. These symptoms, according to his interpretations, pointed to a psychic origin, which were in some profound sense contained within the mind, when in fact they were bodily expressions of emotional trauma. But because he worked as a dualist and consequently restricted his vision to the unconscious psychic reality, he demarcated these "mental expressions" from brain states and certainly the soma itself. Instead of anchoring the ego in some melding of mind and body, "an ego that would be body, of a body that would be ego—he dissociates it. He makes it into a 'mental projection' of the corporeal surface, its transposition on the psychic plane" (Rogozinski 2010, p. 73) and thereby forsakes any attempt to develop a unified theory that would integrate the emotions (the body) with the mental. This is perhaps his deepest commitment to a Cartesian understanding of the subject, namely, the mind-body divide. And there, at the base of modern Western metaphysics, Freud's theory was most vulnerable. That affections are immediately known does not mean that they then can be related to oneself (much less to others) as representations. Here, the cognitive character of emotion, the problem of how emotion is represented, and what such representation signifies are matters that underlie some of the later critiques based on revising Freudianism along Nietzschean lines.

At the most basic level of his theory, Freud conceived emotions as a physiological component of animal behavior, and in this regard, the id, as the repository of id-instincts in the last formulation, was firmly placed within the biological domain. However, we must not construe Freud's idea as the same "bodily feelings" William James ascribed to emotions; on James's account, emotions as *feelings* are derivative of physiological responses and thus have no motivational force.[25] Freud offered a radically different account: The linchpin of psychoanalytic theory is that conscious or not, emotions have intentions, whose elucidation provides the meaning to the feelings and behaviors of the ego. After all, psychoanalysis is devoted to uncovering those intentions and thus explaining the motivation of unconscious drives.

Although instincts, drives, and emotions are typically construed as expressions of some primitive psychic apparatus, Freud regarded emotions as part of the conscious cognitive mind (Freud 1915a), whereby an emotional response is either a discharge of energy caused by an idea or the awareness of the discharge (Lear 1990, p. 87).

> Strictly speaking . . . there are no unconscious affects as there are unconscious ideas. But there may very well be in the system Ucs. [unconscious] affective structures which, like others, become conscious. The whole difference arises from the fact that ideas are cathexes— basically of memory-traces—whilst affects and emotions correspond to processes of discharge, the final manifestations of which are perceived as feelings. In the present state of our knowledge of affects and emotions we cannot express this difference more clearly. (Freud 1915b, p. 178)

Simply put, James assumed a physiological orientation where feelings reflected underlying emotion, whereas Freud intellectualized emotions by linking them to ideas and thus subject to other conscious mental processes. While Freud acknowledged that emotions may be conscious or unconscious, we could only know affections—the conscious aspects of emotive life expressed as moods or feelings. If this distinction is maintained, then Freud's notions of hate, love, anger, and so on must be understood as *ideational* states, and when associated with trauma, repression is the requirement for maintaining emotional homeostasis.

Repression, working to control emotion, actually processes the idea associated with that affect (Freud 1915a). To repress the idea is to deal with the emotion. In this psychic calculus, emotional life is construed only in conscious terms, and "what analysis does, then, is to rescue the rationality of an emotion" (Lear 1990, p. 90). Note that Freud does not maintain that unconscious emotions do not exist but rather we cannot gain access to them, whereas in studying their linked ideas, a psychic mapping might be achieved. Simply, his science structures his psychology, and what he can *know* is what there *is*.

On this account, the representational structure of his (Kantian) theory becomes quite clear: Only when an idea is attached to a drive or to the emotion is it perceived as such, that is, it can become conscious, for if the emotion remains inaccessible to conscious processes, then its motivational effects must remain mysterious. The consequence is that the unconscious becomes a construct of the rational psychoanalytic ego, which identifies the ideas associated with the emotion. While the Freudian target is the emotion, repression works on ideas, and the ideas, or at least the representations posing as ideas, then become the conduit to the unconscious: Uncovering the repressed idea uncovers the emotion.

The approximations, metaphors, elliptical reference, and poetic allusion employed to capture affective states reflects their essential ineffability. Accordingly, the unconscious cannot be truly represented, but more, psychoanalysis invariably misrepresents unconsciousness by forcing affections into a translation composed of concepts, symbols, and complex interpretations of instinct-linked "ideas" contextualized within an intellectualized story. *Understanding* the affective is part of the psychoanalysis, but in service to the essential emotional engagement that results from the analytic strategy of identifying the repression, the conflict, and finally the "cause" of anxiety. Thus, the traditional analytic fulfills one function; the transference fulfills another.

The "work" of psychoanalysis occurs in transference and countertransference, where the emotional ties established between analyst and analysand allow for reenactment, identification, and eventual release of psychic trauma, repression, and guilt. There, the "sharp split between subject and object" vanishes (Schafer 1983, p. 255) and reason recedes, for in the transference, psychoanalysis enacts a transformation of psychic reality, not its domination. With this emotionally based strategy, unconscious drives would be met on their own grounds in the transference, whose effective enactment became the ultimate goal of psychoanalysis. Here, human subjectivity—redacted, redirected, reformed—might find its fuller expression.

In line with the disjunction between the representational mind and the affections, Freud observed (an insight amply confirmed by his psychoanalytic followers) that conscious recognition and recollection are insufficient for psychic cure. He claimed that psychoanalysis ultimately requires a corresponding affective response linked to recall and insight, because the reconfiguration of psychic conflicts and their history must occur within the emotional domain for effective therapy. Accordingly, transference leads to some emotional resolution, whether in catharsis or less dramatic transformation. In short, interpretation alone fails to penetrate the defenses surrounding emotional trauma to modify the analysand's *emotional* life.

Thus, Freud's psychoanalytic strategy required two stages to achieve a resolution of psychic conflict. The first, based on the rational autonomy of the ego, employs an *analytical* approach modeled on a scientific philosophy to discern a natural object, the unconscious. Freud invented an interpretive method in the attempt to "capture" the unconscious through symbols, slips of the tongue, jokes, dreams, and so on. In the second *therapeutic* stage, the conscious ego functions are bypassed and the analysand is placed in direct confrontation with past emotional trauma. In this recognition phase the conflict of conscious and unconscious psychic centers putatively realign, and in the process the analysand achieves improved emotional harmony. Note that distinction must be made regarding the obvious centrality of rational analysis and the role emotion plays in psychoanalysis. For Freud, the scientific approach served only as a means to an interpretation that, potentially at least, would lead to "redemption." Indeed, therapeutic relief depended on both some inner logic based on rational insight and an emotional recalibration coupled to that understanding. So once the analytic portion of psychoanalysis reaches maturity, the therapeutic process advances on a very different basis through transference dynamics. In short, according to orthodox Freudianism, psycho-*analysis* serves as a ladder to the emotional platform, where the curative psychodynamic work occurs. At that transition, Freud moved from philosophy to psychology.

IV

With the theoretical elements of psychoanalysis in place, a brief accounting is due:

1. The unconscious is *noumenal*, and emotions are ("strictly speaking") conscious;
2. the drives have ideas attached to them, which may be discerned through interpretations of various manifestations, for example, dreams;
3. such phenomena are then considered as derived from the unconscious, but in such representation, the direct expression of the unconscious (the emotion) is not represented, only the idea coupled to the drive, which appears as an affection (the conscious awareness of the emotion or mood or feeling);
4. the idea thus displaces the primary emotion, which has no standing as such until it reaches consciousness.

With this schema, Freud presumed that the conscious ego would interpret the unconscious mind as it engages the world— as another object, albeit with special qualities requiring new stratagems. Because only the epiphenomena of unconsciousness (dreams, parapraxis, etc.) appear to consciousness, psychoanalysis, as *"the science of the unconscious mind"* (Freud 1923b, p. 252; emphasis in the original), finds itself describing unconsciousness through a language of consciousness.[26] Following a Kantian model, Freud had no qualms that the "noumenal" unconscious might be discerned and analyzed as any other natural object. Ironically perhaps, the emotional constituents found no place in his epistemology. So broadly regarded, the unconscious of psychoanalysis is a construction, one devised as a derivative of representational modes of thought. The critical corollary: Freud recognized the noumenal character of the unconscious, and in that recognition, he tacitly accepted the philosophical fault lines of his theory (Tauber 2010, pp. 63–69).

The same subject-object divide that appears so clearly in the scenario of capturing external reality also applies to representing psychic life. Rather than more accessible, inner states are different in character from knowledge of external reality. One difference pertains to the product of the cognitive process: Physical objects may be objectified, by which we mean that different observers might agree on what the object is. Of course, that agreement may or may not correspond to the same assessment, and in the end, knowledge rests on shared experience and the debate concerning its validity from different points of view. With subjective states, one's representation (even to oneself) has no such objective standing, and while that experience might be expressed in the same representational language used to discuss the external world, the feeling or emotion exists as such, in some sense experienced outside language. However, Freud denied this epistemological conundrum. Simply, he posited the same empiricist subject-object relationship he employed as a neuroanatomist studying neurons for accessing inner psychic states. Both brains and mental states would be treated as natural objects of scrutiny subject to an autonomous epistemological agent perceiving, synthesizing, categorizing, and assessing that object.

However, reason's capacity to fulfill its role in psychoanalysis rests on an astonishing claim. At the end of his 1915 acknowledgement to Kant, Freud writes,

> [L]ike the physical, the psychical is not necessarily in reality what it appears to us to be. We shall be glad to learn, however, that the correction of internal perception will turn out not to offer such great difficulties as the correction of external perception—that internal objects are less unknowable than the external world. (Freud 1915b, p. 171)

On what basis could Freud make such an assertion? It certainly breaks strict Kantian orthodoxy. If viewed from the broad perspective of Freud's therapeutic goals, this epistemological "intimacy" provides a possible basis for the transference mechanism, which would serve as the key to the emotional resolution of psychic conflict. By positing a smaller "space" separating the conscious cognitive faculty from the affective unconscious, is Freud perhaps suggesting a unique cognitive bridge? He provides no comment and leaves his assertion as self-evident. In any case, by making the intimacy of psychic experience a special case, he sidesteps the problematic status of objectifying mental states. That he blurs the distinction between the analytical interpretation he has taken such pains to establish and the immediacy of personal feeling is, at best, a philosophical sleight of hand. In fact, there is no basis for assuming that one has more direct epistemological knowledge of inner mental states than of exterior nature, and more specifically, by assigning idea representations to the affects, he forsakes dealing with emotion on its own terms.

Considering Freud's philosophical sophistication (Herzog 1988; Fulgencio 2005; Tauber 2010, pp. 40–48, 155–59), he might have been more critical, for his complacency left psychoanalytic theory in a profound philosophical imbroglio. If one accepts that "Being is not [directly] visible and does not represent itself" (Roustang 1993, p. x), then the relationship between mind and nature looms, and those critical of representational modernist philosophy have concluded that "no ontology of representation can be developed except to demonstrate its impossibility" (ibid.). The remaining chapters of our study address in various ways how key philosophers have addressed this challenge, so here suffice it to observe that for any representational system some underlying stratum beneath the phenomenology of the visible, or the conscious, an underlying essence exists—what Descartes called the "Soul"; Schopenhauer, "the body"; Nietzsche, "the will to power"; and Freud, "the unconscious." In the psychoanalytic context, Michel Henry calls this primary or original stratum "affectivity," which he presents as the "sole ground of true thought" or "absolute subjectivity" (ibid., p. xi). On that view, the representation of the affects, their mediation as it were, constitutes a distortion (at best) or a violence (at worst). As a primordial origin, affectivity has only its own expression, and no representation can capture its reality.

Accordingly, two different meanings of the unconscious must be delineated. When regarded from the representational universe of consciousness, the unconscious becomes an object of consciousness and thus attains meaning as it is deciphered to some conscious understanding. A second meaning refers to a deeper ontology, where the essence of the psyche lies ineffably beyond the realm of faithful representations and thus fundamentally inaccessible. When the second meaning is subordinated to the first, the unconscious, originally the ego's radical other (not representable), now has, through representation, lost its thorough alterity, and "the aberrant concept of an 'unconscious representation' is born" (Henry 1993, p. 298).

The Freudian depiction of the unconscious mind necessarily constructs (and thereby falsifies) the object of inquiry. For example, the manifest dream can only be a partial and altered or translated recollection of the primary dream contents. All unconscious primary material ultimately remains restricted to its own domain, and the counterpart, the contents of consciousness subject to the strictures of its own phenomenal contents, "has first been thoroughly trimmed, simplified, schematized, interpreted—the *real* process of inner 'perception . . . is absolutely hidden" (Nietzsche 2003, p. 221). And Freud admitted in his reflective "Autobiographical Study" that the basic question concerning the ultimate nature of the unconscious "is no wiser or more profitable than the older one as to the nature of the conscious" (1925, p. 32).[27] The admission that his representations were inadequate for his ostensible task is an ironic fault, for the affections are there to behold in direct subjective experience. However, Freud did not develop a means to describe what lay at the heart of his inquiry in its own *affective* terms.

Others followed a strategy different from Freud's, one that began with Nietzsche, who held the line between the conscious/unconscious domains more securely and recognized the unbridgeable gulf separating them: "The 'inner experience' only enters our consciousness after it's found a language that the individual understands . . . i.e., a translation of a state into states *more familiar* to the individual—(2003, p. 271; emphasis in original; see also p. 107).[28] This orientation derived from Nietzsche's effort to drive all human life relentlessly to bedrock "will," where the "will to power" captured the incessant drive of the inner *Triebe* of which we are ignorant:

> Assuming that nothing real is "given" to us apart from our world of desires and passions, assuming that we cannot ascend or descend to any "reality" other than the reality of our instincts (for thinking is merely an interrelation of these instincts, one to the other), may we not be allowed to perform an experiment and ask whether the "given" also provides a *sufficient* explanation for the so-called mechanistic (or material) world? I do not mean the material world as a delusion, as "appearance" or "representation" [*Vorstellung*] . . . but rather as a world with the same level of reality that our emotion [*Affekt*] has. (Nietzsche 2008, p. 35)

Of course, he asserted that his thought experiment concluded with a monolithic drive at the core of human life, and with that assertion, Nietzsche consistently pursued the logical consequences of recognizing the primacy of the affects to chart a course that

Freud might well have followed. After all, both agreed that given the character of consciousness, it was

> essential that one make no mistake about the role of "consciousness": . . . [W]hat becomes conscious is subject to causal relations entirely concealed from us—the succession of thoughts, feelings, ideas in consciousness tells us nothing about whether this succession is a causal one: but it gives the *illusion* of being so, in the highest degree. Upon this *illusion we have founded our whole notion of mind, reason, logic,* etc. (none of these exist: they are fictitious syntheses and unities). . . . And these in turn we have projected *into* things, *behind* things! (Nietzsche 2003, p. 228)

Denying consciousness as the highest stage of organic development, Nietzsche would insist that (1) the unification of the diverse multiple instincts and the affects are the most astonishing product of evolution (ibid., pp. 29, 113); (2) affective life employs consciousness only as a tool for its own goals (p. 45); and (3) ultimately the affects themselves interpret (p. 96), leaving consciousness the illusion of its own autonomy (pp. 8, 228). Nietzsche discarded science (another illusion of knowledge) to validate and celebrate emotional life. He regarded the denial of the primacy of affective life as a cardinal feature of Western nihilism, and thus he sought to sunder the chains of consciousness and an illusory morality. Reason in his context became a tool of enslavement, both to control instinctual life and to impose social conformity.

These themes will resurface in our discussion of alternatives to Freud's theoretical investment in reason (and consciousness) at the expense of a philosophy more closely aligned with his erstwhile competitor.[29] Redefining and then reforming the rational, self-conscious ego lies at the heart of Nietzsche's critique. And Heidegger's own influential effort to create a philosophy that might effectively address the impasse of the Cartesian mind, full of authority and penetrating insight, begins with Nietzsche's identification of the will to power as the underlying malady affecting Western culture (Heidegger 1977a, 1982). On this view, they join a powerful current of romantic sentiment that would valorize nature, place humans *within* the world they scrutinized with such scientific precision, and free the expressive affections to achieve a life full of exuberance and emotional fulfillment. To oppose the indomitable will of the ego, the constricting forces of mass society, and the restraints of a tyrannical rationality sets the agenda Nietzsche, and then Heidegger, expressly addressed, and they did so with nothing less than a radical dismemberment of the Enlightenment project. Anyone caught on the other side of the line they drew in the sand was assigned to a discarded metaphysics. And Freud, despite contributing to their agenda in ways he could not have predicted, remained committed to the authority of the ego and the reason that would govern the unruly passions.

Although we have emphasized how Freud's scientism directed his theory construction, we must acknowledge that he also accounted for psychic drives as being experienced *directly* through the affects that express them qualitatively (Laplanche and Pontalis 1973, p. 13). As already mentioned, these found their place in the domain of emotional transference between analysand and analyst and thus serve a critical role in the therapeutic process: "If the instinct did not attach itself to an idea *or manifest itself as an affective state*, we could know nothing about it" (Freud 1915b, p. 177; emphasis added). The alternative to the idea (namely, a conscious idea), the affect itself, presents directly as experience without representation, and the affect is included as a way of knowing.[30] The affect (feelings, emotion) displaces representational knowledge with something else, a direct visceral experience. Indeed, the unconscious *is* affect, and to the extent we know the unconscious, it is by this direct affective experience. Freud himself knew as much: When distilled through psycho-*analysis*, the "affective or emotional impulse is perceived but misconstrued" (1915b, p. 177), precisely because of the distortion imposed by the attachment to an idea, that is, a representation that has, for defensive purposes, been displaced from the initial emotional event. So an inner tension divides psychoanalytic theory: On the one hand, the analytic is required to gain insight; on the other hand, only with emotional recognition would therapeutic progress ensue.

In sum, Freud, while steadfastly holding on to an epistemology that would serve his science, understood the limitations of his theory. The representational lies superficial to, or by the side of, affective life, so to observe that we do not know the unconscious becomes the inadequacy of representations to capture that reality. Instead, an altogether different kind of knowing is required. The transference hardly constitutes knowledge in the usual sense, but Freud recognized its critical role in his psychotherapy, and in terms of our concerns, he understood the limits of rational analysis and emphasized the importance of transference and countertransference as modalities of experience that were uniquely evidential (Wollheim 1971, p. 195). Instead of some derived, analytic interpretation, the emotional experience of the transference phenomenon demanded a kind of receptivity and understanding, linked but separate from the intellectual processes generated in the analysand-analyst exchange.[31] Formally, transference/countertransference is the portal through which the affective gains entry to the consultation room, and it is in that emotional exchange that psychoanalysis commits, and fulfills, its true labor. Affectivity is expressed directly through passion, mood, surges of emotion, and instinct, all of which fall well beyond the control of reason and its progeny. Freud, stepping outside his scientific ambitions and accepting the pragmatic therapeutic requirements of his method, emphasized this cardinal fact and taught the analyst to be sensitive to his or her own unconscious as a receptacle of affective transmissions of the analysand. Accordingly, the analyst

> must turn his own unconscious like a receptive organ towards the transmitting unconscious of the patient . . . so the doctor's unconscious is able, from the derivatives of the unconscious which are communicated to him, to reconstruct that unconscious. (Freud 1912, pp. 115–16)

The translation of those feelings into language was to heighten awareness of emotional content, but in the end, this translation only served a deeper affective recognition process.

To conclude, Freud employed or designed representations— myths, mechanisms, interpretations, and so on—to portray the dynamics of an underlying affective life, which, in final analysis, serves as a language that points to the affections one feels but may not *know*. Accordingly, the tyranny of the despotic unconscious would be broken by analysis mediated by reason's autonomy, reason's ability to free itself from disguised or hidden psychic forces. Interpretation would thus discern deterministic causes of overt behaviors and thoughts that hitherto were inaccessible, and putatively some form of psychological release would then be achieved. In acknowledging that "reason includes in itself that which is not known" (Steuerman 2000, p. 17), Freudianism places at the heart of its theory the asymptote of analysis and then provides an inflection into the emotional domain. This transition from insight to transference, from intellectual recognition to emotional experience, provides a strategy of fulfilling Freud's original aspirations. Freud and his followers each have endeavored to find the crossover point and establish the means by which the transition, an endless exchange of insight and lived experience, might be opened and made more accessible. Although reason serves a crucial role in that venture, the therapeutic result requires an *emotional* resolution. The merits of that strategy do not directly concern us, but we note that the same skepticism of reason's authority, which fueled the philosophical attacks on psychoanalysis, find responses within contemporary psychoanalytic theory as well.

However, in balancing the relative roles of reason and emotion in psychoanalytic theory, Freud, in the end, based his theory on the power of analysis and the ultimate authority of reason, for "there is no appeal to a court above that of reason" (Freud 1927, p. 28). "Knowledge leading to freedom" goes to the heart of the

Enlightenment project, which in the Freudian scenario takes the form of "reason in service to the ego." Accordingly, successful psychoanalysis ostensibly strengthens the ego's self-determination, which, in this view, follows a modernist (Kantian) ideal of recognizing the authority of reason in its struggle against the forces of enslavement (Tauber 2010, pp. 141–45). And here we find the thrust of those who attacked Freud's project and the larger context in which it resides. In parallel assaults, Freud's philosophy of mind came under severe challenge, and in each case, the domineering ego became the target of radical revisions of psychoanalytic theory: Lacan would celebrate the affective over the rational (the unconscious other over the ego); and Adorno, regarding Freud trapped in bourgeois culture and psychoanalysis as a tool of social repression, would topple the ego's rational authority and the moral ideals invoked as its *telos*. Each argued that the Freudian portrait of the human psyche arose from a philosophical "mistake," albeit a fecund one. We begin with the dialectic of Enlightenment diagnosis proposed by Adorno and Max Horkheimer.

2   Prospects of Enlightenment

Human reason has the peculiar fate . . . that it is burdened with
questions which it cannot dismiss, since they are given to it as problems
by the nature of reason itself, but which it also cannot answer, since
they transcend every capacity of human reason.
                    —IMMANUEL KANT, *Critique of Pure Reason*

In modernity, the rational ego as a detached agent scrutinizes the
world. Because of its steadfast autonomy, which extends to itself
through self-critical appraisal, this conception of the ego grants
to humans the capacity to discern reality and to act morally.
Despite this Kantian self-critical stance, the august standing of
representational reason suffered immediate attack by numerous
romantics (Helfer 1996), and the genealogy of twentieth-century
assessments may be traced to these sources. Our account begins with
Horkheimer and Adorno, who, in the *Dialectic of Enlightenment*
(1993),[1] charged that the ego could not escape the spell of its own
representations. Indeed, given the various political, historical, and
cultural forces that configure "enlightened" reason and employ it
for larger social requirements, Kant's formulation, as regarded by
their critical optics, appeared as a vulnerable site for manipulation
by mass forces, which conspired against individual choice and
freedom. However, with their diagnosis they provided an antidote

grounded in a self-appraisal in which the ego itself is understood as a representation, and most saliently for our theme, the modality in which reason is cast determines both psychic and social "health."[2]

This compound position embeds both moral and epistemological imperatives: To recognize representations as such (as opposed to some final reality) provides an epistemological perspective that at a minimum cautions how one's point of view provides only a singular and limited perspective. Instead of an unattainable view from nowhere, subjects are restricted by the unavoidable limited mediation of their vantage point, which Nietzsche celebrated and positivists lamented. But further to their critique, the individuality posed in its perspectival epistemology also brings along with it a self-awareness of a moral perspective and the concomitant sense of autonomy from which the responsibility of self-initiated, self-governed actions commence. Thus, the individuality of the knowing agent places herself within a universe where consciousness grounds the potential redemption from all those forces that conspire to limit individual freedom. In short, representation serves both as the epistemological métier of mind and the moral vehicle for liberation through self-conscious appraisals.

Adorno and Horkheimer used the Freudian template to critique the oppressions of mass society and the capitalism shaping individual desire and limiting individual choice. By setting the ego's reason as the target of their scrutiny, the logic of self-assessment took a new turn and much fell before their analysis. The clarion call of the Frankfurt School proclaimed that lies (masked as truth), folly (masked as reason), and fantasy (veiled as insight) inevitably lead to the collapse of rational society with widespread moral and social failures (Sherratt 2002, p. 3). Their conclusion, derived from an assessment of Enlightenment reason, categorically asserted that versions of autonomous rationality had been proven inadequate to the task of orienting and ordering mass cultures. The failure could not be quelled by further enthroning reason, either through scientific methods or the objectifying orientation enfolded in scientism.

Reason, at least in its most rigidly austere "rational" pose, was unsuitable for understanding the social world, and more particularly, instrumental reason prevented any kind of reflective thought or formulation of goals; rather, it served only as a means to achieve the conquest of outer and inner nature (Horkheimer and Adorno 1993, pp. 32, 54–55).

The *Dialectic of Enlightenment* was composed as a social critique (as well as a philosophy of history) originating in Marxist political thought. It bypassed the clinical dimension of psychoanalysis and engaged Freud's own social theorizing by twisting the psychodynamics he described from what they concluded depicted an inevitable self-destructive process to one in which a liberation politics might emerge. Their critique focused on the ego as Freud conceived it and, more particularly, the exalted place reason held in the mediation with social reality. Here Freudianism received the first of a series of grievous blows, which began (in the case of Adorno and Horkheimer) to resurrect the Enlightenment but was soon followed by critics who sought to overturn the metaphysics of the ego altogether and dismantle modernism in the process. Before examining the resuscitative efforts of the Frankfurt School, let us briefly summarize Freud's depiction of the rational ego, which is best discerned in the psychoanalytic description of how individual psychodynamics are enacted in the social arena. And from there, the dynamics of the ego are most readily explored in revisionist thought.

I

Freud's cultural theory claims standing as an important resource of political theorizing in its own right (Tauber 2012a); however, for our purposes, the ego placed in its social setting offers crucial insight about the ego's Kantian character in psychoanalytic theory. A seamless line extends from Freud's theory of individual psychoanalysis to the extrapolations that would characterize society: the therapeutic promise to balance the pull of a destructive past that burdens the present and limits the future; the reason upon which analytic insight is based; the shared psychological conflicts of individuals and the social group; and combining each of these components, the articulation of social reform in which progress and perfection might be embraced. Directed over a broad spectrum, Freud's hopes for reform must be measured against his own deep appreciation that discord and aggression were inextricable from human congress. The balance between cautious hope and an abiding skepticism marks the to and fro of Freud's complex deliberations on the application of psychoanalytic theory to social dynamics, yet in the end his therapeutic orientation places him in the role of reformer. And that quiet optimism was based on his own investment in the ultimate autonomy and rationality of the ego conceived in the modernist modality.

Psychoanalytically informed social theory followed a basic template: Applying the psychic dynamics discerned in patients, Freud then extrapolated the individual drives to the selfsame forces that operate in the collective aggregate. In the simplest scenario, repression of the erotic caused psychic conflict, instinctual imbalance, misplaced objects of emotional investment, and ultimately self-destructive effects. The Freudian prescription, based on *analytic* insight, modeled social reform on psychoanalytic success: Identify the repression, and free it to allow a healthy expression of the erotic. On the basis of exposing the psychoanalytic dynamics, the lessons learned from that endeavor should then guide social reform, which would have a firm, rational (scientific) basis. On this view, the very structure of psychoanalytic thinking embeds a utopian revision of Western culture, inasmuch as individuals might marshal their destructive drives to a better balance with the erotic. Accordingly, a utopian society would flourish if organized around a proper balance of work and pleasure, as opposed to repressive control.[3]

Unraveling psychic mechanisms is one thing; to establish another relationship between individual and society is a different matter, or at least one drawing from a vast set of assumptions and characterizations of culture. How, in fact, better balance and healthy release would be achieved, and how such a massive reformation of obstructive social forces might be accomplished, Freud did not predict. In this sense, his utopianism, for better or worse, is "iconoclastic" (Jacoby 2007, p. xiv) and hardly prescriptive in any concrete terms. Yet a general prescription is offered and, more important perhaps, his moral message could hardly be clearer.[4]

Freud's assertions were bold. He promoted psychoanalysis as potentially redemptive for both individuals and the collective, based on investing the ego with an authority that would become the target of Adorno's critique:

> The ego learns that there is yet another way of securing satisfaction besides the *adaptation* to the external world. . . . It is also possible to intervene in the external world by *changing* it, and to establish in it intentionally the conditions which make satisfaction possible. This activity then becomes the ego's highest function. (Freud 1926a, p. 201)

Thus, from the psychoanalytic perspective, the therapeutic thrust of Freud's theory placed the rational ego at the center of his meliorism. And with that orientation, Freud becomes an apostle of humanism (Tauber 2010, pp. 219–26), albeit others view him with different moral valences (for instance, Rorty 1991a). After all, reason drives the therapeutic endeavor and thus serves as Freud's lodestone, for like Kant before him, he sought a path toward freedom guided by the promise of rational discourse and the liberalism at the heart of the Enlightenment.[5] However, reason alone did not suffice. We have already discussed the emotional transference component within the psychoanalytic scenario, but beyond the couch, Freud regarded effective sublimation as the means for achieving healthy social adjustment.

On Freud's view, sublimation offered the best strategy for countering destructive forces by providing a conduit for the liberation of "desire" with the least disruptive consequences. He thus advocated finding a balance between conformity with society's demands and libidinal release in the face of persistent repression. For him, the good life addressed each need by advocating productive work and meaningful love. For all the subsequent commentary and attempts to revise this prescriptive account, none of the post-Freudian accounts are more than elaborate variations on this dual-pronged approach (Tauber 2012a). Indeed, post-Freudian approaches have taken each of these paths, and some have converged on the promise of "the aesthetic," which combines both the sexual vitality of unconscious drives and the sublimation required for ego fulfillment to provide a "middle ground" within the original spirit of Freudianism. (This is the path Adorno will develop, as discussed later.)

Following either pathway, the discussion intertwines the character of reason and whether a modernist-conceived ego might achieve the psychological liberation Freud envisioned. After all, Freudian-based social theory must confront the problem of how the insight of reason might be coupled to some realignment of human desire to offer cogent responses to the challenges he declared so pressing. Nowhere is this theme better elaborated than in *Future of an Illusion* (1927), where Freud states the central challenge that organizes all of his social theory. Having begun his critique in 1898 and now continued with the same orientation thirty years later, he condemns society for its excessive controls, and more specifically, he bewails the psychic imprisonment imposed by excessive repression, not only for the toll on individual human happiness but for the inevitable failure of that repression. The resulting damage of excessive regimentation ranges from emotional disquiet, to neurosis, to social self-destructive behaviors, and most catastrophically, to war. In targeting illusions that aid those forces and imprison the psyche, Freud prescribes reason. The very promise of psychoanalysis builds upon the ability of the ego's rational analysis to reveal the secrets of unconscious drives and thereby better control them. And on this basis he offered a reserved hope in an ultimate belief in the promise of reason:

The voice of the intellect is a soft one, but it does not rest till it has gained a hearing. Finally, after a countless succession of rebuffs, it succeeds. This is one of the few points on which one may be optimistic about the future of mankind, but it is in itself a point of no small importance. And from it one can derive yet other hopes. (ibid., p. 53)

And from that position, Freud mused about a utopian psychology, whereby a liberation politics might emerge from psychoanalytic insight:

One would think that a re-ordering of human relations should be possible, which would remove the sources of dissatisfaction with civilization by renouncing coercion and suppression of the instincts, so that undisturbed by internal discord, men might devote themselves to the acquisition of wealth and its enjoyment. That would be the golden age. (ibid., p. 7)

This anthem to the Enlightenment carries philosophical baggage that Freud perhaps did not consider. And more, he left the ego, whom he himself robbed of self-confidence, exposed to scathing criticism from both Adorno and Lacanian-inspired postmodernists. The domineering reason of an oppressive ego characterizes each approach.

Reason's authority rested on a Kantian configuration in which the ego, utilizing its autonomy, observes the world objectively as the lawgiver to Nature (Kant 1998, p. 109) and self-reflects rationally for moral deliberation (Fogelin 2003, pp. 70, 93; Tauber 2010, pp. 125–27, 136). That epistemology and moral philosophy were so closely linked was no accident. Science for Kant claimed the most obvious success of rationality, and for Enlightenment thinkers, political systems and social programs were to model themselves on the rational ideal, that is, the notion that optimal human reasoning and due deliberation yield the best social result. Freud conceived reason closely akin to Kant's own formulation (Tauber 2010, pp. 131ff.), that is, reason "followed its own laws" to serve as the base of knowledge, objectivity, truth, and rationality. More broadly, reason functioned within a set of normative values oriented toward human perfection, freedom, and social progress. And when Freud wrote about the hope enlisted in reason's authority, his message clearly articulated these ideals. Indeed, the promise of psychoanalysis was based on the integrity of rational understanding (Freud 1927, p. 28), and from this position he mused about a utopian psychology whereby a liberation politics might emerge from psychoanalytic insight.

Ironically, who could be more suspicious of the ego's rationalizations, explanations, and interpretations than Freud himself? For after all, what is rational depends on a host of contextual elements, and as these are altered, choices based on certain options must correspondingly change. Further, particular choices become more or less important as decisions are made with varying intentions in mind. In this sense, reason is instrumental, a tool to achieve a goal, and goals may not be explicit, consistent, or conscious, and oftentimes, not rational (e.g., Cherniak 1986; Kahneman and Tversky 2000; Hanna 2006; Peter and Schmid 2007; Skorupski 2010). Freud opined that the ego was not master of its own house, where he might have added, the ego may not even know in which house she or he lives.

Obviously, Freud built a complex calculus of components composing his theory, of which the most prominent concerns reason's own standing. That vulnerability became the focus of later theorists who based their own critiques on Freud's initial presentation. Staunch modernist that he was, nevertheless, his psychology became the portal that opened onto postmodern conceptions of the subject.[6] Thus, while holding on to the deep irrationality of human motivation and action that was driven by unconscious desire, Freud still placed reason in an insular portion of the mind, where its autonomy might assess and direct. From this latter perspective, reason exercised by a free agent becomes a grammar by which the conscious person judges options and choices. Such human self-awareness fulfills an important cognitive (and moral) function of observing itself in a challenging environment.[7] Adorno and Horkheimer recognized reason's vulnerability and launched a critique that would reconfigure the ego in ways Freud hardly could imagine.

II

Adorno and Horkheimer argued against Freud's naïve Kantian-inspired notion of reason for a more historically self-conscious mode of thinking and thereby reiterated in a different voice the refrain of historicists of previous generations (Bambach 1995). For them, reason is grounded in neither the transcendental realm nor universal laws but in human history and, thus, historically developed and bounded by human nature. Reason stood not before its own self-critical tribunal but before "human nature." Their skepticism of analytic or logic-based forms of reason separated them from the positivists of all stripes, and in rejecting systematic or grand metaphysics, they joined almost all of their contemporaries in shunning post-Hegelian theorizing. Instead, they embraced, albeit with a most critical eye, a view of psychology based on psychoanalytic theory that placed human drives at the base of behavior and thereby underlying the character of the social aggregate. For them, a post-Freudian analysis offered the opportunity to revisit Kant's original premise that reason would examine itself and might do so in line with understanding the limits of human psychology.

The themes developed in *Dialectic of Enlightenment* build upon the central motif of the history of the West as a series of oscillations between *enlightenment*, defined in terms of seeking and enacting truth, against the countermovement toward regressive *myth* (a negative phase) characterized by the absence of aims; animistic in character (nonrational, delusional, and ignorant); and organized by social domination, fear, and barbarism. Placed in an antipodal position, Enlightenment can never be free of myth, and reason itself, as witnessed by modern societies, is characteristically contaminated with mythic features and thus co-opted for ventures antithetical to Enlightenment ideals.

Writing during the Second World War, Adorno and Hork-heimer offered this model of ceaseless oscillations between mythic and Enlightenment prototypes to illustrate the commingling of enlightened and barbaric features of the twentieth century. However, their treatise served not only to diagnose the social chaos of their era but also to offer a therapeutic alternative. Although they rejected Marx's teleological view of history, as well as a Hegelian developmental construct, their interpretations do point to Enlightenment ideals as a series of aims ("being enlightened"), which in turn are based upon the human capacity to reason and to attain maturity. Despite their circumspect view of reason, they sought the same goals espoused by earlier Enlightenment thinkers, to achieve freedom and security and, ultimately, to arrive at peace and social progress through the power of a revamped reason. While such goals are left in vague vapors, their work as a whole offers an ethical orientation.

Adorno and Horkheimer began at the same place as Freud, a diagnosis of sickness that masqueraded as health, where the ratio-nalization of the current "normal" life might be better realized by a different rationality. The claim could not be presented or justified scientifically but was posed as a moral inquiry. In this sense, they closely followed Freud's humanistic orientation (Tauber 2010, pp. 219–26), and more, on this reading, their project resists enlistment in later postmodernisms (Wellmer 1985; Whitebook 1988; Sherratt 2002, pp. 11–13).[8] In short, their "deconstruction" was meant to be constructive.

In the reconstruction of the historical dialectic of reason pre-sented by Adorno and Horkheimer, the vector of true social prog-ress repeatedly encounters diversions and blockades. If we utilize the psychoanalytic construction of the historical agent, mythic ascen-dancy inevitably results, because, despite the potential for rationally establishing social goals and strategies to achieve them, the subject is waylaid by an instrumental reason that poorly resists degeneration. So for Adorno and Horkheimer, the challenge is not only to understand this degenerative process but also to submit a remedy to the regressive dialectic they describe. To achieve that goal, they offer a Marxist-inspired critique of the progressive technical mastery of nature, the mechanization characterizing that relationship, and the subsequent deleterious social and economic effects. However, *Dialectic of Enlightenment* not only presents a philosophical analysis of the relationship of culture and nature (Vogel 1996, pp. 51–99), it also offers a major extension of Freud's own psychological constructions to create a new conceptual extrapolation of social theory. For them, the social and the psychological meet at the depths of psychic self-renunciation, where in the end, reason turns "against the thinking subject himself" (Horkheimer and Adorno 1993, p. 26). Overall, the work subordinates the Marxist concerns and utilizes a revamped Freudian formulation to advance a utopian prescription for the twentieth century.

Dialectic of Enlightenment begins with a basic Freudian premise: The id and ego are locked in opposition, exhibiting different drives and distinct objectives. However, unlike Freud's preoccupation with the arationality of the unconscious in pursuit of its own release of tension, and the requirement of ego control, Adorno and Horkheimer focused upon a repressive ego that diverts the id's object of desire and thus turns those forces toward inner objects. That introversion ultimately results in the ego's own dissolution. In short, they diagnosed a psychic disorder, a narcissistic disease, as the affliction of Western societies, where the collective reflects the dynamics of the individual. So, following Freud, thwarted desire becomes the focus of the cultural *dis-ease*. And as we will see reiterated with Deleuze, this same basic malady—the frustration of desire by repressive social strictures—is assigned the etiology of unhappy Western culture. However, the portrayal of conflicting drives—pleasure drives (based on id satisfaction) oppose the ego's interests (of self-preservation)—is too simple.

Although the Freudian conflict schema initially pitted pleasure and reality principles against each other, as psychoanalytic theory evolved, the demarcations separating ego and libido drives changed. In the metapsychological turn of the 1914–17 period, Freud (1914a) recognized narcissistic targets as active competitors for outer-directed cathexis, and in this inflection a process of introgression was recognized. The basic construct now includes a struggle between intrapsychic domains with opposing fulfillment requirements with a concomitant shift in the very objects of desire. In the loss of clear demarcations and divided strategies, id-drives might find their targets of desire not only in the exterior world but also within one's own body and psychic ego. The neurotic afflicted with such an inversion finds gratification only narcissistically, and reason suffers rationalization and regression in service to fulfilling those misplaced desires, which are inimical to the ego's original goals in navigating the external world.[9] Enlightenment ideals of work and love—the ostensible goals of healthy psychic life—thus suffer displacement, and psychic development falters.

These dynamics found their place in social theory as well: Just as the narcissistic neurotic is caught in a spiral of psychic degeneration, so too does the body politic suffer from unrequited resolution of this pathology. So, according to Adorno and Horkheimer, whereas id happiness is object directed (and pleasure oriented), the ego uses knowledge and reason to control, dominate, and discriminate. When that control extends to the id-drives, they are incapacitated and thereby prevented from recovering healthy objects of pleasure. And with the redirection of the id-drives to interior psychic objects, psychic balance is disrupted, which results in the ultimate dissolution of an effective ego that might have pursued the Enlightenment project. The dialectic of Enlightenment, then, is a self-defeating process whereby the reason that serves Enlightenment ideals squanders its prospects because of misplaced goals and uncontrolled domination of pleasure-seeking objects of desire. The question posed then is how that ego function might be transfigured or properly directed to fulfill its own original agenda.

Dialectic of Enlightenment describes four stages of the Enlightenment's regressive, self-destructive psychic cascade by citing Odysseus as the prototypical Enlightenment figure, a hero who seeks to attain security and steer his ship safely home (Sherratt 2002). In the first stage, *impoverishment*, Odysseus is depicted as always restraining himself, for self-control is key. However, the cost of impoverished joy leads to the poverty characterizing this initial insult to psychic health and reason's effective practice. The episode of the Sirens' song illustrates how pleasure (aesthetic experience) must be compromised, for Odysseus knows the dangers of losing himself in ecstasy. The subordination of beauty and loss of sensual pleasure lead to restricted imagination and appreciation of beauty and, ultimately, meaning (Horkheimer and Adorno 1993, pp. 34, 59). Subjectivity thus suffers a regression as id-instincts recede from reality because pleasure finds no ready object and is stymied. Note that the id's instincts, while restrained, are not dampened or controlled, only diverted.

This renunciation then leads to the second stage, *fantasy*. Further regression results from the id turning away from the world to illusion, where wishes and projections replace external objects of desire. The id then must seek a more immediate object, which then leads to narcissistic desire. As Freud observed, narcissism fails to discriminate the inner and the outer worlds, and the self is thus split. The episode of Odysseus and the Lotus Eaters illustrates the illusion of happiness disconnected from reality (Horkheimer and Adorno 1993, pp. 62–63). (In modern society, the Lotus Eaters are the culture industry, which induces a state of apathy and passiveness.) This primitive state offers no substantive meaning, for the lotus cannot provide constructive industry. Thus, illusion replaces reality as a source of both pleasure and meaning. In the dialectic of Enlightenment, a false utopia has appeared and the movement to mythic life inexorably continues.

In the third stage of regression, *totalization*, the id-instincts become even more restricted by the ego and cannot generate id-objects directly; imagination atrophies, and the ego-objects (technical and material) become the id's objects as well. The original sources of imagination and vitality are lost, as the ego has "totalized" the experience of reality, that is, all knowledge has been reduced to the instrumental (Horkheimer and Adorno 1993, p. 85), both totalitarian and mythological (p. 24). Odysseus engaged in heroic ordeals personifies the world as dangerous, which imposes limits on the pursuits of pleasure. Thus, reality becomes only a source of fear ("enlightenment is mythic fear turned radical" [ibid., p. 16]), and the self is threatened by what is different and consequently postures itself to dominate or destroy and thereby eliminate all heterogeneity. In short, fear leads to barbarism.

In this scenario, the self *becomes* a self as it exerts control over the world, which in turn requires knowledge. The operative key is the need to control. Myth and science originate in human fear, the expression of which becomes explanation (ibid., p. 15); identifying the object in human terms makes the unknown like himself, or at least linked/mediated in human terms. But this distorts the object (and reality more broadly) and thus eliminates all heterogeneous being. Because separation causes fear/anxiety, the subject seeks to overcome this difference through a strategy of domination.[10] However, control is never complete, and the process becomes a cascade of increasing efforts to tighten the grip over that which cannot be restrained and manipulated. The system consequently regresses to rigidity, through the ego's ultimately regressive drive for organization and comprehensiveness. In short, the ego ossifies into a dysfunctional "bureaucracy" (Sherratt 2002, pp. 115ff.).

In classic psychoanalytic theory, ego formation requires a boundary about itself and the differentiation of object relations to discriminate the inner and the outer. If narcissism does not mature, the self is deprived of the world for pleasure and the loss of the boundary. For knowledge acquisition as well, a strong sense of self is critical for reason to effectively be directed outward to yield discriminatory knowledge and control (the prototype of Odysseus steering his ship). Note that in an enlightened state, the subject, through the id, experiences objects as pleasurable and substantively meaningful, and instrumental objects and knowledge thereby become psychologically significant. Thus, in health, a balance has been achieved between ego- and id-instincts, where a coordination of interests occurs: The subject allows the id to identify and satisfy itself through the products of the ego, but in the regressive condition just described, freedom has been eclipsed, because the only relationship with reality is through the ego and the restraints it imposes (i.e., instrumental control serving domination). With the narcissistic turn, the ego itself becomes an object of its own control, and thus the subject suffers restricted freedom as it increasingly becomes enslaved to a narrow instrumental pursuit.

In the final (postmodern) *fragmentation* stage, the only remaining object is the ego itself. Fantasy objects have been radically restricted, and pleasure can only turn inward to find its objects of desire. The id, now totally self-contained, no longer has external objects of pleasure and dries up as a reservoir of imaginative vitality (Horkheimer and Adorno 1993, p. 36). Consequently, in this completed narcissistic shift, the ego turns from external reality as a source of pleasure to itself, an objectless condition (Freud 1914b). This immature state leads to a decline of the id-instincts (contra Freud, where they are only repressed), and the ego-instincts lack a capacity for the experience of pleasure and substantive meaning. Instead of taking pleasure in the external world, the ego (through the preservation instincts) can only be defensive and domineering. And when the only object is the ego itself, the ego becomes a target of fear and attack. The self then suffers from an "auto-immune" disorder as identity becomes fragmented.[11]

In this last stage, the ego itself becomes a fiction, an imagined lie, and its logic, which drives instrumental reason, collapses—and with that fall, control and, ultimately, survival ironically fail. Texts,

systems, theories, concepts are likewise deconstructed into fragments and linear structure of thought, and reason is undermined
or dismantled altogether. Knowledge then has no substantive reality, certainly no foundations or logical imperative. In the end, the
dialectic of Enlightenment is a self-destructive degeneration back
to myth. Adorno and Horkheimer did not regard the dialectic as
inevitable, but by exhibiting the psychic dynamics and showing the
consequences of the ego's hegemony, they offered an explanation
of Enlightenment's seemingly inevitable eclipse, a process "decided
from the start" (1993, p. 24). Consequently, to reverse the obdu-
rate logic they described would require a radical therapy, one that
would rehabilitate the ego.

III

For Adorno, "identity thinking" (a term coined to describe the
process of categorical thought in modern society) comprised the key
epistemological culprit. In this view everything becomes an example of an abstracted representation, a "mathematization," in which
nothing individual in its actual specific uniqueness is allowed to
exist.[12] Accordingly, identity thinking systematically *misrepresents*
reality by subsuming specific phenomena under general abstractions and thus fails to attend to the specificity of any given phenomenal entity; everything becomes a mere exemplar (Fagan 2005).
"[W]hat began as a critique of myth and religion continues with the
elimination of value and secondary qualities until only the mind's
own forms (method, logic, and mathematics) remain. These identi-
tarian forms are the Enlightenment's own mythic spell on nature"
(J. Bernstein 1997, p. 206). Obscuring or omitting qualities or
properties of any given object necessarily misrepresents its object,
or "what can be penetrated by science is not being" (Horkheimer
and Adorno 1993, p. 26). Reality is thereby reduced to expressions
only within positivist products of thought (representations), turning "thought into a thing, an instrument" (ibid., p. 25) and thereby

excluding meaning and subjectivity. Simply, "subjectivity has given way to logic" (ibid., p. 30). Instrumental reason is not "rational" in human terms, that is, meaningful. In this wider context, to be rational is to conform to a theory of meaning or understanding, and for Adorno, *significance* derives from the aesthetic (discussed in Chapter 3).

Adorno developed an alternative logic to the identity thinking by which he characterized Enlightenment thought. This became nothing less than a full assault on representationalism. His so-called negative dialectic described a process of dialectics without identity, an alternative non-identity thinking. For Adorno, the concept fails to fit the object, which means that the object/concept cannot be fully captured by any re-presentation. Indeed, the represented composes only part of the original, and therefore its representation is fractured, distorted, or fantasized. The remaining unknown portion of the object, the missing aspects, then corresponds to that which is beyond the concept and thus unidentified (i.e., the non-identity).[13] This hidden residue, the so-called "excessive space," became the target of Adorno's epistemology.

The excessive space is the site of the *not-yet-represented*, which offers the cognitive space for creating modified or new concepts. Basically, *excess* addresses the limits of a representational conception of mind and the consequences of subject-object predicate thinking to offer a means for creativity and freedom of thought. Adorno's logic proceeds as follows: A representation is the product of a signifier. Adorno rejected this epistemological structure. He conceived that the mental product, which results from carving objects (or representations of those objects) out of mere being, implicitly and unavoidably includes an "excessive" component. In any experience, the mind selects, sorts, and orders objects from an undifferentiated state of being. Indeed, objects become objects only as differentiation occurs, and mere being must be transformed into objects; this reduction, as it were, occurs by a selective negation, one that has formal properties. Specifically, negation refers to the process by which subtraction occurs to transform the mere state of being (through the imposition of order, identity, difference, relation, etc.) to fashion a human-perceived object (concept), something with distinguishing characteristics.

Negation, in which minimal difference is discerned, precipitates the object from the plenum of being, and a residual remains left behind. In the process, where the "thing-to-become-objectified" emerges, an undifferentiated space is left behind. This inevitable remainder is the excessive portion of the set. So, as a result of the formal negation a set emerges, which consists of the object and the excessive residua, or what Rothenberg calls the "empty set" (2010, p. 36).[14] (The empty set has no positive properties, and in a sense it cuts into the state of being by adding its own emptiness, which then unglues and separates objects from the undifferentiated plenum.) This additional capacity (or an undisclosed appendage) serves as a reservoir for further development of the concept. Asserting that representations can never be closed or complete allows for emendation, addition, and interpretation of concepts. Because such mental objects are only part of a larger set, the unused capacity (the so-called empty set or remainder) may then feed the development of the represented concept. As the process propagates, the identified object changes, for the excess from which such modification might occur serves as the ambiguous and imaginative component for the subject to frame and signify the world with a dynamic lacking from the simpler, and distorting, "mirror of nature" identity (correspondence) model.

Non-identity thinking opens the system, in acknowledgment that it cannot be organized into a coherent whole. This move prevents closure (because in principle such thinking is noncomprehensive) and staves off domination/control/distortion (projection) of the object. The negative dialectic "confirmed neither concept nor reality in itself. Instead, he [Adorno] posited each in critical reference to the other. Put another way, each was affirmed only in its non-identity to the other" (Sherratt 2002, p. 63). Thus, Adorno sought to counter the "mathematization" of thought, which like a machine can only reproduce itself, and consequently, in its adjudication and dominance of thought, such identity thinking limits knowledge and ultimately stultifies experience.[15]

In sum, non-identity thinking, in the terms of the dialectic of enlightenment, employs an interactive logic to demythologize and pursue open criticism through a replacement of the representational modality of thought. This philosophical construction, however, constituted only the first phase of Adorno's program, because non-identity thinking continues the process of thought in a second-order dialectical process with identity thinking. While he believed that a more comprehensive intelligence in the representation (instrumental) realm would emerge with such a dialectic, this expansion would hardly end the matter: Non-identity thinking remains in the instrumental sphere, and because such rationality is derived from the same ego-instincts as identity thinking, it thus remains wrapped into the same instinctual imbalance that causes regression of the Enlightenment in the first place. His philosophical ambitions required a radical reformulation of the ego.

3   Adorno: Reconceiving the Ego

At this point, psychoanalysis has complied with the demands of the
ego (and its will to power) seeming without reflection. . . . But it cannot
be a given that psychological categories should offer the best means
for locating and conceptualizing the unconscious. In fact, this very
inclination constitutes a danger in that it threatens psychoanalysis with
a dead-lock. For ultimately, when one has preordained the unconscious
to be a representative of the categories familiar to consciousness, it will
be very difficult to discover and investigate anything other than the
already well-known and reasonable world of the ego.

—JURGEN REEDER, *Reflecting Psychoanalysis*

The Adorno-Horkheimer dialectic identifies the self's emergence
as a *self* through its control of its world, or better, the *need* to
control the world. The degeneracy described in the previous chapter
depicts a distorted and ultimately self-destructive process, where
the subject's instincts withdraw from external reality (due to ego
deflection) as narcissism displaces exterior objects of desire. With
this weakening sense of the self, the boundary discriminating
internal and external fades and projection ensues. Instrumental
systems are then projected onto the external world and actually
supplant it (Horkheimer and Adorno 1993, pp. 24–25). On this

view, the distortions arising from the ego's hegemonic need to control eventually displace real objects with the projection of ego-objects. In other words, the self mistakenly identifies objects derived from the ego for reality, which of course replaces the object of outer-directed intention and ultimately the representation of the world. In some sense, the subject-object split dissolves, not in the romantic aspiration of personalizing knowledge (Tauber 2001) but rather as a distortion, inasmuch as the object exists solely as the result of its identification and conceptual assignment by the ego. Furthermore, returning to our earlier discussion, the signs employed for the subjugation become the object, not its representation (Sherratt 2002, pp. 105–25), and thus the object cannot be captured. Identification fails because of the rigidity and closed character of the system itself, leaving the knowing subject trapped within his own system, only to project his own objects; thus, fantasy displaces reality.[1] Kant's categories of understanding have been taken to an extreme limit where the effectiveness of constructing reality has been nullified. In effect, *Dialectic of Enlightenment* pronounced the death of the Enlightenment itself. How would the Phoenix rise from its ashes? Might a prescription for the ailing ego be made?

I

Adorno attacked the very foundations of agency bestowed by the Enlightenment: the belief that human knowledge can fully capture reality and that rational understanding can be determinant. Accordingly, this fundamental epistemological error impoverishes rationality and finally ends in a collapse, which dismantles the notion of ego autonomy upon which the entire edifice rests. One challenge of Adorno's thesis then becomes, How might such an agent be reformulated?

Because a representational model of the mind cannot capture the "logic" of the null space, other kinds of knowing are required. Adorno's aesthetic prescription, which has been dubbed "the redemption of illusion" (Zuidervaart 1991), was just such an attempt. Illusion not only refers to the illusion of the aesthetic as opposed to the realness of the objectified object (i.e., illusory because of the subjective, evasive character of the depiction relative to an objective epistemology) but also is ironically ascribed to representations themselves for the illusory conceit that they capture reality realistically or truthfully. In other words, mental representation's putative correspondence to reality suffices to claim their *truth*. On this latter view, Adorno's approach is nothing less than a frontal attack on the Freudian representational model of the mind, and in the course of that development, the understanding of selfhood also shifts alignment.

The irredeemable subject-object divide characterizing modernist epistemology separates the self from the world. The division, in its positive modality, provides for freedom, inasmuch as "the conditions of representation reside in the domain of knowledge rather than the world itself—it is possible for the subject to imagine what is not given" (Colebrook 2005, p. 16). So the result of this separation opens subjectivity and its accompanying freedom to go beyond the given, or in another formulation, the subject enjoys an "excess." The basis for this construction directly tracks back to Adorno's conception of non-identity thinking, where the concept cannot fully capture its object, leaving an excess or remainder, that is, "objects do not go into their concepts without leaving a remainder" (Adorno 1973b, p. 5). Because the concept fails to fit the object, its representation is necessarily partial and even distorted.

Humans navigate the world, not because knowers see the cosmos as it *is* in any first-order way but because they construct the universe in which they *live* by employing their cognitive capacity to parse, relate, and discern the world's contents. This process requires ascension to higher cognitive functions that knit together sense perception and the processing of that information. The information that lies in the world is latent and does not exist as information until the mind makes it such. In other words, the indeterminacy of how that world is understood depends on some process (e.g., conversion, distillation, refraction, representation) of perception (already a second-order presentation dependent on cognitive faculties, requiring integration of both analytic and emotional faculties [Ben-Ze'ev 2000]) and a tertiary functional capacity that arises from the excessivity of the cognitive process itself. The information, the world as it were, is all there but in a latent form, waiting to be seen and organized by the mind according to its own dictates. For instance, as one looks at a painting, different perceptions are appreciated; as one watches an accident, different reports emerge; walking into a room, different observers will mark different elements of interest. This basic constructivist phenomenological precept has been extended from the differing perceptions of individuals to contrasting cognitive strategies practiced by different cultural groups.[2] Reality thus becomes a synthesis between mind and nature, and mind, in the context of this discussion, draws upon its excessive capacity to make the imaginative refractions of the world from which new language, representations, and models are drawn. In short, no prescribed reality exists as such, but rather it is constructed by active human knowing, where the mind's excess becomes the creative resource for those constructions.

And agency (connoting moral choices and social behaviors), to capture the metaphysical freedom Kant originally posited, is likewise marked by the excessivity of empty-set or null-space potentials from which higher orders of imagination and judgment draw resources for their own functions. This epistemological schema may be extended to reformulate the subject, where the self is not so much decentered or empty as reconfigured into two components: (1) the known sense of *the I* or *me*, a conscious or possessive function, and (2) the excessive space or potential (function) (previously referred to as the unconscious) from which mental revisions are made.[3] *Excess* in this context refers to how the representational structure of knowledge is expanded and leads to a self-determining subject, whose own boundaries are left open to possibilities—epistemological and moral. From this perspective, the hermeneutics of the interpersonal encounter and self-reflective inner dialogue allow for a nebulous cloud of meanings for both the subject and her other. "No object simply means what it is; every object becomes a site of excessive meaning" (Rothenberg 2010, p. 111), and correspondingly, one cannot control the meaning of oneself for another, and for that matter, one's own self-meaning—representation of self to self—because in each orientation irreducible excessivity precludes closure of signification.[4]

One might consider that psychoanalysis implicitly employs such a formulation, for excessivity holds potential or undeclared meanings for interactions with others, as well as self-analysis of one's own actions and feelings. Simply, selves cannot define themselves in any final sense, for this "Möbius subject" finds herself both inside and outside her own agency.[5] Tracing the inside surface leads to the outside surface, so from an individual point of view, an apparently two-sided figure has only one surface, and from this geometry a metaphorical description emerges:

> One can define each point on the band as here or there, but each point is *excessive* with respect to the determination of its "sidedness." . . . This excess alters the apparently rigid boundary between sides (or between cause and effect): nondeterminate sidedness means that causes are not quarantined from their effects because the excess brings them into congruity. At the same time, these points and their relations have a certain specificity; they do not merge into one another. (Rothenberg 2010, p. 31)

In the psychoanalytic context, "excess" captures the indeterminacy of cause and the elusiveness of identity in the unconscious domain.

Excessivity refers to the *indeterminate* potential of each subject in terms of accounting for the causative forces—both internal and external—that shape and determine identity and action.[6] After all, psychic dynamic causation, with all of its disputed and problematic epistemological standing, requires a conception that breaks the strictures of mechanical explanations to become a basic template in which all knowledge might be schematized. So beyond the excess of options that arise from self-conceiving personal identity through imaginative creativity, moral opportunity, and judgment, some degree of indeterminacy is introduced, which highlights the limits of knowledge (analytic knowledge, more specifically). With this formulation, the subject cannot be confined to any definitional procedure or prescribed causative channels as understood from either the perspective of inner psychodynamic factors or outer social dynamics.

In terms of the previous discussion, the undeclared *un-represented* is that vacant space in which identity and action expand, albeit still subject to external deterministic factors and internal configurations, but overdetermined to an extent that bursts linear lines of causation (and understanding). With this conception, opportunities beckon well beyond the universe of possible representations, which, by their very nature, can confer only narrowly depicted coordinates of identity and choice. Thus, the target of this formulation is representation itself. And now we appreciate the theoretical composite offered by Adorno's conception of non-identity thinking, where in its latest iteration, extimate causation both configures subjects as structured by the social yet allows for degrees of personal autonomy to redirect (or even break) the causal effects of the personal psychological past and intrusive social present. The very excessivity that so characterizes the subject provides a place in which creative meanings are devised and actions exercised.

Through "formal negation," the world emerges in the process of signifying both self and other. And if we apply this conception to psychoanalysis, Freudianism becomes a particular method of exploring that excessive space from which meanings may be derived. However, the questions remain, How are such meanings created (i.e., by what methods), and what is the status of such truth claims? A conceptual framework has been provided by excessivity, but the dynamics of its functions have not been advanced, and this lacuna leaves the Freudian project with the same charges leveled by its many critics essentially unanswered. Perhaps another approach is warranted, one that fundamentally changes the entire philosophical structure of the subject. To achieve such a reconfiguration, we must reconsider, if not radically reformulate, the notion of agency itself. Adorno offered an option.

II

Adorno's effort to rescue the Enlightenment sought not to eliminate myth but rather to place myth and reason in better balance with each other. With that effort he hoped to formulate an invigorated, more complete mode of thinking, one that would go beyond the limits of dialectics in the usual sense. Because the separation of the ego- and id-instincts results in regression, a strategy to rectify this state required appropriately placing the id-instincts within the psychic economy. More particularly, inasmuch as part of reason's foundations resides in the id-instincts, he sought to establish their cognitive standing. To complete his reconstruction, Adorno complemented the negative critique with a positive dialectic, a noninstrumental kind of knowledge acquisition, which he placed in the aesthetic realm, and in that move, he turned from epistemology to aesthetics (Adorno 1973b, 1997, 2007; Buck-Morss 1977; Zuidervaart 1991). This strategy of broadening subjectivity would empower the id-instincts with a cognitive role and thereby place the ego and the id in a positive dialectical relationship. If successful, enlightenment would then incorporate an intensified subjectivity (Horkheimer and Adorno 1993, p. 18).

For Adorno, the "aesthetic"—typically associated with the Dionysian—is not destructive or irrational but rather orients and leads to the ego's employment with the world and thus strengthens the ability of the self to engage the other (the world/reality). The basic move shifts the ego's defensive, introverted narcissism to outward participation by revising the modality of thinking to an aesthetic-based encounter with the object, one mediated through different kinds of emotive cognition. On Adorno's view, instead of representation, manipulation, control, and dominance, the aesthetic builds on enchantment, or a balanced "receptivity" with the object. The term "aura," introduced by Walter Benjamin and adapted by Adorno for his own program, evokes this notion of absorption to establish a different kind of identification, a non-identity form of thinking or experience outside the instrumental sphere.[7] Here, Adorno finds his antidote to identity thinking and the misrepresentation associated with it. For him aesthetic refers

> not in the first place to art, but, as the Greek *aistesis* would suggest, to the whole region of human perception and sensation, in contrast to the more rarefied domain of conceptual thought. The distinction which the term "aesthetic" initially enforces . . . is not one between "art" and "life," but between material and the immaterial; between things and thoughts, sensations and ideas, that which is bound up with our creaturely life as opposed to that which conducts some shadowy existence in the recesses of the mind. . . . That territory is nothing less than the whole of our sensate life together—the business of affections and aversions. . . . It is thus the first stirrings of a primitive materialism—of the body's long inarticulate rebellion against the tyranny of the theoretical. (Eagleton 1990, p. 13)

On this reading, myth expresses the aesthetic in ways that leaves analytics waving her arms in disarray.

As discussed, *Dialectic of Enlightenment* uses the myth of Odysseus, which, not ironically, illustrates the theme of instrumental reason's inadequacy. Specifically, the episode of Odysseus and the Sirens shows how the conflict and ultimate impasse between the allure and need for "the song" is countered and repressed by the fear of the loss of control. Odysseus, aware of his entrapment in desire ("Men have always had to choose between the subjection to nature or the subjection of nature to the Self" [Horkheimer and Adorno 1993, p. 32), sees only two routes of escape: His men plug their ears with wax and row on, oblivious to the temptations of

the Sirens' song, while he, tied to the mast, hears without consequence: "Temptation is neutralized and becomes a mere object of
contemplation—becomes art" (ibid., p. 34). Art is the tamed distil-
late of the pleasure denied by the need for control, which remains
grounded in the danger of the ego's precarious state in a world
mediated by limited reason—a rationality that restricts experience
and forfeits the fulfillment of desire:

> The strain of holding the I together adheres to the I in all stages;
> and the temptation to lose it has always been there with the blind
> determination to maintain it. . . . The dread of losing the self and of
> abrogating together with the self and the barrier between oneself and
> other life, the fear of death and destruction, is intimately associated
> with the promise of happiness which threatened civilization in
> every moment. Its road was that of obedience and labor, over which
> fulfillment shines forth perpetually—but only as illusive appearance,
> as devitalized beauty. (ibid., p. 33)

If we put aside the regressive movement of taming art, the basic
scenario of the aesthetic, which allows for a mediation with the
object that is neither domineering nor distorting, offers the
noninstrumental mode of thinking Adorno would employ to
emancipate humans from their self-destructive psychologies.

The unity of absorption (with the external object) through aesthetic experience putatively negates the unity of (inward-directed)
narcissism. So while appearing as a threat to the self, absorption
with the exterior pleasurable object (through aesthetic experience
and knowledge acquisition) actually negates the loss of the self that
occurs in the narcissistic spiral. Accordingly, proper integration of
subject and object is a "to and fro" of integration and separation.
Subjectivity is thereby strengthened (contra Freud, who saw unity as
regressive), albeit the relationship of subjectivity and expression is a
complex one: "[I]t is a gross simplification to equate expression and
subjectivity. What is subjectively expressed does not need to resem-
ble the expressing subject. In many instances what is expressed
will be precisely what the expressing subject is not; subjectively, all

expression is mediated by longing" (Adorno 1997, p. 276). Expression "comes from the space or difference between things as they are and how they might be" (Ryle and Soper 2002, p. 87), and in articulating that desire, imagination is exercised. Whether successful or not, it is the process itself that confers a liberation. And with that move, Adorno hoped to rescue the ego.[8]

The aesthetic element in Adorno's thought must be regarded in concert with the general historical approach he adopted, as opposed to a biological, ontological, or moral one. In this sense, he situated human being as the product of ongoing historical forces, and these must be turned, if not tamed, to allow for human flourishing. On this reading, he follows Nietzsche, whose *Übermensch* stands for desublimated art that has been returned to life. No longer passive, the aesthetic is creative in its receptive mode of experience (Früchtl 2008, pp. 152–53). To achieve this heightened subjectivity, Adorno turned to expanded thinking that must include the emotive: "The assumption that thought profits from decay of the emotions, or even that it remains unaffected, is itself an expression of the process of stupification" (2005, #79, p. 122). In that move, Adorno wished to capture what often is reduced to emotion, and thus irrational. The ironic failure of Freud to offer a theory of the affects demands a response, and in the aesthetic, Adorno offered a candidate, one in line with Nietzsche's own philosophy of the *Übermensch*.[9] In the end, the discussion must address the ego, whose metaphysical underpinnings structure the entire project.

III

Adorno's criticism of Freud's version of reason displaces knowledge acquisition as exclusive to ego function (and control) and expands it to include the id and thereby make a fuller accounting of reason itself in the instincts—ego and id *combined*. Here he follows Nietzsche. While celebrating the sensuous, Nietzsche recognized that only through the "bond of brotherhood" between Apollo and Dionysus might the supreme goal of all art be obtained (1999, p. 104). In fact, for Nietzsche the issue is not the sensuous per se but rather *art*, which is a product of reason and order, on the one hand, and the expression of the emotions and the sensuous, on the other hand. Nietzsche's exalted view of art, the "saving 'sorceress' with the power to heal" (ibid., p. 40), placed artistic creation and participation at the center of his program promoting a vital and healthy life: "Art is the highest task and the true metaphysical activity of this life" (p. 14). Accordingly, art not only affirms life but also becomes "the unvarnished expression of truth" (ibid., p. 41) and thus bestows meaning, "for only as an *aesthetic phenomenon* is existence and the world eternally *justified*" (p. 33). Nietzsche would accuse a hegemonic rationality as sapping the vitality of Greek tragedy, and art more generally. He described Socrates as "an instrument of Greek disintegration, as a typical decadent," who destroyed tragic vitality by asserting "'Rationality' *against* instinct, 'Rationality' at any price as a dangerous force that undermines life" (1967, p. 271). Obviously, Nietzsche's philosophy radically opposes the centrality of rationality in Freud's own theoretical configurations (Tauber 2010, pp. 161ff.), and we see reiteration of this basic orientation in Adorno's own expositions and again with the Anti-Oedipus program pronounced by Deleuze and Guattari (discussed in Chapter 6).

Another way of understanding the superstructure of Adorno's project is to place it within a larger philosophical discourse, which for our purposes follows the Kantian consideration of the self in a threefold manner,

> as a relation between the dimensions of self-knowledge, of self-determination . . . and self-experience. But the dimension of self-determination is fractured by an inner conflict, namely, that between autonomy and authenticity, between (deontological) morality and (eudaemonist) ethics, between self-determination in a strict sense and self-realization in general. "Enlightenment" in the properly Kantian sense is directed essentially toward the first alternative in each case,

toward autonomy and morality, while the Romantic approach is primarily concerned with the second, with self-realization, self-creation, and self-expression of concrete individuality. (Früchtl 2008, p. 140)

On this framework, Adorno's thesis is placed most readily within the romantic modality, for the realization of the self in experience for maximizing self-determination, self-knowledge, and ultimately self-fulfillment best orients his claims for the aesthetic alternative he presented. After all, he "emphasizes the independent character of thought and one's own 'experience' above all else" (ibid., p. 148). Note that Adorno does not advocate sublimation, which he regards as a limit imposed by bourgeois controls: "[A]rtists do not sublimate. That they neither satisfy nor repress their desires, but transform them into socially desirable achievements . . . is a psycho-analytical illusion" (Adorno 2005, #136, pp. 212–13), which, of course, is only the product of the "vacuous sublimity of bourgeois consciousness" (Adorno 1973b, p. 205).[10] Freud's proposal of sublimation as a means to harness the erotic forces of the psyche is, for Adorno, simply a misplaced control arising from Freud's own bourgeois entrapment.[11]

Adorno's criticism points to a deep inconsistency in psychoanalytic theory arising from a dual view of the instincts, which codifies an oscillation between lamenting the renunciation of the drives as repressive and praising their repression as sublimation and thus beneficial for culture. This "dual hostility towards mind and pleasure" results from "Freud's unenlightened enlightenment" that "plays into the hands of bourgeois disillusion. As a late opponent of hypocrisy, he stands ambivalently between desire for the open emancipation of the oppressed, and apology for open oppression. Reason is for him a mere superstructure," and thus he discards the only purpose in which the means of reason "could prove . . . [itself] reasonable: pleasure" (Adorno 2005, #37, pp. 60–61). Whereas Freud regarded id-instincts as primitive, Adorno championed them as constitutive to enlightenment—not as a complement to instrumental reason but rather in a positive dialectical relationship, which would establish an expanded intelligence (Sherratt 2002, pp. 209ff.). What would become a theme reiterated again and again in post-Freudian theorizing, psychoanalysis in its original formulation appears as an arm of social repression and control.[12] So Adorno's argument is not over the particularities of psychoanalysis, but rather his critique goes to the very heart of Freud's depiction of the psyche, one whose own inner conflict gives rise to social aggression. For Adorno, at best, psychoanalysis only describes Western psychodynamics and in that description offers a rationale for acceptance of a status quo, one that Adorno utterly rejects.[13]

IV

Of our philosophical protagonists, Adorno most directly confronted psychoanalysis on its own terms. His evaluation of Freudianism led to alternative interpretations that support a skeptical assessment of the very basis of psychoanalysis: the reliance on reason as the therapeutic tool of failed repression. Instead, Adorno places the onus of failure on the ego's mode of reason as the psychic culprit, and from that basic move, all else falls into place for his own philosophical agenda. By taking Freud's basic psychological depiction and reconfiguring key elements to draw another scenario, Adorno led a coup to dethrone the ego's modernist standing.

While Heidegger posed his task in reconfiguring metaphysics, Adorno followed Freud (albeit without the clinical apparatus) by writing a social theory in terms of a diseased ego. He did not try to discharge the ego altogether, as Heidegger, Lacan, and later postmodernists attempted, but rather sought to rebalance a psychic disequilibrium. Adorno saw contemporary sickness consisting in a supposed normality, which not only inhibits freedom within the narrow confines of thwarted sensual pleasure but also stymies the potential to live a fuller libidinous life in cultural industry. In this sense, Adorno extended Freud's moral agenda (Tauber 2010, pp. 212ff.). Couched in positivist terms, conceited with empirical data, adjudicated by strict interpretive criteria, psychoanalysis remains grounded in a humanistic vision for mankind. Adorno joined Freud's ethical project, and despite their divergent interests and methods, they converged on ways of thinking about the nature of the human subject and the relationships that characterize social being (Tauber 2012a). Given the current penchant for defining human nature scientifically (e.g., E. Wilson 1999, 2004; Pinker 2003; Buller 2006), this "enlightened" way of approaching this complex issue seems strikingly out of step with the prevailing zeitgeist.

Adorno's approach employed aesthetics as the antidote by which he hoped to purge the toxicity of instrumental reason. Based on the psychic architecture described in the *Dialectic of Enlightenment* and the alternative required to counter identity thinking, he argued for liberating the id-instincts by directing them through a conduit to the aesthetic. He thereby proposed that a different kind of knowledge be acquired and experienced. So whether knowledge is placed within a primitive Dionysian ecstasy or a complex atonal symphony, Adorno draws a distinction between this kind of cognitive mediation and that of instrumental reason. And by introducing the aesthetic, the exclusive ego-defined role of reason has been opened to other cognitive modalities. Holding fast to his own philosophical system, he sought to meld the aesthetic with non-identity thinking, both to offer a specified redemptive strategy to the dominance of identity thinking and to add a dimension of human fulfillment stifled by instrumental reason. Accordingly, the aesthetic expands reason and transforms thinking to fulfill a larger humanism. By deploying the full id-instincts upon reality to putatively complement and enhance the subject's engagement with the world, Adorno hoped to counter the impoverishment resulting from the exclusive engagement of the ego.[14] Furthermore, the id-instincts are thereby strengthened because they find pleasure in the exterior object and require no inner substitute. Thwarting introgression (or illusory projection), the ego and id would then converge on objects in the world and subjectivity, thereby enriched. And as a consequence, maturity is defined as the balance between the id- and ego-instincts, or in other terms, the true reality principle reflects a healthy equilibrium between the pursuits of id-directed pleasure and the restraints imposed by the ego's awareness of danger. If we enable a fuller engagement with reality (i.e., the world no longer seen only as dangerous), a revised dialectic emerges, one in which the interplay of id- and ego-instincts becomes the dialectic between an unbounded and bounded self. We are thus presented with a utopian revision of the Western psyche by resolving the irreconcilable tension described in the regression of the id-instincts. While Freud and Adorno regarded a better marshaling of the id-instincts, not in sexual license but rather as the means to a healthier, more robust existence, they radically differed in regard to their views of reason and objectifying science, their respective diagnosis of the pathology leading to neurosis, and their proposed strategies for social reform and individual liberation. Freud's circumspect views on what he regarded as the inevitable calculus of human aggression led him to considerations of reform narrowly based on psychoanalytic emancipation. Through a process of remembrance, recognition, reconciliation, and responsibility, the analytic procedure placed the ego's interpretive reconstruction of one's psychic history as the linchpin of the entire enterprise. Reason was never enough, but analysis is, after all, *analysis*.

Adorno's key move was directed at a particular kind of instrumental reason, which rests at the base of Freud's inquiry. Adorno had no such allegiance to reason in this form and instead expanded "thinking" to include that which fell well outside the scientific domain. Reason's character thus assumed a dimensionality that more directly addressed the emotional basis of encounters with the world.

The aesthetic became the experience around which a different kind of knowing challenged the hegemony of what Adorno called the "mathematization" of knowledge. By disallowing the reduction of human understanding to such a restrictive mode of logic, he erected an epistemology to fulfill a moral agenda, namely, the emancipation of Man, whom he characterized in light of the capacity for *creativity*. For Adorno, the domain of the imagination represented human vitality and the *telos* of life. He would free its expression as the means to fulfill human potential and flourishing. For that project he discarded thinking restricted by a conception of reason based on a particular formula of rationality and substituted a form of reason specifically designed not to be complete in its representations.

Adorno attempted to characterize the "unexplainable" of human thought, and for that he required a reconceived conception of the ego, one not lodged within the walls of what one knows but what one might aesthetically experience and creatively imagine. On this vision, science has little relevance, when modernist forms of knowledge have been displaced as the pinnacle of human accomplishment and romantic imagination has taken its place. Indeed, the subversion initiated by Freud (that self-knowledge was based on fantasy) has been radicalized. Not only were humans portrayed as being deeply ignorant and deceived as to their true longings; that ignorance actually pointed to the source of human potential. Instead of capturing desire through the mathematization of the mind, humans would, according to Adorno, better celebrate its mystery and receive its blessings. The task of psychoanalysis then becomes the effort to uncover the psychic wellspring and draw from its waters. Instead of control governed by fear, reception guided by wonder must orient the wanderer in the world. From that point of view, Adorno serves as a key architect of postmodern subjectivity in large measure because he, perhaps ironically, aligned himself in this respect with Heidegger (an archrival with whom Adorno sought no kinship).

In the next chapter, we will follow the path taken by Heidegger, which proved radically different from Adorno's; however, their respective end points found the self firmly embedded in the world both for gratification and for social ends. The subject-object dichotomy characterizing modernist thought was blurred by each of their philosophical analyses, so despite their vast philosophical differences, each turned the inner-peering ego out into the world; each endorsed a form of receptivity that clearly marks a dividing line between the Kantian construction of cognition based on an autonomous agency and the subject contextualized within the world, one open to very different ways of knowing.[15] In this sense, they join as an odd couple to confront an ego confined to self-reflection and narcissism. While both had recognized the same fundamental challenge of configuring a post-Cartesian agent, they had posed divergent strategies, with long-standing repercussions in moral and social theory still not fully developed or understood.

4   Heidegger's Confrontation

> Dasein is an entity which does not just occur among other entities. Rather it is ontically [i.e., factually] distinguished by the fact that, in its very Being, that Being is an *issue* for it. *Understanding of Being is itself a definite characteristic of Dasein's Being.* Dasein is ontically distinctive in that it *is* ontological.
>
> —MARTIN HEIDEGGER, *Being and Time*

In the spring of 1929, as Freud was about to embark on writing *Civilization and Its Discontents*, a celebrated debate between Heidegger and Ernst Cassirer at Davos enacted a clash of philosophical visions with profound impact on European philosophy. Heidegger had published *Being and Time* two years earlier after a relatively long academic dormancy. Much like Zarathustra descending from the mountain, he projected himself as the herald of a new era in which metaphysics would be utterly reconceived, if not discarded. The theme of the meeting, "What Is the Human Being?" (Gordon 2010, p. 111), allowed him to further develop his reconception of agency, which had already been detailed in his portrayal of Dasein in his magnum opus (1962).

Being and Time sought to overturn the modernist subject-object construction altogether. Instead of there being an agent conceived as the master of nature, who would define the cosmos in terms of human reason, Heidegger argued that Man is that which acknowledges Being. Facing the wonder of existence (the *there is* as opposed to *not*) requires making the ordinary extraordinary by recognizing the unfathomable incomprehensibility of the *is*. *Da-sein*—a "being-there" or "is-there" ("English will not weld the requisite amalgam" [Steiner 1978, p. 82])—conceives the encounter with Being as constituting *the* authenticity of human being. Dasein would reside in the world and instead of seeking knowledge (as usually construed), he would seek another kind of existence in which the endeavor to "unveil" Being constituted Man's quest for truth (*aletheia* = "the unconcealed"). Such a revealing required a new kind of philosophical deliberation, because the concealment (and distraction) of beings had become the exclusive focus of modernity. Thus, more than a capacity of a "privileged listener and respondent to existence" (ibid., p. 32), Dasein enacts a moral *imperative*. To achieve this existential stance, Heidegger argued for a reconception of subjectivity, one that required discarding the Cartesian ego altogether.

During the 1920s Cassirer had also published his own defining work, *The Philosophy of Symbolic Forms* (1953, 1955, 1957), in which he extended the Kantian project by elaborating on Man the Symbolist. He saw the representation of the world as the fundamental human function and product, whether configured in language, myth, or science. The mind comports nature and existence in various modalities, and this melding of the world and knowledge instantiates an ego set apart to scrutinize its world and control it. Such a cogito represents the world to itself and thereby orients existence about its own concerns (the "beings" of Heidegger's lexicon). For Heidegger, that positioning entirely misses the imperative of facing Being, with the dire consequences of modernity's nihilistic crisis. The argument may have appeared to be over epistemology and metaphysics, but at its heart, the Davos debate was the stage for a struggle over the *psyche*, the human soul.

Freud clearly would have sided with Cassirer's Kantianism, and more specifically a modernist notion of agency, but that argument passed him by. Sitting in the middle of the philosophical turmoil, he was apparently completely unaware that psychoanalysis would become a part of the argument and that ultimately he would contribute to undermining the very tenets he held dear. While Freud apparently never read Heidegger or engaged him in any way, he might well have been shocked by such a confrontation. As outlined here, Heidegger most clearly defined the alternative to the modernists' sense of reason and, more specifically, their defense of traditional rationality. He would turn from their concern with reason and its preoccupation with the self (where "to reflect upon modernity is inevitably to reflect upon the self" [Früchtl 2008, p. 138]) and move the agenda to confronting Being. He would thereby attempt to radically replace traditional philosophical theory and practice.[1]

Confronting Cassirer, Heidegger moved from his phenomenological portrayal of *Being and Time* to a frontal critique of Kant's notions of reason, which Cassirer had reformulated (and defended) as part of the general neo-Kantian effort to reform Kantian idealism. Extending his argument against predicate thinking, Heidegger left his neo-Kantian opponent bewildered and most likely alarmed at the enthusiastic response generated by the radical turn proffered (Gordon 2010). Later we will explore the details of that confrontation, which in many ways swept Freud's own modernism into the whirlwinds that would eventually be known as postmodernism. To understand these later developments, we must place Heidegger's cardinal contributions in juxtaposition to the Kantianism he attacked.

I

Much of Heidegger's philosophy may be tracked back to his reading of Nietzsche. In respect to the suspicion of reason's hegemony, the central role of art, the dissatisfaction with modernity's embrace of science and technology, and the Cartesian subject standing as the master of nature—metaphysically sovereign, exerting its will as it will—Heidegger embraced Nietzsche's deconstruction of agency and with it, Western metaphysics (Heidegger 1982). The election of the "I" with "its random desires and abandoned to an arbitrary free-will" (Heidegger 1977a, p. 70) focused Heidegger's critique of modernity, and more particularly the ego's very standing. Indeed, Dasein would displace the "I-ness" of the self-reflective ego. In this scheme, the self-conscious rational subject would be rendered neutral by the assertion that "the way in which man is man, that is himself . . . by no means coincides with I-ness" (ibid., p. 79), by which Heidegger referred to the autonomous ego.

The basic structure of Heidegger's philosophy thus begins with undermining the Cartesian cogito, in which the ego stands as "the only 'underlying' reality," that which establishes the foundation for certainty that Descartes required to build his own system. In "conformity between *ratio* and object . . . everything is referred back to the human viewer. . . . The *cogito* comes before the *sum*; thought precedes being; and truth [actual perception] is a function of the certitude of the human subject" (Steiner 1978, pp. 69–70).[2] "From then on, 'subject' progressively became the term for I. Object now became all that stands over against the I and its thinking," which in turn becomes the scientific attitude and ultimately the basis for "the true being" (Heidegger 2001, p. 118). Heidegger utterly rejects this construction, and it is within this context that his criticism of Freud became part of the general barrage against the subject-object thinking characteristic of objectifying science, and more broadly the scientism applied to human beings. As already mentioned, the particularity of *being* (and more particularly, specific beings) obstructs Dasein's confrontation with existence as such. Arguing that the entirety of Western metaphysics rests upon the displacement of philosophy's encounter from Being ushered in by Plato, Heidegger sought a conception of subjectivity that would allow, indeed, accomplish, a radical shift in philosophy's entire agenda. In that shift, the ego would be displaced for an understanding of agency that permitted such an encounter, which, in turn, meant nothing less than a novel epistemology.

With his outright rejection of Kant's objectifying representationalism and replacement with the "receptivity" of Dasein in the world, Heidegger attempted to dissolve the predicate mode of knowing. Obviously, knowing is one modality in which Dasein lives, but for Heidegger, such knowledge is subordinate to a more authentic kind of experience: "The perceiving of what is known is not a process of returning with one's booty to the 'cabinet' of consciousness after one has gone out and grasped it" (Heidegger 1962, p. 89), but rather knowledge is part of a generalized being-in-the-world. For Heidegger, Western metaphysics had initiated a displacement, which would be corrected by an altogether different epistemological posture: "Dasein is 'to be there' and the 'there' is the world: the concrete, literal, actual, daily world. . . . A philosophy that abstracts, that seeks to elevate itself above the everyday of the everyday is empty. It can tell us nothing of being, of where and what *Dasein* is" (Steiner 1978, p. 83). So Heidegger moves from a predicate structure of knowing the world—the world seen as a collection of objects, processes, or a world-picture (1977a, 1977b)—for an agent embedded in the world (1997). As he explained,

> as distinct from the traditional thought of metaphysics, a totally different question is asked in *Being and Time*. Until now, beings *have* been questioned in reference to their being. In *Being and Time* the issue is no longer *beings as such*, but *the meaning of being in general*, of the possible *manifestness* of being. (Heidegger 2001, p. 119; emphasis in original)

Oriented toward being, *Man* would emerge, not as a subject or as an object but rather as enveloped in discovering Being and in the process, himself, as part thereof. Or in other words, "My thesis is that the unfolding essence of the human being is the understanding of being" (Heidegger 2001, p. 208). And from that perspective, psychoanalysis, with few exceptions, was engaged in a different venture altogether.[3] However, Freud was caught in the philosophical crossfire, when Heidegger signaled him out as failing to fulfill the deepest agenda of human being: "Freud's approach . . . specifically neglects to determine the human being's character of being" (Heidegger 2001, p. 224). One might fairly object that Freud, after all, was a psychologist, not a philosopher, yet Heidegger clearly saw him as a worthy target, given the cultural importance of the psychoanalytic understanding of human subjectivity and agency. Indeed, psychoanalysis aptly serves Heidegger's critique.[4]

Heidegger's agenda thus distinguishes the world of being and that of Being. The former is the world depicted by the ontic sciences (e.g., physics, psychology, physiology, etc.), which are devoted to the elucidation and control of nature. The ontic orientation underwrites an ethical vision of humankind's reduction to scientific scrutiny that offers, at best, a narrow depiction and, at worst, a dehumanizing distortion. Psycho*analysis* rests firmly embedded in an objectifying scientism and thus suffers all that which Heidegger would hope to overturn. Instead of an agent who constructs beings, where grasping concrete phenomena becomes an ontic exercise, Dasein engages phenomena ontologically by its openness to the ground of possibility, allowing the phenomenon to be a phenomenon. Simply put, Heidegger's philosophy is of Being, not Man. Thus, "Dasein is in-the-world and constitutes the being of the world by a network of meanings through which the ontic world is disclosed, revealed (passively, receptively)," or in other words, Dasein is "the ontological ground of beings and as that which constitutes Being" (Needleman 1967, p. 123). For Heidegger, "to endow meaning is to endow being—and, therefore, the Dasein, as the unique source of meaning in the world, is the unique ground of Being" (ibid., p. 122). Meta-issues—the overcoming of nihilism, the seeking, or establishing of meaning, the rehumanizing of culture—all fall into place as products of this basic orientation (Heidegger 1977a, 1977b, 1979, 1982, 1993a).[5]

Forsaking the dominance of the world and a conception of Man as the measure of all things, Heidegger would espouse a different humanism, where the philosopher must find a humanistic ground-ing for the "study of man." In this regard, Freud and Heidegger shared the general moral agenda of recapturing a besieged *humani-tas*, but they assigned radically different views as to how such a task might be accomplished. In the "Letter on Humanism" (Heidegger 1993a),[6] Heidegger articulated terms of authenticity but defined as the turn toward Being and thus quite askew from the meanings associated with traditional understandings of humanism (Rock-more 1995, p. 97). A direct confrontation thus appears with Freud, who had deliberately retreated from an unknowable Being (Freud 1927) to a positivist-inspired object of study, the neurotic human portrayed in a new science. After all, thinking for Freud followed a scientistic subject-object orthodoxy; for Heidegger, thinking became the engagement with Being, whose ineffable character pre-cluded modernist modes of thought (Heidegger 1976).[7] Thus, the paths Heidegger and Freud followed radically diverged, of which the most obvious differences concerned the role of representation as an intrinsic product of the predicate reasoning process. After all, Being represented becomes a world of beings.

Assuming a cosmological orientation,[8] where the existential state of Man in relation to Being framed Heidegger's philosophical enter-prise, the question of how human thinking might again confront pre- (or perhaps, post-) representational reality focused his radi-cal turn. Indeed, the revision of Kantianism required a new means of expression that sought to capture a realm left unaddressed by predicate thinking, and thus the symbolizations of Cassirer and the mechanical lexicon of psychic energies became relics of a discarded metaphysics. In sum, both Cassirer and Freud built their respec-tive epistemologies on the self-conscious agent, which embraced an anthropocentrism Heidegger forcefully rejected (Askay and Far-quhar 2006, pp. 190ff.).[9] Regarding the particular context of our concerns, having reconfigured the infrastructure of the Kantian system, Heidegger left the self utterly deconstructed and altogether reconceived the notion of truth that oriented such a knowing agent.

II

If truth is no longer conceived as the best (even ultimate) condition of knowing, because knowing is no longer conceived as a representation of the world, then on what basis might truth be defined or even configured? What is the relationship of normative reason to truth, which in turn must address both the basis of normativity and the definition of truth? Revising the subject-object epistemology that would define truth in terms of human knowledge, that is, the rightful correspondence between the ego's representation and the world represented, Heidegger declared that truth was determined by Dasein's authenticity. And authenticity is the faithful turn toward Being. Thus, the encounter with Being, which, by its very nature cannot be represented, upturns modern notions of truth altogether (Dahlstrom 2001). In an astonishing reversal of the usual meanings, Heidegger asserts that Dasein's recognition of the ultimate mystery of Being (its essential hidden and unknowable character) represents the truth function. Dasein *exercises* its freedom in a perpetual "unveiling" of truth, that is, the true is that which emerges in the light of the openness, a presentation or offering of Being (Borch-Jacobsen 1991, pp. 105–6). Yet the endeavor of unveiling perpetually faces a reciprocal veiling, for the *what* of the unveiled is *nothing*, for "Being in its very disclosure, withdraws into veiling" (ibid.). Heidegger summarized these "mechanics" in his inaugural address at the University of Freiburg (delivered a few months after the Davos disputation)—a credo of truth, authenticity, and the basic character of Man.

> Da-sein means: being held out into nothing.
>
> Holding itself out into the nothing, Dasein is in each case already beyond beings as a whole. This being beyond beings we call "transcendence." If in the ground of its essence Dasein were not transcending, which now means, if it were not in advance holding itself out into nothing, then it could never be related to beings nor even to itself.
>
> Without the original revelation of the nothing, no selfhood and no freedom. (Heidegger 1993c, p. 103)

This metaphysical structure in which Dasein finds itself presents a basic existential (insurmountable) veiling/unveiling oscillation, which requires the leap just described: The leap is a leap into that which has no representation, which in fact is a leap into *nothing*, and thus doomed to failure from a rational point of view (as assessed by any objectifying criteria, much as Kierkegaard's leap of faith is a leap into absurdity). But it is precisely objectivity that has been discarded, a casualty of the rejection of subjectivity as determined by the Cartesian construction. Instead, Heidegger presents the fundamental character of Dasein as "a way of thinking, which, instead of furnishing representations and concepts, experiences and tests itself as a transformation of its relatedness to Being" (1993b, p. 138), which requires facing the unknown, death, and finitude. In that *presentation* to the void of nothingness, Dasein constitutes its authenticity, or truth.

Thus, Heidegger turned his earlier work on psychologism from an inquiry about truth as defined within the Kantian construct to something entirely different. He joined an ongoing dispute. By the end of the nineteenth century, a diverse and complex reevaluation of the status of logic fractured philosophy into competing schools largely formed around how one regarded reason. The debate took form during Freud's own period around the relationship of psychology and philosophy. With the charge of "psychologism," Gottlob Frege and Edmund Husserl in distinctive ways sought to purge logic of any psychological determinants, and in their effort, they were instrumental in delineating philosophy from the new discipline of psychology. Placing Freud in this setting highlights the issues that later organized the philosophical attack on his theory of mind.

The polemic over psychologism was about the extent rationality is a matter for *psychological* study, which reflected a much deeper philosophical problem, the relation of mind and nature. The original dispute centered on the question of whether logic and epistemology were subject to psychology, which in turn arose from the newly contested views of philosophy's character and purposes. From that base, various philosophies of science emerged, including, most prominently, a more austere positivism (Tauber 2009c). In this scientistic milieu, an alliance composed of advocates of empirical philosophy and a new science, psychology, placed sensory experience as the basis of all knowledge. Two strategies organized their collective effort: Experience would be understood in terms either of some kind of introspection of conscious experience or by some naturalistic extrapolation of neurophysiological processes. Accordingly, logic is a record of the laws of thought (discerned psychologically), which in turn rested upon physiological processes, which could be discerned by observation of human inferential patterns. Simply, the normative, grounded in human biology, would take its bearings from a form of naturalism, which then joined the reductionism that had captured all the sciences—natural and social—to forge an attack against a defunct idealism propounding schemata of transcendental conditions from which knowledge would be derived. In the process, philosophy underwent a major transformation.

The attack was led by Frege, who "argued that mathematics and logic are not part of psychology, and that the objects and laws of mathematics and psychology are not defined, illuminated, proven true, or explained by psychological observations" (Kusch 2011). He maintained that mathematical truths are not empirical truths, and thus he drew the opposition between "truth" and "what-is-taken-to-be-true" to distinguish logic from psychology:

> People may very well interpret the expression "law of thought" by analogy with "law of nature" and then have in mind general features of thinking as a mental occurrence. A law of thought in this sense would be a psychological law. And so they might come to believe that logic deals with the mental process of thinking and the psychological laws in accordance with which this takes place. That would be a misunderstanding of the task of logic, for truth has not here been given its proper place. Error and superstition have causes just as much as correct cognition. Where what you take for true is false or true, your

so taking it comes about in accordance with psychological laws. A derivation from these laws, an explanation of a mental process that ends in taking something to be true, can never take the place of proving what is taken to be true. . . . In order to avoid any misunderstanding and prevent the blurring the boundary between psychology and logic, I assign to logic the task of discovering the laws of truth, not the laws of taking things to be true or of thinking. (Frege 1977, pp. 1–2)

For Frege truth is objective, so the laws of truth (logic) are also objective, and correspondingly, logical laws are not only descriptive but also normative: "Logic is concerned with the laws of truth, not with the laws of holding something to be true, not with the question of how men think, but with the question of how they must think if they are not to miss the truth" (Frege, quoted by Maddy 2007, p. 201).[10] Husserl, building his antipsychologism on a different set of issues, also regarded the crucial problem of establishing truth's insularity from psychology the basis for logic's independent standing.[11] And joining them from the neo-Kantian perspective were those like Wilhelm Windelband, who similarly regarded psychologism as a grave danger to philosophy, because of the reduction of "the principles of reason to mere temporal and psychical conditions independent of any transcendental source" (Bambach 1995, p. 78; Anderson 2005; see Windelband 1921, pp. 181–82, and his relation to Freudianism in Tauber 2010, pp. 105–15).

The fate of the fin de siècle discussion about psychologism projects the later analytic-Continental divergent approaches, which followed from a key nodal point of Kant's philosophy. Kant had sought to solve the twin demands of understanding how logic depends on the general structural features of the world and at the same time how logic is embodied in human cognition and laws of reason. His transcendentalism made logic a form of judgment, while his empiricism corresponded logic to the underlying structure of the world. Placing logic within the structure of human cognition is psychologism; and following an empirical naturalistic course, logic presents human cognition as seeing and representing the world as structured. The argument follows a naturalist line: Because brains, as natural entities, evolved in a world so structured, logical truth reflects this homology. And at this joint, the Kantian project was attacked, at the hinge separating intuition and sensibility. Without logic in its own transcendental realm, what is its philosophical status? Into the fray stepped Heidegger.[12]

III

For Kant, the human mind set the a priori conditions for experience; for Heidegger, humans must first have some understanding of the Being of those beings, or in other words, the conditions for experience were not mental but *practical*. This move from the rational to the existential marked Heidegger's attempt to interpret Kant's first *Critique* as preparatory to an ontological investigation as opposed to the neo-Kantian contention that it represented the basis for an epistemology. This issue focused the Davos confrontation with Cassirer.

The direct antecedent of the dispute begins with Hermann Cohen, Cassirer's predecessor at Marburg, who had rejected Kant's separation of a receptive perceptive faculty from the faculty of understanding and insisted on the autonomy of the latter. The *noumenon* then became only a marker for the "task" of epistemological investigation, that is, no longer a metaphysical unknown. Transcendental idealism was thus transformed to a project for scientific explanation on the basis of scientific method. For Heidegger, this view of the mind omitted its most crucial feature, the mind's receptivity to the world. For Heidegger, knowledge (and ultimately truth) is a product of an orientation to the world based on a set of intuitions, and to capture that alignment, the ego in its subject-object configuration would be displaced—with all of its Cartesian-Kantian baggage—for a radically reconceived agent, Dasein.

The philosophical project then became an understanding of how Dasein exists in the world (open to experience) in order to be receptive to those conditions: Dasein exists as a "potentiality-of-Being," one that has abandoned itself to "possibilities because it is an entity which has been thrown" into the world and open to it (Heidegger 1962, p. 315). This constitutes a particular characteristic, for unlike other beings, "Being is an *issue* for it" (ibid., p. 32). Dasein is thus determined not by reference to a "what" but rather as that being that "always understands itself in terms of its existence—in terms of a possibility of itself: to be itself or not itself" (ibid., pp. 32–33). In other words, Dasein, its very essence, is concerned with its own potentialities, and to the extent it remains "open," its authenticity is assured. Thus, the truth function for Heidegger is governed by Dasein's commitment and ability to confront Being. This portrait depends on Dasein's recognition of its own finitude, and in fact, recognizing and facing its own death is the basis for its self-consciousness and placement in Being. Facing the nothing of Being is, in a sense, to face human finitude, which in turn presents the utter otherness of infinitude.[13]

So, according to Heidegger, the centrality of subjectivity in the modernist sense must be revised from a subject-object relationship to one that recognizes (and philosophically builds from) the subject's direct (preconceptual) presence in the world, where subjectivity emerges without mediation of processed perceptions, that is, representations. That effort required a revision of modernity's metaphysics, namely, nothing short of the demise of the ego, or Man:

> Western history has now begun to enter into the completion of that period we call *modern*, and which is defined by the fact that man becomes the measure and the center of beings. Man is what lies at the bottom of all beings; that is, in modern terms, at the bottom of all objectification and representability. (Heidegger 1982, p. 28)

Heidegger's program struck at the very heart of the modernist subject-object relationship by declaring the weakness of that epistemological structure. The self, no longer an object, is now conceived as a life unfolding in the world. So, instead of an entity, "a thinking thing," the self is better conceived as an engagement with Being. No longer a mind (cogito) at the center of consciousness, Dasein finds itself in *what* it does (Heidegger 1962, p. 155). This then becomes the existentialist Heidegger, where "there is no pregiven 'human nature' that determines what we are. Instead, we are what we make of ourselves in the course of living. . . . '[E]ssence' *of Dasein lies in its existence'* [ibid., p. 67]" (Guignon 1993, p. 223; emphasis in original).

This interpretation radically opposed the modernist view of reason and, more particularly in the Davos debate, the representationalism marking subject-object thinking. So for Heidegger and Cassirer, the respective vectors of thought diverge at the point of how reason might be conceived. For Heidegger, reason ultimately obscures Being by presuming to represent that which lies beyond comprehension in human terms. Representation thus *mis*-represents; reason not only mistranslates Being but also distorts the ultimate reality Heidegger sought. And for the modernist Cassirer, reason is the instrument for human imagination to discover the world and, in a sense, master it. Reason then becomes the instrument of *human being*, not in relation to the cosmos but in relation to oneself. Thus, Heidegger directly attacked Cassirer on the basic premises from which Cassirer had recently completed his project of characterizing human knowledge (and ultimately cognitive experience) through various forms of symbolization. Thought, according to Cassirer, was structured by representational cognitive structures, which developed in characteristic forms—language, myth, and science (1953, 1955, 1957). Because reason was not the final arbiter of knowledge in Heidegger's scheme (1997, pp. 117–19), an entirely different epistemology emerged, one based on receptivity as opposed to reason's capacity for symbolic creation. Where Cassirer and the other neo-Kantians had moved away from metaphysics, Heidegger had embraced ontology as the basis for re-creating philosophy altogether. Whereas Cassirer intended to establish a philosophy of symbolic forms, Heidegger dismissed the effort as superficial to, and distorting of, the essence of man. The clash of philosophical purposes could hardly be clearer. The upheaval in philosophy that resulted from Heidegger's revision of Kant's program can not be overestimated, and not surprisingly, repercussions were immediately felt in psychology.

To comprehend the philosophical basis for Heidegger's attack, we must unpack the central argument he employed, which radically appropriates Kant for his own purposes or, as he readily admitted, did "violence" to Kant's philosophy (Heidegger 1997, pp. xx, 141). Continuing his earlier dissertation about psychologism, Heidegger launched his critique at Kant's theory of sensibility, which begins with the central question, *"[H]ow are synthetic a priori judgments possible?"* (Kant 1998 [B73], p. 192). The neo-Kantians absorbed "intuition" into the "understanding," a move that precipitated a series of philosophical responses of which Heidegger's was the most radical. In Kantian epistemology, *understanding* must be distinguished from reason and sensibility and has several meanings: a spontaneity of knowledge, a power of thought, a faculty of concepts comprising the categories, a faculty of judgment, and the faculty of rules (Caygill 1995, p. 406). Simply, the understanding is given the materials of experience by the sensibility, which it then processes. And *intuition* stands for the direct, unmediated character of sensations, the immediate presentation of a particular object in space and time. However, this is not Lockean empiricism, for the intuition also possesses an a priori status. This dual character (sensuous and intelligible) was essential for addressing the general problem of transcendental philosophy, where judgments function to synthesize concepts with sensible intuitions. Kant argued in the *Prolegomena*,

> If our intuition had to be of the kind that represented things *as they are in themselves*, then absolutely no intuition *a priori* would take place, but it would always be empirical. For I can only know what may be contained in the object in itself if the object is present and given to me.

> Of course, even then it is incomprehensible how the intuition of a thing that is present should allow me to cognize it the way it is in itself, since its properties cannot migrate over into my power of representation; but even granting such a possibility, the intuition still would not take place *a priori*, i.e., before the object were presented to me, for without that no basis for the relation of my representation to the object can be conceived; so it would have to be based on inspiration. (Kant 2002, p. 78)

Here then is the linchpin of representationalism, and Kant goes on to make the argument about synthetic judgment:

> There is therefore only one way possible for my intuition to precede the actuality of the object and occur as an *a priori* cognition, *namely if it contains nothing else except the form of sensibility, which in me as subject precedes all actual impressions through which I am affected by objects.* For I can know *a priori* that the objects of the senses can be intuited only in accordance with this form of sensibility. From this it follows: that propositions which relate merely to this form of sensory intuition will be possible and valid for objects of the senses; also, conversely, that intuitions which are possible *a priori* can never relate to things other than objects of our senses.
>   [4:283] §10
> Therefore it is only by means of the form of sensory intuition [space and time] that we can intuit things *a priori*, though by this means we can cognize objects only as they *appear* to us (to our senses), not as they may be in themselves; and this supposition is utterly necessary, if synthetic propositions *a priori* are to be granted as possible, or, in case they are actually encountered, if their possibility is to be conceived and determined in advance. (ibid., pp. 78–79; emphasis in original)

The complex relationship between understanding and sensibility brings together intuitions and concepts, where intuitions originate in the receptivity of human sensibility and concepts develop from the spontaneity of the understanding. And noteworthy for our general consideration, both intuitions and concepts are representations.

For Kant the object of knowledge cannot be known solely on the basis of the a priori logical structures of judgment alone (Friedman

2000, pp. 27–29). Some mediation is required between the pure forms of judgment composing Kant's general logic and the conceptualized manifold of the impressions supplied by the senses. These so-called mediating structures are the pure forms of intuition—space and time. So the transition to knowledge from sensory impressions requires an underlying spatio-temporal determinant. For instance, *substance* is schematized in terms of the temporal representation of permanence; *causality* is schematized in terms of temporal representation of succession, and so on. Thus, in this epistemology, "pure" logic must be supplemented by a "transcendental" logic, whereby logical forms become schematized in terms of spatio-temporal representations as mediated by the independent faculty of pure intuition.

Following post-Kantian idealism, twentieth-century neo-Kantians rejected the very notion of a faculty of pure intuition in order to close the gap between knowledge and its object. Instead of a dualism comprising a logical, conceptual, or discursive faculty of pure understanding, on the one hand, and a receptive sensory faculty of pure sensibility, on the other hand, they collapsed this duality to a single logical faculty. Since space and time no longer function as independent forms of pure sensibility in this revision, experience described by "transcendental logic" must proceed solely on the basis of purely conceptual a priori structures. The issue then became how to define such a logic (Willey 1978, p. 81; Könke 1991, pp. 89–90).[14] Heidegger claimed instead that sensibility should be granted its foundational role not merely as a "sensual" or "psychological" faculty but truly as a "metaphysical" foundation for experience. Accordingly, he read the first *Critique* as an inquiry into finitude itself as the birthplace of ontology (Gordon 2010, pp. 128–29).

The key to understanding the relation between finitude and ontological knowledge lay in Kant's claim that time is the a priori condition of all appearances, which implied that ontological knowledge was bound to temporality. Heidegger found support for this view in Kant's own assertion that the "transcendental imagination" mediated between the faculties of sensibility and the understanding by providing a temporal synthesis and thereby creating "schemata" that were then applied to pure intuition. The schemata remained undefined, and this became a pivotal point for Heidegger's own interpretation of the place of reason in the Kantian system.

Heidegger's interpretation of Kant rested on an innovative comparison of the first and second editions of *Critique of Pure Reason*: In the 1781 edition, Kant described the transcendental imagination as a third faculty, one independent of the sensory and the understanding. Reading the *Critique* as a metaphysical work seeking to establish the ontological basis of knowledge, Heidegger probed the first edition to find the faculty upon which the final synthesis of perception and understanding occurs. He argued that the representations must be joined through "judging" (Heidegger 1997, p. 81), and such "mere thinking" remains with only what is "represented" and thus forms an "analytic." Heidegger interprets the meaning of the analytic as a "dissection" of the faculty of understanding,[15] which then requires a synthesis between (1) sensory *perception* (mediated by the "transcendental aesthetic," whose transcendental condition of time and space is processed by thought or experience), and (2) a second component of knowledge, *understanding*, which is addressed by transcendental logic. This faculty is analytic "in the sense that Kant traces the conditions for the possibility of scientific experience back to a unified whole, that is, the faculty of understanding" (Heidegger 2001, p. 115). Thus, for Kant, analytic is a dissection of the understanding not to its elements but to an unfractured

> unity (synthesis) of the ontological possibility of . . . the objectivity of the objects of experience. . . . Therefore, the goal of "the analytic" is to expound the original unity of the function of the faculty of understanding . . . the articulation of the [a priori] unity of the composite structure. (ibid.)

Heidegger directly extends this formulation to an "analytic of Da-sein"—the ontological basis for being-in-the-world.

Because a final synthesis is yet to occur with the "function of the understanding," thinking does not constitute full knowing. That final step requires a recognition or posture relative to the world from which representations are constructed. Here a distinctly Heideggerian move is made: Not only does the predicate relate to the subject but also the subject-object composite, together, must relate to "something wholly other" (Heidegger 1997, p. 81).[16] *Knowing* goes beyond *thinking*, because the final synthesis must include facing that which is presented as other and the truth of that knowledge is in "accordance with the Object" (ibid., p. 83). Moreover, being-in-the-world is required both to constitute knowledge and to authenticate human being. So the epistemology, built on an ontology of being-in-time, becomes the standard of authenticity, and truth, of Dasein.

For Heidegger, the more radical view of the first edition suggested that the transcendental imagination was independent of reason, and it enjoyed this independence because it was grounded in temporality. The "concepts of the understanding give order to experience; the principles of reason are the standard by which it is judged" (Neiman 1994, p. 6). By removing reason from the sensory and placing it within the understanding, reason might function within its own domain unto its own laws independent of the natural world of appearances and causation to structure reality according to a human perspective, that is, in reason's own terms. In other words, human minds are "the lawgivers" to nature.

> Reason, in order to be taught by nature, must approach nature with its principles in one hand, according to which alone the agreement among appearances can count as laws, and, in the other hand, the experiments thought out in accordance with these principles—yet in order to be instructed by nature not like a pupil, who has recited to him whatever the teacher wants to say, but like an appointed judge who compels witnesses to answer questions he puts to them. (Kant 1998, p. 109)

Indeed, beyond the reach of the sensuous and time, reason has "complete spontaneity [to] make its own order according to ideas, to which it fits the empirical conditions and according to which it even declares actions to be necessary that yet have not occurred and perhaps will not occur" (Kant 1998 [A548 / B576], p. 541). Kant goes on to describe how reason possesses its own ordering principles and thereby distinguishes itself from the world that it examines (ibid. [A550 / B578], p. 542). Further, unlike certain human behaviors that have an obvious empirical content and thus deterministic causality, reason possesses no temporality (or what we perceive as natural causality), "and thus the dynamical law of nature, which determines the temporal sequence according to rules, cannot be applied to it" (ibid. [A553 / B581], p. 543).

In sum, to fulfill its *autonomous* function, reason must be free of experience, and, in this view, the ability to survey the world and make judgments depends on reason's independence from that world. Reason, accordingly, resides outside the natural domain, free and autonomous, to order nature through scientific insight and regulate human behavior through rational moral discourse. This allows for creative judgment in science and freedom of choice in the social (ethical) domain. The autonomy of both theoretical and practical reason serves as the bedrock of Kant's epistemology, enabling the synthesis and apprehension of the natural world and the discernment of the moral universe. And Heidegger, in dramatic contrast, built a philosophy based on the receptivity of Dasein to the world encountered. Ordering is thereby replaced by existential experience.

Heidegger pinpoints his divergence from Kant to a critical juncture between the first and second editions of *Critique of Pure Reason*, where the placement of the "transcendental power of pure imagination" assumes a revised placement in Kant's scheme. In its mediating role of forming schemata, this faculty serves as an intermediate between sensibility and understanding (Heidegger 1997, p. 92), and as a third faculty (ibid., pp. 94ff.), it was assigned the task of "forming" time as the basis from which knowledge is constructed, and more, it was "original time" (Gordon 2010, pp. 130–31). But Kant abandoned that construction in the second edition, where the power of pure synthesis was transferred to function exclusively within the domain of the understanding. In that move, Kant had transformed his argument from a psychological doctrine (a mediating role for the transcendental imagination) to the more logical conception of the 1787 (second) edition in order to protect Reason's mastery (Heidegger 1997, p. 119). And here we discern the outlines of the psychologism debate a century later.

According to Heidegger, the transcendental power of pure imagination is essentially a rootless, mysterious faculty, which, while fundamentally unknown, is still intuited. In other words, it is not something "we simply know nothing" about, but rather it is "what pushes against us as something disquieting in what is known," that is, an undefined presence (Heidegger 1997, p. 112). And "Kant shrank back from this unknown root" (ibid.), having brought metaphysics to an "abyss. He had to shrink back. It was not just that the transcendental power of the imagination frightened him, but rather that in between [the first and second editions of the *Critique*] pure reason as reason drew him increasingly under its spell" (ibid., p. 118). For Heidegger the price paid to preserve the autonomy of reason as the essential ground of ontological knowledge was too dear. Indeed, for him the chief question then became, "What and how much can understanding and reason know, free from all experience?" (ibid., p. 116). In forsaking a direct and sustained commitment to engage in the world (as opposed to a subject-object separation based on reason's autonomy), reason becomes a veil to the primary (authentic) encounter with Being. Simply, knowledge has been compromised, truth diluted, authenticity sacrificed. Heidegger's entire project focused upon reversing this retreat: "Kant knew of the possibility for and necessity of a more original ground-laying, but it was not part of his immediate purpose" (ibid., p. 117), which was to preserve reason's autonomy not only for its epistemological chores but even more important, for Kant's moral philosophy.[17]

As discussed, Kantian Reason, because of its autonomy, serves as a functionary of knowledge acquisition and discernment; however, by instantiating the subject-object divide, authentic engagement with the world is obscured, if not prevented. Heidegger (1991), in a lecture course given in 1955–56, devised an ingenious genealogical analysis of *ratio* to argue that the development of Western metaphysics drove a wedge between man's self-consciousness (in the form of thinking) and his grounding (in the form of being), which had been unified in ancient Greek philosophy. The argument commences with a discussion of Leibniz's adage *"nihil est sine ratione*: nothing is without reason." Inasmuch as all is accounted for by cause, "every being necessarily has a reason" (Heidegger 1991, p. 9), *reason* establishes *being*. The principle of reason does not deal with reason as such, that is, it "already presupposes that what a reason is has already been determined" (ibid.), and further, the principle of sufficient reason itself has no reason, so it stands alone to assume a primary or fundamental character. Because

> nothing is without reason . . . everything counts as existing when and only when it has been securely established as a calculable [represented] object for cognition. [Thus, this principle] becomes the fundamental principle of all cognition, and cognition then becomes unmistakably Rational and governed by Reason. (ibid., p. 120)

For Heidegger, the principle of reason determines all cognition and behavior, and by extension, the ontological ground or being of traditional Western metaphysics. And here we come to the Heideggerian inflection: He asks, What might the difference be between reason and being? Inasmuch as all being seemingly must conform to the cognitive structure of objects discerned in the world, reason and being have been conflated. But if a differentiation is considered, a radically different metaphysical posture appears.

Language ensnares Heidegger's efforts in this regard—"What these words say can never be drawn together and packaged in a definition" (1991, p. 94); nevertheless, he attempts to draw a philosophical genealogy about these concepts.[18] Echoing themes discussed previously, he asserts that we distinguish experience that "comes to presence in what is over-against us and what comes to presence in objectness" (ibid., p. 87). The "object" exists as a product of the principle of reason, but the "over-against" us is only intuited as a presence. So Heidegger suggests that a leap be performed "from out of the principle of reason as a fundamental principle about beings into the principle of reason as an utterance of being concealed" (ibid., p. 89). This domain of the concealed, being-as-such, may be approached if we attempt to discern the modern difference between being and ground/reason with a second "tonality" of the principle of reason, one that "speaks a truth, a truth whose import we can hardly imagine" (ibid., p. 90). However, being shackled by language, our lexicon fails. Heidegger insists (as he does throughout his philosophical opus) that philosophy miscarries principally by forgoing the attempt to make that discernment. Instead of retreat or acceptance, he would offer a response to that challenge.

IV

In conclusion, Heidegger's Dasein, conceived specifically in contrast to an anthropological conception of Man, emphatically focuses on how humans might be thrown from the everyday social and psychological life into *existence*, toward Being. This is in contrast to the process of objectification, one that requires a subject to assume a perspective of, or distance from, the object of experience. That construction is built from a Cartesian self-consciousness that must order the world according to its own terms, experience the world as the representation of that reality:

> All this is, is now either what is real as the object or what works the real as the objectifying within which the objectivity of the object takes

shape. Objectifying, in representing, in setting before, delivers up the object to the *ego cogito*. In that delivering up, the ego proves to be that which underlies its own activities. . . . The subject is subject for itself. (Heidegger 1977c, p. 100)

Consequently, "consciousness is self-consciousness," and thus, "everything that is, is therefore either the object of the subject or the subject of the subject." Accordingly, Descartes effected an "insurrection," where the "world changes into object" and is thus put at the "disposal of representing" and subjected to "human positing and analyzing." Consequently, "the earth itself can show itself only as the object of assault . . . of unconditional objectification" (ibid.).

Without further delving into Heidegger's reconstruction, we have discerned enough to draw the dramatic lines of confrontation, which emerged with his challenge to Kantianism, a challenge that would sweep up Freud's own theory in the ensuing debates about the place of reason and representationalism more specifically. The space opened by redefining the character of reason left an opportunity for a species of post-Freudian theorizing to thrive, and in the next chapter we will discuss how Lacan, assuming the general philosophical posture Heidegger championed, translated that orientation into a revision of Freudian psychoanalysis with profound repercussions. His ironic "return to Freud" would not concede even a compromised ego with the epistemological characteristics that Freud bestowed upon it.

5   Lacan's "Return to Freud"

From an analytical point of view, the only thing of which one can be guilty is of having given ground relative to one's desire. Whether it is admissible or not in a given ethics, that proposition expresses quite well something we observe from experience. In the last analysis, what a subject really feels guilty about when he manifests guilt at bottom always has to do with—whether or not it is admissible for a director of conscience—the extent to which he has given ground relative to his desire.

—JACQUES LACAN, *The Ethics of Psychoanalysis*

Psychoanalysis in its therapeutic construction seeks to recognize and then assign meanings to affective experience underlying psychic life. The analysis per se is but the means to reach back to repressed emotional experience, and through its apprehension, "identification" of a neurosis is made. Because "representability as such allows only one of all available psychical contents to be 'known to consciousness'" (Henry 1993, p. 288), widened approaches have been sought to achieve that goal. Indeed, the commitment to the affective domain shifts Freud's therapeutic strategy from a primary focus on the rational reconstruction of psychic trauma to the *instrumental* use of reason as a step toward establishing a reliable interpretation of psychic trauma that has been repressed through its association with a psychic "idea." Or put another way, the affect leads the analysis. Following this orientation, the effort to represent the unconscious introduces a philosophical challenge. Instead of applying ideas to the unconscious, which is essentially a (mis)translation of affective effects, some critics have argued that emotion must be accounted for on its own terms. Specifically, the ontology of the unconscious psyche requires its own grammar and lexicon to explore its structure. The question then, given the centrality of the transference mediated by emotional exchange, is how to place the affective in the *philosophical* structure of Freud's theory. Finding the affections gathers together much of post-Freudian understanding—inspired by Heidegger, developed by Jacques Lacan, and enacted by those who still seek their desire.

Lacan's sophistication and proficiency in using philosophy to develop his own version of psychoanalytic theory have generated a large secondary literature. The assessment that "no writer in the history of psychoanalysis has done more to bring Freudian theory into dialogue with the philosophical tradition than Jacques Lacan" is well supported (Shepherdson 2003, p. 116), and many have observed Heidegger's influence on Lacan (they met in 1955), which has both particular and general aspects (for example, Richardson 1979; Lee 1990, pp. 208–9; Dallmayr 1993; Rockmore 1995, p. 128; Shepherdson 2003, pp. 117–18, 131–32; Rogozinski 2010, pp. 52ff.). Most apparently, Heidegger's philosophy of language ("[L]anguage speaks, not humans. Humans only speak inasmuch as they respond to language" [1991, p. 96]) found a ready home in Lacanian theory, which espoused a psychoanalytic thesis on the tenet that "the unconscious is structured like a language" (Lacan 1978, p. 20).[1] Indeed, not only does the unconscious "speak" but it displaces the ego as the center of psychoanalytic interest that characterizes object-relation psychologies. That rift among psychoanalytic theorists is not of direct concern here; rather, we seek to understand how Lacan conceives psychoanalytic agency in contrast to Freud, specifically, one indebted to Heidegger's revisionary philosophy. On this view, Heidegger opens the space into which Lacan places his own efforts to revise Freudianism, and, as we will see, this restructuring will prove indispensable in postmodern reconfigurations of thinking and moral agency.

I

Acknowledging the limits of self-knowledge, Freud nevertheless accepted the potential of rational insight and the salutary effects of analysis as a means toward progress, at both the individual and social levels. Lacan denied that the conscious ego is either the author of his own acts or the meaning and value one assigns to them (whether before psychoanalysis or afterward). To think otherwise results in illusion (Lacan 1991, p. 243). An intimate stranger, an Other, resides within the subject; Lacan places the *true subject* not in the ego but in the unconscious: "[T]he self is understood to be spoken in discourse rather than the self being the sovereign agent of enunciation" (Halliwell 1999, p. 10), and with that move, Freud's scientific perspective has been replaced with the primacy of the subjective voice, and psychoanalysis then becomes the means whereby the self-deception of a scrutinizing, domineering ego retreats before an "uncovering" or "revealing" of the true self. This formulation, heavily indebted to Heidegger's conception of Dasein, conceives "authenticity" as the recognition of the ongoing oscillation between the veiled and the unveiled encounter with Being. In a psychoanalytic Sisyphean drama, such a characterization refers to an agent doomed to ever presenting itself to that which cannot be recognized. For Heidegger, and for Lacan, the process of facing the unknown, the *nothing*, is quintessentially human, and by adopting this metaphysical posture, Lacan organized his revision of Freudian theory around the persistent search for the *lack*, the absent, the beyond, which orients the vectors of desire. He would thus transform psychoanalysis into a Heideggerian quest for Being, albeit translated into the psychoanalytic lexicon.

The origins of Lacan's formulation may be tracked back to Freud's own conception of the ego and its relation to the larger psychic structure. For Freud, the unconscious dominates the psychic economy, and he describes the "arrogance of consciousness" (1910a, p. 39) as a jockey atop a blinkered horse (1923a, p. 25). The rider, astride his unconscious other, may think he may direct it, but that control is largely illusory. And as we watch the ongoing dynamic of horse and rider, we may well ask, Who is the Self and who is the Other? For Freud, the unconscious constitutes the psyche's center, and the relationship between consciousness, with its armory of rationality, resides in both a conceptual and psychological no-man's-land; thus, selfhood (in its classical discourse) remains largely undeveloped (Tauber 2010, chap. 6). That Freud held to the ego's authority represents a moral position, not one necessarily consistent with his psychological depiction of psychic dynamics. As such, an inconsistency looms, which Lacan targeted.

When Freud presents the realization of a wish as something divorced from some distinct social reality, and the ego becomes the agent that creates and presents those series of representations that would mediate the wish, the self disappears in the endless reproduction of those representations generated to address unfulfilled desire. Accordingly, "the wish has exchanged its being for a procession of symbols and imaginary fixations whose proliferation lends itself to the play of analysis, which is itself endless. The 'ego' must now be sought in the forest of signs and illusions" (Henry 1993, p. 303). If this is the residual basis of selfhood, a function that represents a deeper psyche, then Freud justly leaves the issue, for what might the ego then *be*? What does it represent beyond a representing faculty? On what grounds would any autonomy upon which psychoanalysis rest then be based? The implications of this representational construction of the psyche leaves unanswered fundamental questions about agency that seem to abdicate a coherent philosophy of personal identity and the moral structure upon which it might rest (other than the internalization of social mores and strictures within the superego). Indeed, when posed in these terms, we again ask, Who, in fact, is the subject? Nietzsche posed the question and offered a reply, which closely resonates with Lacan's position:

> I don't concede that the "I" is what thinks. Instead, I take the *I itself to be a construction of thinking*, of the same rank as "matter," "thing," "substance," "individual," "purpose," "number": in other words to be only a *regulative* fiction with the help of which a kind of constancy and thus "knowability" is inserted into, *invented into*, a world of becoming. . . . [U]p to now philosophers have believed . . . that this "I" was the given cause of thinking. . . . However habituated and indispensable this fiction may now be, that in no way disproves its having been invented: something can be a condition of life and *nevertheless be false*. (Nietzsche 2003, pp. 20–21; emphasis in original)

In sum, the "I" of the subject-object structure of conscious thinking divides the unity of psychic life into a conscious-unconscious artifice, whose structure conforms to a theoretical model but fails to offer an adequate manifold for personal identity. Thus, the attempt to capture unconscious "thought" must fail, inasmuch as this aspect of psychic life does not conform to the imposed structure of conscious predicate thinking. Following Nietzsche, it is unconscious psychic life that constitutes human being, and the affects of that domain are demonstrably present and directly available in various modalities of emotion and feeling.

Desire, emerging from psychic sources well below consciousness and indecipherable in reason's terms, becomes the radical other only as the result of a relationship imposed from above, that is, from a conscious ego that would clamp its own mode of knowing upon a psychic domain that follows a different language and a different logic—a mind of another kind. Lacan sought to remedy this psychology. He built his position from a deep suspicion of the representational modalities Freud employed in psychoanalytic theory (e.g.,

Kernberg 1980, p. 17). Following that "the unconscious is not susceptible to colonization by Knowledge," yet to become "accessible to the introspective psychological eye" (Reeder 2002, pp. 18–19), the unconscious is rendered in representations, a *mis*representation must result. In short, the unconscious has been "harmonized" with (and for) the ego (ibid.).

Lacan, offended by this compromise, propounded a major revision to Freud's entire approach in asserting that the unconscious cannot be *known* by any of the ego's representations. For Lacan, what is discovered is an absence, where "the reality of the unconscious . . . is not an ambiguity of acts, future knowledge that is already known not to be known, but lacuna, cut, rupture inscribed in a certain lack" (Lacan 1993, p. 153). Anticonceptual and thus inassimilable, its domain is always "other" and no symbolization can contain it (Winquist 1998, p. 313). Accordingly, not only does the analytic misrepresent the unconscious and thereby distort it but also the endeavor to uncover the sources of unconscious desire lies beyond the tools of psychoanalysis. In this regard, Freudianism becomes a basic instantiation of ego domination. Lacan would denounce this therapeutic ethos and decry its goals of an adaptive psychotherapy. Echoing Adorno's sentiments, Freudianism imprisons the subject in a web of misrepresentations that justifies an oppressive social order. So "insight" is ultimately doomed to frustration, for analytic tools come to a void "at the heart of our object world" (Reeder 2012, p. 35). In this view, another formulation is required to achieve the aspiration of liberating the shackled. And Lacan set his sights precisely on establishing that new theory.

The metapsychology from which Lacan builds his case begins with his appropriation of Freud's schematization of the drives into their *source* (somatic process), *aim* (tension reduction), and *object* (person or thing through which the drive is satisfied). The "empty core" (Reeder 2012) that Lacan identifies as the lost object of desire transforms Freud's *das Ding* (the *thing*) into *the* quest of the Lacanian psychoanalytic process.[2] The mother's abandoned breast, as a paradigmatic case,[3] ultimately must be substituted with something or someone else, and while the original object is given up, the desire associated with the primordial feeding (or any other primary desire) remains unrelinquished. When desire moves from its primary object to a substitute, the attempts to find what has been lost persist. Thus, the process of substitution (or in another parlance, representation) becomes a fundamental feature of psychic life.[4] Once retrieved (as image, fantasy, word, *Vorstellung*), such memories become objects within the subject's cognitive realm as representations (Lacan 1992). The dynamics of this process will be discussed later, so suffice it to note here that as a representation, the original entirety of the object has been fractured, leaving a residual, an excess, which is created as a residue of the representation itself. That missing remainder becomes the focus of Lacan's theory.

Freud's introduction of *das Ding* is the beginning of Lacan's own theory, in which this moment in subjective development marks the infant's shift from the biological to the mental domain. For Freud, this speculative event cannot carry his theory. Although *das Ding* approximates Kant's *noumenon* (*das Ding an sich*) and thus sets a rough conceptual framework, it has little direct contribution to Freud's representational schema. However, for Lacan, *das Ding* assumes a pivotal role to become the focus of his theoretical musings from which he builds a new metapsychological foundation for the clinical practice of psychoanalysis (Boothby 2001; De Kesel 2009; Reeder 2012). For him, *das Ding* organizes the subject's psychic life in relation to her desire. Upon the movement from the original object of desire to its representative, Freud's *das Ding* is presented in another form (and thus not itself) and a portion of its identity (character, nature) is left unaccounted altogether. And as the process of identifying, sorting, parsing, remembering continues in ever-widening associations, the sequential excesses (the nonrepresented) grow and the original wish-object becomes increasingly lost, obscured by the various manifestations of a representational cascade that has no delimiting features.

The movement of *das Ding* from its primary status to its various secondary manifestations is the wedge upon which Lacan will drive his own theory. Lacan commences with two basic steps. First, he emphasizes the character of desire as essentially incapable of being fulfilled:

> [W]hat is supposed to be found cannot be found again. It is in its nature that the object as such is lost. It will never be found again. Something is there while one waits for something better, or worse, but which one wants.
>
> The world of our experience, the Freudian world, assumes that it is this object, *das Ding*, as the absolute Other of the subject, that one is supposed to find again. . . . One doesn't find it, but only its pleasurable associations. (Lacan 1992, p. 52)

Second, given desire's ultimate frustration (due to the realities that block and intrude upon fulfillment), the original object must be exchanged and thus represented by others. In this movement, the "coordinates of pleasure" ("pleasurable associations" established by the initial object of desire) orient the subject toward fulfillment (or at least potential satisfaction) by determining points of reference established by previous pleasurable experience. In directing desire to its immediate—newly represented—object, displacement naturally occurs, but the new object, fundamentally incomplete, thwarts desire in a psychic compromise from which there is no escape. Lacan identifies this "gap" as the beginning of a new conception of psychodynamics.

Whereas for Freud, *das Ding* is something in reality that simply disappears, Lacan characterizes *Ding* by its ability to concern and engage, constituting a point of reference for a desire always aiming at something that is *not* there. Accordingly, the "lost object" is lost only retroactively as other representations are recognized. "*Das Ding* designates an unencompassable aspect of every representation, a kind of ungraspable center of gravity that lends coherence to the various manifestations of an object while remaining itself ineluctably out of reach" (Boothby 2001, p. 204). Only through interpretations does *Ding* become recognized as represented through some selected object, which a psychoanalytic narrative organizes into its own context of understanding.

> *Das Ding* is a void that arises because a chain of representations *is representation* and not the represented. In this view, *das Ding* stands out as an effect of the subject's symbolic function and the retrograde projection of a *no-thing*, an empty core at the center of the object world that can be substituted only with the series of representations that have made it appear in the first place. In this capacity of a locus without proper content *das Ding* constitutes a point of reference for (the coordinates of) desire and the subject's realization of its existence. (Reeder 2012, p. 39; emphasis in original)

In the encounter with *das Ding*, a dynamic that articulates a representation of some kind where an object is, in a sense identified, the undifferentiated "the real" is fractured or cut. The result forms the represented object and a residue. This remainder is both outside (represented) and inside—a structure that holds, in a sense, the original place of the Other. Structurally, the Other orients the subject and the object, and dynamically, it serves as the nexus for the drives and thus the locus of desire. This Other has various forms in Lacanian theory, but the aspect that orients desire is called *objet a*.[5] This something at the heart of the subject, a presence that serves as a doppelgänger of the self-conscious ego, remains mysteriously silent and alien, yet present. Lacan can well ask, "Who, then, is this other to whom I am more attached than to myself, since, at the heart of my assent to my identity it is still he who agitates me?" (2001, p. 130; 2006, p. 436). Whereupon he responds that psychoanalysis becomes the project of uncovering (Heideggerian unveiling) unrequited desire as the expression of this Unknown Other.

For Lacan, to support psychic health and self-fulfillment, desire (the psyche's vital "motor") must be recognized as such and its various obscuring representations exposed. However, to live out one's desire, to fulfill the potential of one's fate in the reality of persistent and remorseless frustration, portrays a tragic view of an ethical life: Once *das Ding* exists—leaving only traces of the original object in various displacements—the lost object per se vanishes as the object of desire (be it the breast, the mother, or reality itself), and the various substitutions, partial (and thus dissatisfying) replacements, must fail the role *das Ding* had originally fulfilled. Accordingly, the ultimate object of desire is *das Ding*—and that object of desire is precisely that which a world of objects (a web of representations) cannot furnish. In a very literal way, then, the object of desire is acquired as a product of the human apparatus for thinking. And the product of this representational mind must leave desire unfulfilled.

Because *das Ding* is lost to our understanding, substitutions are made and fantasy replaces reality:

> [T]he libidinal being bonds with a fictional object and constructs for this bond an equally fictional bearer: a subject. The gap—and accordingly, the relation—between the two will not only be imaginarily misconceived, it will also and primarily be symbolically repressed, that is passed on from signifier to signifier. (De Kesel 2009, p. 88)

Thus, Lacan takes the psychic vectors originating with *das Ding* as the basis for a representational process that by its very nature must misrepresent and, in its fantastic construction of imaginary signifiers, creates substituted, that is, fabricated, objects of desire. As a result the subject herself (in her capacity of judgment) lives within an imaginary psychic reality of signifiers, and in that illusory subject-object identity, not only does the subject pursue displaced primary desire but also the object-relations of subjectivity have been fundamentally distorted. Thus, the imperative to address desire in the Lacanian construct becomes the task of redeeming subjectivity from the falsifications of misrepresented desire. The therapeutic task thus emerges: Breaking through the web of representations—the complex of derivative signifiers—requires recognizing the primacy of the primordial desire that lies at the base of a distorted subject-object psychic reality.

II

For Lacan, the ego is another object, with a powerful self-deceptive facility that cannot effectively preside over desire. This disenfranchisement became the key tenet of Lacan's earliest theory of subjectivity, according to which the ego is an *imaginary* construct and thus differentiated from the (true) *subject* of the unconscious. Accordingly, the ego forms as a result of a misleading identification, which in the famous mirror trope is the process that occurs as a result of the introduction of the imaginary upon the infant's first recognition of itself as a "specular image" (Lacan 1988, p. 282; 2006, pp. 75ff., 853; Fink 1995; Evans 1996, pp. 114–16).[6] According to Lacan, this primordial, imaginary identification occurs as a result of an unconscious adoption of an external image, which, in effect, "irredeemably 'traps' the subject" (Chiesa 2007, p. 15) in the misrecognition (or imaginary misidentification) of some new object. In other words, as a result of the imaginary identification, the ego becomes another object (and, accordingly, the subject cannot be reduced to the ego). In that identification, the ego assumes that image, a representation of itself as it were. While the initial encounter is a moment of jubilation since it leads to a feeling of mastery, this so-called mirror stage also is accompanied by a misunderstanding (*méconnaissance*) and alienation. After all, the mirror image is not the ego, or as René Magritte noted of his painting of a pipe, "Ceci n'est pas une pipe." At the very least, a tension develops at the root of identity, and for Lacan, the ego perpetually struggles to break its own self-representation, or in later developments, the self-consciousness of identity.[7]

This psychic structure derives from Lacan's understanding of the Cartesian ego, which in effect is the ego's representation of itself as divided by its own self-consciousness. Lacan argues that a gap appears between the

> "I" of the "I think" and the "I" of the "I am," which follows as a logical conclusion from the "I think." That is to say, either these two "I's" are not the same thing or the second is already assumed in the positing of the first. "I think" already entails the subject "I" and, thus, the conclusion, "I am" is strictly superfluous. Descartes has not really proved or substantiated anything beyond what he had already presupposed. (Neill 2011, p. 15)

Thus, to communicate with oneself already entails a division. The very nature of such a monologue is, in fact, a dialogue, that is, one who speaks with another, or in the Cartesian framework, with oneself.[8] So the "I" that is said to think is already marked off from the "I" that affirms the thinking, as the result of the ego having represented "'himself' to 'himself' or . . . he imagines himself but such imagining can only come about on the basis of him *symbolizing* [representing] himself" (ibid., p. 17; emphasis in original). In other words, subjectivity swings between the self-consciousness of "I think" and the being of "I am." And the authenticity of "I am" drives toward identifying and living the true subject, unconscious desire. When I am not consciously thinking, when "I" is not (re-) presented in thought, the subject extends in the world, unmediated by the self-consciousness of its own thought. Here, despite the very different discourse, we recognize Heidegger's presence.

Following this divisionary practice to its logical end, Lacan posits the ego as "dis-unified, as duplicated, as, in some sense, impossible, insofar as, in positing itself, it presents, and only presents, itself as an image of itself for itself" (Neill 2011, p. 19). Simply, for Lacan, "I think, therefore I am" attests strictly to conscious thought, and such thought for Lacan is illusory. This leaves the unrepresentable unconscious as the true subject, which Lacan describes as "[only] an apparatus. This apparatus is something lacunary, and it is in the lacuna that the subject establishes the function of a certain object, *qua* lost object" (1978, p. 185). Lacan thus took Freud's original formulation, where the unconscious is an "acephalic subject . . . who no longer has an ego, who doesn't belong to the ego" (Lacan 1991, p. 169), and bestows an authenticity upon that presence, which he describes as the "'barred' subject that is no longer anyone, an X, an empty place, a 'subjectification without subject'" (1978, p. 184; Rogozinski 2010, p. 53). In short, the ego not only is an illusion in the calculus of psychic dynamics but is, at best, a placeholder, which, from the Lacanian perspective, is only to be purged in the "therapeutic" triumph of unconscious desire.[9] And here we again see Lacan's appropriation of the psychoanalytic trope in which the lost object of desire, *das Ding*—the thing—is sought.

This analysis inverts Freud's own understanding of psychoanalysis, where an ego probes its own psyche to conduct a private language of inquiry. According to Lacan, such a private language has no standing, for in employing some form of language or signifying system, the ego splits itself (i.e., thinking), and following his schema, the ego in representing itself to (or for) itself is enmeshed in a falsifying representational language. Thus, psychoanalysis becomes "the science of language inhabited by the subject. From the Freudian point of view, man is the subject captured and tortured by language" (Lacan 1993, p. 243). There is no ego without thinking, and there is no thinking without language: "[T]he signifier of the subject [language] comes to take the place of the subject and, as such, constitutes the subject as extinguishable" (Neill 2011, p. 21), and because humans are represented in language, language is constitutive to, and formative of, the ego (ibid.). Thus, the ego "is nothing but language while, at the same time, the subject is nothing because of language. It is only through being represented that the subject can be said to exist at all and yet, at the same time, in being so represented, the subject is strictly not there. The signifier is there" (ibid., p. 23). So what is the *signifier*?

The Lacanian universe is made up of three components—the real, the imaginary, and the symbolic register—in which the signifier functions as a mediator of sorts. The *real* is that which cannot be symbolized; "the signifier is a unique unit of being which, by its very nature, is the symbol of but an absence" (Lacan 2006, p. 17). This absence, a constitutive lack, requires signification in the *imaginary* realm, so in this construction the absence of the signified in its real dimension causes a transference as a signified into the imaginary dimension. There, in the *symbolic register*, as a result of the play of signifiers, signification (meaning) ultimately emerges. According to this tripartite schema, the signifier is the psychic function that basically moves the unknowable real to the imaginary, where it assumes representational signification in the symbolic register and obtains meaning as the product of its relation to other signified representations. In this view, the psyche is a dynamic field of "significants." The crucial element of this psychic calculus is the failure of representation itself. The signified is never complete. Something is always missing in the signifying chain, for the signifiers cannot eliminate an ever-present absence, the lack of the real. Something thus remains "radically unassimilable to the signifier" (Lacan 1993, p. 179), and consequently the order of language (i.e., representation) must be incomplete.

By making representation the focus of his psychology, Lacan sought to show the limits and essential inapplicability of a Cartesian schema to create a psychology in which representations must fail in the attempt to construct a stable identity. Indeed, "identity is possible only as a failed identity" (Stavrakakis 1999, p. 29). Accordingly, in this formulation, the ego's representational function misrepresents precisely because it endeavors to represent the unconscious, that which cannot be represented. In short, the failure is constitutive to the ego's mode of thinking.[10] However, more than offering only a diagnosis, Lacanian psychoanalysis provides a prescription as well, one that required the dismantling of the ego's authority. Thus, Lacan based his so-called return to Freud on positing that his revision of psychoanalysis "sets us at odds with any philosophy directly stemming from the *cogito*" (2006, p. 94). And then an ethical component is added: "The point is not to know whether I speak of myself in a way that conforms to what I am, but rather to know whether, when I speak of myself, I am the same as the self of whom I speak" (ibid., p. 340). He would seek a psychology that reconfigured authenticity, again by displacing the ego for another notion of agency. To achieve that new state, he sought to expose the ego's origins and thereby identify the hegemony Freud himself understood as "the arrogance of consciousness" (Freud 1910a, p. 39).

Lacan considered the cogito a "mirage" (2006, p. 340), and with its dissimulation, he deduced that the subject cannot be represented by itself to itself and subjectivity consequently must have a different understanding. He saw the template from which identity is first achieved occurring at the mirror stage. As already discussed, no longer an individual or conscious subject, this initial establishment of a sense of unity and identity (the so-called spatial imaginary identity) serves as a representation to the ego *of* the ego. To the extent the image is incorporated, that doppelgänger precipitates a tension in the disjunction created by the fragmentary, incomplete character of this alter ego as compared to the lived, bodily experience of the subject. This becomes the crucial philosophical locus for Lacan: The ego cannot claim, because of its dependence on an *imaginary* (perhaps less radically, *constructed*) identity, a stable subjectivity, one based on some notion of epistemological autonomy, insular self-consciousness, and certainty.

The "gap of alienating tension" provides the space in which "the symbolic order comes in" (Lacan 1991, p. 323), where "everything that is human has to be ordained within a universe constituted by the symbolic function" (ibid., p. 29). The symbolic order is constitutive for the subject, because in the linguistic representation a symbolic register confers identity, which draws from language and all that is embedded therein—cultural, historical, gender, family normative structures. In the psyche's evolution, the child learns and submits to language in order to stabilize her identity: "[T]he child becomes a subject in language, it inhabits language" (Stavrakakis 1999, p. 20), and thereby navigates the world through the representations of words. The subject, in "its constituent relation to the signifier itself" (Lacan 1978, p. 43), becomes the subject of the signifier. Indeed, the signifier dominates the subject (Lacan 2006, pp. 28, 45). The structural difference is critical: Because no unity or direct reference relates signifier to the signified, "meaning is produced by signifiers; it springs from the signifier to the signified and not vice versa (as argued by realist representation)" (Stavrakakis 1999, p. 25). Note that the signifier is not something that functions as a representation of the signified, that is, "the symbolic is not the order of the sign, as in Saussurean linguistics, but the order of the signifier" (ibid., p. 26). In this schema, the signifier "creates the field of meanings" (Lacan 1993, p. 292), and herein a new psychology emerges—the subject becomes an *effect* of the signifier (Stavrakakis 1999, pp. 19ff.).[11] And as already mentioned, signification—the becoming of a subject—resides within a lattice of signifiers signifying other signifiers. The signified achieves its meaning only as a product of a linguistic process in which the signifier signifies to the subject.

> What, then, is the subject for Lacan? It is "what the signifier represents to another signifier." Always absent from discourse, the subject is the element missing from the signifying chain, and it is never able to be said, to be articulated in spoken language without letting itself be represented by the signifier substituted for it. This certainly does not mean that I existed as a subject *before* being displaced by the signifier: the "priority of the signifier over the subject" implies that I am *nothing* before the signifier "I" . . . calls me to exist as subject. (Rogozinski 2010, p. 65; emphasis in original)[12]

And more, identity becomes the product of endless failure, in which a process of incomplete, if not falsifying, identifications emerges from the symbolization of the imaginary. That miscarriage is due to the constitutive failure of representation to capture the real, which then leaves no grounding to support the construction of identity.

Lacan thus reframed the scaffolding of the psyche by presenting the subject as what the signifier represents to another signifier and thereby removed the subject as such. That inner signifying language, of course, cannot be confused with overt public dialogue, for Lacan dismissed inner dialogue and interpersonal encounters to a reduced superficial, imaginary plaster over the vibrant reality of the symbolic unconscious, where the subject, in essence is "being spoken."[13] This signifying psychology thus displaces the Freudian ego for an unconscious that has assumed new authority, one that no longer vies for dominance in a tripartite psychic structure but one that radically ordains all functions. The repercussions of this formulation extend to the very depths of psychoanalytic theory by redefining the status of the ego and its relation to the unconscious. Simply, the ego (even in its circumspect Freudian incarnation) has lost its self-knowing pretensions, and in its fall from Cartesian grace, Lacan would sing its requiem.[14]

One might well agree with Lacan that the ego "evolves" from the unconscious to serve the psyche for certain purposes, but Lacan's opponents argue that to conceive the ego as only an illusory subject is to misconstrue the ego's undeniable presence of itself as a subject. That this self-consciousness is lodged in its own locus of psychic activity does not necessarily consign its legitimacy to some indenture to its origins. The two domains—conscious and unconscious—engage in an interior dialogue (whether conceived as Freud did or otherwise; see Tauber 2013), and in that exchange the just claims of each are developed. In other words, as Jacob Rogozinski (2010) charges, not only is the mirror trope erroneous as Lacan employed it in terms of theorizing about the origin of the ego but the disingenuous dismissal of the ego's own certainty as a cognitive agent aware of the world and itself in it misconstrues agency with wide-ranging ramifications. And so the debate is posed.

III

The Lacanian therapeutic ethos seeks to displace the ego's (falsifying) authority and thereby express the true subjectivity of the unconscious (expressed as desire). By understanding the ego's agency, Lacanian psychoanalysis thereby shifts from rational interpretation linked to potential control (through understanding) of unconscious drives to a therapy of rediscovering and liberating unconscious desire. As opposed to imposing another (conscious) moral structure upon personal identity, Lacan would pursue unconscious desire in order to fulfill itself. And with that move, the ego's autonomy is forfeited. Freud had concurred about the compromised standing of the ego's own sovereignty, while at the same time holding to a modernist concept of a normative ethos by which the ego governs the psyche; Lacan goes further. His theoretical portrait emphasizes the ego's constraints, not its freedoms. Like Adorno and Heidegger, Lacan would displace the hegemony of the ego for what he devised as a more authentic identity. The question of course looms, *What* is authentic?

When Lacan observed that "the only thing one can be guilty of is having given up on one's desire,"[15] he summarized a critique that went to the very roots of Freudian psychoanalysis. In the opening of his seminar on ethics, Lacan drives home the theme of his entire endeavor, in which he extends the very presence of the unconscious not as a destructive counterforce to "the good life" but rather as a presence whose calling imposes a *moral* command. Lacan interprets Freud's "Wo Es war, soll Ich werden" (Where id was, there ego shall be [Freud 1933, p. 80]) as a duty—an ought, an imperative—whose exhortation, while a search for truth, fundamentally expresses a "moral experience" (Lacan 1992, p. 7).

Beyond a challenge to conventional notions of ethics (indeed, Lacan is not concerned with ethics per se), desire organizes psychic health, and by orienting toward both recognizing and following desire, Lacan would effect a radical revision of subjectivity (De Kesel 2009, p. 49).

Doing things in the name of the good, and even more in the name of the good of the other, is something that is far from protecting us not only from guilt but also from all kinds of inner catastrophes. To be precise, it doesn't protect us from neurosis and its consequences. If analysis has a meaning, desire is nothing other than that which supports an unconscious theme, the very articulation of that which roots us in a particular destiny, and that destiny demands insistently that the debt be paid, and desire keeps coming back, keeps returning, and situates us once again in a given track, the track of something that is specifically our business. (Lacan 1992, p. 319)

Psychodynamically, one does not forgo an object of one's desire, that is, some specified goal, for

human desire, strictly speaking, has no object. Indeed, it doesn't quite know what to do with objects. . . . Desire disappears when it attains its ostensible object. . . . Desire thus does not seek satisfaction; rather, it pursues its own continuation and furtherance—it merely goes on desiring. (Fink 1997, p. 51; emphasis in original)

As the subject balances the restrictions of reality with the call of desire and unrequited yearning, two options appear, both of which claim legitimacy: In a minor key, a refraction of the tragic image of humanity looms, but this is not Lacan's position or concern. He asserts the more optimistic alternative, an implicit hope, which follows the Nietzschean anthem of renewal, where the struggle itself sustains vitality. The ethics of psychoanalysis then becomes the endeavor to save desire. Accordingly, psychoanalysis becomes the proponent of freed yearning and the advocate for the legitimacy of the unconscious as the locus of human being. (Here, echoes of Adorno's own anthem resound, albeit in a very different register.)

The import of Lacan's interpretive schema is far more than a description of psychic development. For him, the symbolic or representational function occasions the loss, that is, the establishment of *das Ding* that desire unremittingly seeks (Reeder 2012). And if postmodernism has a cardinal lesson, it is the demand that we attend to true desire, the expression of one's true self, which for Lacan is the unconscious itself. Simply, the psyche is organized and functions to capture that which has been forever lost, and in that quest, desire must follow an available course, one, however, that cannot attain its true object and thus is ultimately doomed to failure. Repression (leading to conflict and then anxiety) becomes the central motif in the Freudian force field of this psychic drama, but Lacan sought an alternative, as did all those who would take the Freudian deterministic psychoanalytics in another utopian direction. Following Adorno and Heidegger, he devalorized the ego constituted by values and cultural determinants that had been imposed for social expediency at the expense of individual happiness. As Freud noted, "[C]ivilization is largely responsible for our misery" (1930, p. 86), but instead of a strategy based on sublimation, Lacan advocated "authenticity," the pursuit of desire.

Psychoanalysis, while recognizing its "impossible" task of uncovering the real, nevertheless, in its pursuit of discerning the unconscious domain, seeks to deliberate on the identifications that characterize ego formation. On Lacan's even more wary view of self-knowledge, Freudian doubt assumed a more radical orientation: Because symbolization must be incomplete, we do well to define the limits of those symbols (political and social) and attempt to differentiate the most egregiously false representations from those that hold more promise for human flourishing. In other words, with Lacan's implicit understanding that psychoanalysis must fail in representing psychic dynamics, he lay the groundwork for a skepticism, which informs a moral scrutiny absent from more confident views of human autonomy.

Beginning with an ego lacking autonomy, Lacan challenged the ego psychologies that would strive to achieve varying degrees of freedom by strengthening the ego. In his account, the ego in Western societies has become a receptacle of unidentified social forces as part of the identifications that its identity comprises.[16] Strictly speaking, of course, no stable identity as such exists in the Lacanian construct, only identifications, which include political ideologies and other socially constructed objects (Stavrakakis 1999, pp. 30–39). Reality is always a mediated reality, a symbolic construct, and because an objective, knowable reality does not exist, the health of the ego cannot be defined objectively in adaptation to reality. The normative structure having collapsed in the social ether created by historical contingencies, any human-centered perspective loses authority. Lacan derived this position from erasing any real boundary between man and society: "[M]an becomes social with the appropriation of language, and it is language that constitutes man as a subject" (Turkle 1978, p. 74). As the ego incorporates the social, the distinction of private and social, with a Marxist nod, becomes a bourgeois ideology. So instead of adaptation, Lacan stressed personal discovery, and from there a utopian glimmer appears.

Lacan's "return to Freud" interpretation oriented postmodern critiques by shifting psychoanalysis from the medical "cure" model to a "science" of individual "research" and self-discovery. With that move, adaptation to the social has been subordinated to understanding the misalignments of the analysand and her world, which are due to the oppressive cultural environment itself. From this orientation, largely the result of a very different understanding of the ego, both as a psychoanalytic locus and a social construct, Lacan swung psychoanalytic social theory from the ego-oriented psychologies to one positioned to understand and radically reform the social with an agent of different character. He clearly provided an alternative to the ego-based utopian social theories offered by Anglo-American commentators by turning "psychoanalysis into a school for listening to the passions of the soul and to the malaise of civilization, the only school capable of counteracting the philanthropic but deceptive ideals of happiness therapies that claim to treat the ego and cultivate narcissism, while really concealing the disintegration of inner identity" (Roudinesco 2003, p. 33).

The ensemble of critiques, which drew from a synthesis between Lacan and French Marxist theorists (following the events of May

1968 [Turkle 1978]), have been widely influential. Clearly, much of post-Freudian culture criticism has characterized the "decentered subject" and explored opportunities for a psychoanalytic-inspired reconfiguration of social repression from this perspective.[17] Indeed, Marxist reinterpretations of Freudian social dynamics and Lacanian psychoanalytic theory forged an important alliance, which in toto jettisoned Freud's own Enlightenment commitments, and in so doing they challenged the moral standing of the ego. When viewed from the postmodern side of the modernist divide, perhaps Lacan's proclamation "return to Freud!" led his theoretical compatriots to an ideology of personhood that took for its coordinates a radically altered notion of ethics.

From a moral point of view, a schism emerges between the Freudian and Lacanian perspectives. Whereas Freud sought rational insight leading to control as the modus operandi of psychoanalysis, Lacan built an ethics from the subject's liberation of her desire ("do not give way to your desire"), and in the process he indicted Freud at the deepest reaches of moral ideals. According to Lacan, Freud had discovered that "man isn't entirely in man" and thereby had abdicated humanist standing (Lacan 1991, p. 72).[18] So for those who saw an ironic outcome to Freud's endeavor, one that constituted a fundamental philosophical mistake with wide-ranging ramifications, a major revision of his psychology was required. They attempted to construct theories that would give the affects a more faithful depiction of their role in psychic life, one that would free them from what might be called reason's tyranny. That effort centered on characterizing an emotional reality framed by desire, *endless desire*. This, the latest chapter in the long history of the controversy about how to configure the emotion-reason spectrum of thought, witnesses the ascendency of passion in answer to the demise of reason and the controlling ego. And as part of that dynamic, the moral philosophy guiding psychoanalysis has been reassessed. Typical of poststructuralist thought, Lacan's ethical universe dispenses with any normative ideal as the ego has been replaced with a "subject" whose desire trumps all else. The narcissism that Freud so carefully elucidated has ironically come to dominate the ethos of a theory recast with very different presuppositions. Is the Lacanian depiction the inevitable end point of the Freudian Revolution? Has reason's own self-inquiry found itself in an endless regress where the Cartesian cogito can find no resting place? The challenge to post-postmodernists seems self-evident.

From this widened perspective, the contest over Freudianism has become a chapter of a much larger story. The choice offered by Freud and Lacan leads to very different notions of human identity. Freud, the modernist, recognized the precarious place of reason in the psyche's economy, and he understood with profound insight how reason's own subjection to emotion severely compromised claims of autonomy and sacrosanct logic. However, he balanced uncertainty against what he thought the most effective cognitive tool humans possess, namely, reason. So on balance, with all caveats considered, Freud took a *moral* stand on the ethics of a reasoned life, and this orientation required an active response to life's challenges. Perhaps that is his greatest contribution, for having recognized the power of the unreasoned unconscious and the weakness of the ego to direct the forces of the id, he refashioned a humanist program for a psychoanalytically informed world by asserting the standing of reasoned analysis as a moral imperative. In this view, a choice between Freud's thesis of "insight leading to mastery" and a more passive (or "lighter") position demarcates the ethical vision of our times. Indeed, which psychology will dominate in establishing the contours of self-identity and the parameters of freedom? Much is at stake.

In no small measure, the line demarcating the "egocides" differentiates two intellectual and moral communities (Rogozinski 2010). In dislodging the ego under his disingenuous "return to Freud," Lacan assigned the ego an illusory life in order to recognize the being of desire and authenticate its calling.[19] That revisionist interpretation of the psychoanalytic task, which has been subject to seemingly endless comment, belies what Freud actually wrote: "It [referring to "Where id was, there ego shall be"] is a work of culture—not unlike draining of the Zunder Zee" (1933, p. 80), which, at least for Freud, meant the eventual triumph of rational forces over arational desire. His persistent preoccupation with social theory and utopian application of his theory rests on that basic orientation. However, as discussed in the next chapter, that aspiration, following a psychology focused on liberated desire, took a very different turn and ended in a postmodernism he most probably would not have recognized as originating in his own model of the psyche.

6   The *Désirants*: Whither the Ego?

It is a Freudian axiom that the essence of man consists, not, as
Descartes maintained, in thinking, but in desiring.

—NORMAN O. BROWN, *Life against Death*

Post-Freudian philosophical reflections on the ego divide between
those who offered critiques aimed at reforming dysfunctional
ego instincts and rehabilitating reason in service to healthy ego
functions, and those who would celebrate the demise of the ego
altogether and reach into the unconscious for an expressive libido
that would liberate the ego of its excessive restraints (Tauber
2012a). The first group huddles together in the modernist camp,
defensively responding to the second group, who vigorously
attacks the very notion of selfhood. Even though this is an
oversimplification of an obviously complex continuum of thought,
these two competing orientations have framed the discussion about
the ego's philosophical character for the past fifty years, and here
we consider the argument from the postmodern perspective.

I

A vague utopianism orients postmodernists to break asun-
der a restrictive rationality and thus liberate knowledge, expand

experience, and recast morality in their attempt to reformulate personal autonomy. Reaching back to the romantics, and most directly to Nietzsche, they have extended these earlier attempts to emancipate the affects that would allow emotion and feelings to "speak" for themselves. Traditionally, the passions oppose the strictures of reason, and at least in folk psychology, the sense of responsibility imposed by social conformity and the work ethic leave the emotions to find release as best they can. At least that scenario served Freud's hydraulic theory of the libido. With the introduction of the superego, a more complex calculus of control appeared. The superego internalized repressive cultural demands, and rationality suffered further demotion. Later critics took Freud's basic insight of the ego's uncertain self-knowledge and problematic ability to become free of unconscious forces to deconstruct the very notion of a self conceived as a cogito. Whereas Freud directed psycho-*analysis* to the cognizant, rational ego (whose moral agency he embraced), antihumanists contested the very notion of an autonomous rational agent and the moral possibilities attached to such a subject. In that move, they inflicted a potentially devastating wound to Freud's entire moral project. As already discussed, that deconstruction began with Heidegger and was extended in the psychoanalytic context by Lacan, who would displace Freud's preoccupation with the destructive vectors of the unconscious with valorization of a more neutral "desire" and corresponding dethronement of the ego's rationalistic hegemony. Accordingly, social theory was recast with a very different orientation based upon a radically reconceived agency.

In terms of our particular concerns, the standing of reason and notions of personal identity have undergone critiques that have thoroughly altered the Freudian vision of emancipation. The very idea of selfhood has been reconfigured within a domineering social context of "power" and manipulation (Foucault), and concomitant with that move, the arch-principle of autonomy, upon which Enlightenment ideals placed the epistemological and moral agent, has been deconstructed. In parallel, a modernist conception of language, in which an identifiable relation between signifier and signified exists to establish a correspondence theory of truth—based on the validity of the representational system—has been replaced with a pragmatic, holistic understanding (Quine 1990; see Tauber 2009c, pp. 92–100). Rigidified, representational relationships are perceived as fundamentally unstable and characteristically break apart and reconform in new combinations with resulting new meanings (perhaps best developed by Derrida [1978]).

These conceptions of personal identity and the language that constitutes human being reflect a pervasive postmodern ethos: Ephemerality, fragmentation, discontinuity, and the chaotic are accepted as given, and no effort is made (as in classical modernism) to transcend or counteract the lack of structure and the apparent multiplicities at work in all sectors of human experience. Simply, postmodernism "swims, even wallows, in the fragmentary and the chaotic currents of change as if that is all there is" (Harvey 1990, p. 44). And if some unified representation of the world is impossible to fulfill and the complex connections and differentiations can be described only in terms of perpetually shifting fragments and changing relationships, what epistemology *works*? Into the breach falls pragmatism, where local knowledge and practical modes of action replace metastrategies (Harvey 1990, p. 52; Tauber 2009c). And with this move, a different kind of "solidarity" (most influentially espoused by Rorty [1991b, 1991c]) must replace guiding ideals of Truth, Objectivity, and the Real (Hall 1994; Brandom 2000; Malachowski 2002; Auxier and Hahn 2010).

The postmodern theorists have been widely influential in shifting basic epistemological parameters of selfhood from modernist conceptions to something else. In their wide-ranging writings, not only have they offered a new prescription for reading texts but, far more broadly, they have argued how individuals—political, moral, social agents—might be characterized philosophically upon tenets quite different from Cartesian notions of certainty. On a host of issues, they have opined about Freud and Lacan, the role of language, and the character of self-consciousness and how the positions they have charted map onto revised notions of political power and morality. In aggregate, they have attempted to revamp Western metaphysics, and a key element of their attack has focused on the representationalism bequeathed by Kant. Those who find their writings largely outside their concerns might well ask, as does François Cusset, "Why still bother with theory, French or otherwise?" (2008, p. xi). Now, a generation later, the answer rests on acknowledging that these critics have provided an influential challenge to the modernist conception of the ego, and more particularly the Freudian version in terms quite different (and with wide-ranging repercussions) from those who scoff at psychoanalysis writ large. Postmodernism, of course, is notoriously difficult to define, and we do well to differentiate its use to describe a sociohistorical period, a general movement of art in the mid-twentieth century, and for our purposes, a critique of modern epistemology (Harvey 1990; Rose 1991; Best and Kellner 1991). Regarding the demise of the ego framed by post-Freudian critiques, we begin with a short consideration of the contributions made by Lyotard, for in important respects he set the agenda for more frontal deconstructions of the Cartesian-Kantian agent.

II

Lyotard is credited with bringing the term "postmodernism" to prominence and common usage in a short work published in 1979, *The Postmodern Condition: A Report on Knowledge*, where he wrote, "Simplifying to the extreme, I define postmodern as incredulity towards metanarratives" (1984a, p. xxiv). Therein he declared that the grand metanarratives of modernity had been eclipsed by more modest undertakings, which recognized that no overriding historical explanation or structural depiction of culture or language could capture the complexity of postindustrial society. Simply, modernity's narrative framework had failed, and with its rejection, the epistemology employed was also discarded. Modernity for Lyotard equates to modern reason, the Enlightenment, totalizing thought, and philosophies of history, each of which contributes to the three conditions for modern knowledge: "the appeal to metanarratives to legitimate foundationalist claims; the inevitable outgrowth of legitimation, deligitimation, and exclusion; and a desire for homogeneous epistemological and moral prescriptions" (Best and Kellner 1991, p. 165). Postmodern knowledge and its moral orientation oppose each of these conditions, so putatively a new epistemology is required, one that responds to new criteria of knowledge, which value heterogeneity, plurality, and innovation coupled to pragmatic construction of local rules devised by political participants. In short, instead of foundational universals and metanarratives, Lyotard espoused *micropolitics.*

Co-opting Wittgenstein's notion of "language games" (Wittgenstein 1968), Lyotard argued that local domains of knowledge, established by particularized standards and notions of truth seeking, would have to replace the grand theories or final "truths" characteristic of the epistemological aspirations of modernity. Much in the spirit of Nietzsche's struggle of wills, competitors within these local domains would determine knowledge. The most obvious consequence of dispelling Objectivity and Truth as abiding, ideal attainments is forms of relativism, which displace the universality of reason and notions of knowledge. While Lyotard (1984b) focused his conceptual characterization on postwar art and architecture, his major epistemological theses resonated powerfully with antipositivist characterizations of science (joining the Kuhn-Feyerabend rejection of normal science as rationally progressive [Tauber 2009c]) and a revival of pragmatism in law (Lyotard 1988).

Lyotard thus became a pivotal figure in the debate that pitted the forces of Enlightenment against "the other of reason." Although reason became the article of contention, as Lyotard commented, the issue arose from the imbroglio of capturing the world in representations:

> The postmodern would be that which, in the modern, puts forward the unpresentable in presentation itself; that which denies itself the solace of good forms . . . that which searches for new presentations, not in order to enjoy them but in order to impart a stronger sense of the unpresentable. A postmodern artist or writer is in the position of a philosopher: the text he writes, the work he produces are not in principle governed by preestablished rules . . . [or] categories. . . . Those rules and categories are what the work of art is looking for. (Lyotard 1984b, p. 81)

In other words, the artist searches for, or perhaps establishes, the rules by which the work has been created, so postmodern would be "understood according to the paradox of the future [*post*] anterio [*modo*]" (ibid.). By becoming "witnesses to the unpresentable" (ibid.), the modernist conceit that the world is given to humans for their representation (understanding and mastery) has been shelved for another project altogether. Simply, Lyotard would abandon the "fantasy to seize reality" (1984b, p. 82). Much would be lost.

While Lyotard developed a theory of aesthetics to accompany this formulation, more directly pertinent for our consideration is his rejection of "the severe god Logos, dear to Freud" (1974, p. 133). What did he mean? Confusion arises because for both modernists and postmodernists, reason is inseparable from the emotions, the beliefs and values that ground rationality, and the historical context in which reasoning is exercised. On this general view, self-understanding weaves personal histories and their reconstructed stories within cultural myths to fashion a complex fabric. That narrative, created as a product of the power relations of identity politics and the subject's needs established by this larger social context and individual desire, restricts desire to those modes already established by cultural demands. To the extent that reason serves the forces that imprison, post-Freudian critics following Nietzsche, Heidegger, and Adorno reject the hegemony of that which passes as upheld by some unobtainable objectivity or interpretive process. Lyotard (at least at one point in his career) pushed that orientation forward to perhaps its logical conclusion by rejecting reason altogether and asserting an emotive-based mode of human being.

In Lyotard's 1971 commentary, *Discourse, Figure* (2011), he identified psychoanalytically defined desire as configured by the dual aspects of a transgressive force that subverts reality for its own ends and a counteraffirmative force that intertwines Eros and Thanatos (Best and Kellner 1991, p. 150). (Note that this is not a dialectical relationship as formulated by Norman O. Brown [1959].[1]) If this construction serves as a psychic ontology, when desire is then articulated in discourse, the rules of language (or representation more generally) determine its expression. And given the nature of language, *discourse*—rationalized and conventional—"freezes, immobilizes, and paralyzes the flow and intensities of desire" (Best and Kellner 1991, p. 150). Lyotard then proposes in this "proto-postmodernist" work a disruptive literary strategy where the displacement of conventional writing with poetic imagery and ambiguity would provide for a figural language more capable of capturing psychic desire.

In his next major work, *Libidinal Economy* (1993), published in 1974 (five years before *The Postmodern Condition*), Lyotard extended this position and, in doing so, clearly fell into the same circle occupied by Brown (1959) and Deleuze (1983), namely, an adaptation of key Nietzschean tenets that celebrates the emancipation of desire and the demotion of reason as a faculty of human fulfillment.[2] This work, Lyotard's most radical diatribe against theory, reason, and modernity writ large, must be counted as a key text of the politics of desire and one of the most histrionic critiques of representationalism of the period. Following a theme closely aligned with that of *Anti-Oedipus*, the first volume of Deleuze and Guattari's *Capitalism and Schizophrenia* (published in 1972), Lyotard maintains that desire has been co-opted by oppressive forms of family, work, economy, and state. Not only is desire then used to energize its own oppression but the vitality and resources originating in desire are sapped upon its transmutation into nonlibidinal objects. To release desire into fuller, freer expression may be best accomplished through forms of writing and art that moved from a representational modality to what he called a "tensor" modality. Tensor is a "routing" for desire that ends not in a form of representation *of* that desire but rather as a way of expressing, and thus freeing, libidinal forces. In short, a politics of desire is a strategy for liberating creativity and vitality, for both attaining psychic health and achieving a social utopianism.

Libidinal Economy was the apogee of Lyotard's response to Freud, and indeed, there is no reference to Freud or psychoanalysis in *The Postmodern Condition*. Having little interest in the psyche per se, Lyotard soon abandoned the utopian politics of desire to turn to the politics of justice. After all, it was plain that without some guiding theoretical structure for the disseminated libidinal forces, no programmatic effort might be launched.[3] While freeing the libidinal drives as an alternative to the oppression of reason, Lyotard offered little else. Poorly based in an argument or an articulate philosophical tradition, his radical reading highlights the lacuna left by a program that leaves *meaning* aside. With Lyotard's abdicating any reference to understanding and leaving analysis out of psychoanalysis altogether, the unreflective envelopment by the libido leaves nothing for Freudianism or its intellectual progeny to *do*.

Lyotard's dismissal of the Logos and then placing the discourse of the "not-rational," "the other of reason," in the material reality of the body—of desire, of libidinal impulses—without consideration of social theory and a supporting social analysis ironically left him with a philosophy devoid of subjects. Of note, discussion of community and intersubjectivity fails to appear in Lyotard's writings, so an effort to articulate an ethics makes no appearance. His totalizing attack included the attempted destruction of all forms of social theoretical constructions of the commune and the individual, and Freudianism must be included in that devastation. At that juncture, Lyotard parts ways with Deleuze and Guattari, who sought in their own radical reading of Freudian psychoanalysis the means to produce postmodern identities through revised subjectivities that would better oppose the oppressive effects of society. Indeed, *Anti-Oedipus* (Deleuze and Guattari 1977) transformed Freudianism to something well beyond any preamble Lyotard had offered.

III

Following Lacan, Deleuze and Guattari join Lyotard in discrediting foundationalism, representation, unified metanarratives, and hierarchy for a celebration of diversity, difference, and complexity. From a political perspective, these preferences reflected their rejection of the dominance, if not imperialism, of modernist normative discourses and the consequent erasure of variety and pluralistic flourishing. Closely following a Marxist critique of capitalism, their work framed the relationship of a psychoanalytic conception of the individual within a capitalist system they regard as constitutively oppressive. Thus, their reading of Freud, and the alternatives they offer, coalesces around the basic premise that capitalism, and the modernism in which it is situated, helps establish the hegemony of a restrictive social power at the expense of the individual. Their social theory thus revolves around reconfiguring the politics of personal identity with an eye toward this larger Marxist agenda.

Deleuze and Guattari presented a deconstructive theory of the ego, in which a dynamic unconscious assumes a new primacy. The rational subject is thereby rendered as an artifice, and a new psychic identity emerges. This decentered subject has been articulated by various postmodern theorists, most notably Foucault, to present the subject as possessing a fluid identity, unconfined by some rigid unitary notion of the self, whose Cartesian heritage they utterly reject. Deleuze and Guattari offered a different politico-historical interpretation of personal identity structured on a particular normative account of psychological well-being, one in line with the ideals of a society organized around capitalist pursuits. They begin with a far-reaching assessment: Freud was not radical enough in his critique of civilization's discontents because his construction of the subject, based on his universalized reading of the Oedipal conflict, subordinates freedom and the primacy of desire as a revolutionary force in the resistance to social and psychic repression (Deleuze and Guattari 1977, pp. 113–22). The Oedipal conflict enacted within the narrow confines of the Victorian nuclear family "colonizes" psychic life with the psychological adjustment to paternal dominance and the ensuing psychic adjustments then required (i.e., repression and conflict) (ibid., p. 170; Schwab 2007, p. 4). Instead, they offer "anti-Oedipus," a theory that, in essence, overthrows paternal dominance. The revised theory is built to address how the individual might be permitted to pursue desire unencumbered by the traumatic baggage of the family drama enshrined by Freudianism. Offering an alternative psychic configuration, Deleuze radically reconfigured personal identity through a politics of expressed and enacted desire, one that would resonate with Lacan's vision. Sharing a deep suspicion of reason and valorizing desire at the expense of rational control and sublimation, this Lacanian-inspired postmodern revision of psychoanalytic theory has had broad influence on contemporary social theorists.

The germ of what will become a more general philosophical orientation originated in Deleuze's *Nietzsche and Philosophy* (published in 1962), where he read Nietzsche as a postmodernist (Koelb 1990) who heralded the postmodern emphasis of desire (the Will) and the subordination of Reason. There, several key ideas developed around the celebration of desire as productive and creative, as opposed to the tragic constellation of absence, suffering, and loss. The critique begins with Nietzsche's reassessment of consciousness, which is described as servile to the body. And the body, the domain of unconscious forces, is characterized as a field of forces, which cannot be defined beyond their multiplicity. The notion of multiplicity and dynamics of unconscious *active* (vital) forces puts consciousness (and the ego more broadly) into a *reactive* modality

(Deleuze 1983, pp. 39–41). In other words, primary active forces lodged in the body (unconscious) generate reactive forces in consciousness, and science, as the instrument of conscious thinking, cannot access the deeper domain. Moreover, for Nietzsche and Deleuze, the primacy of the body must be recognized as holding authority over the conscious ego. From this basic position, Deleuze then builds a Nietzschean-inspired philosophy on (1) the primacy of the body (the unconscious), (2) the inadequacy of science to discern those psychic dynamics, and consequently, (3) the inability of a representational model to provide an adequate account of desire.

Nietzsche set the ground rules for later attacks against representationalism on the basis of the restrictive perspectivism bestowed by language, culture, and the cognitive strictures inherent to any human knowing. Privileging the body's desire and will dominates attempts at objectivity and those schemes devised around the conceit of neutral representation. Thus, the entire scientific-based Freudian enterprise is discarded (Deleuze 1983, p. 42). Further, not only conceptually inadequate to its self-assigned task, science is "part of the *nihilism* of modern thought" (ibid., p. 45; emphasis in original) and thus part of the moral bankruptcy of modernism. A decade later, following these tenets, three works appear in rapid succession, which propel these ideas into a fully developed philosophy: *Difference and Repetition* in 1968, *The Logic of Sense* in 1969, and *Anti-Oedipus*, written with the psychoanalyst Guattari, in 1972. Of these, Deleuze cites *Difference* as his key text (1994, p. xv).

Difference is an anti-Hegelian, antidialectical work in which Deleuze moves further toward Nietzsche in a sustained critique of representationalism. Using the tropes of "difference" and "repetition," an attempt at redefining identity emerges.[4] Failing to acknowledge Adorno's own anti-identity philosophy, Deleuze opens *Difference* with "identity" defining the world of representation and then the condemnation: "[M]odern thought is born of the failure of representation, of the loss of identities, and of the discovery of all the forces that act under the representation of the identical. The modern world is one of simulacra" (1994, p. xix). From this base, that is, dispensing with a representational identity thinking, Deleuze then goes on to depict the unconscious as following a logic far different from Freud's simple form of opposition or conflict. Psychic conflicts are the result of more subtle differential mechanisms, where desire is better understood as a "questioning, problematizing and searching force" that operates with a calculus of difference to discern its objects of satisfaction (ibid., p. 106). In other words, *desire* (as process) and *satisfaction* of desire operate in different domains, and thus representation, identity thinking—identification—is discarded for another epistemological strategy to discern the dynamics of unconscious desire.

Deleuze would not be judged by old standards, as he forthrightly declared of his central tenet:

> Difference is not and cannot be thought in itself, so long as it is subject to the requirements of representation. . . . It seems that it can become thinkable only when tamed—in other words, when subject to the four iron collars of representation: identity in the concept . . . opposition in the predicate . . . analogy in judgment and semblance in perception. (1994, p. 262)

And following Nietzsche's lead, he concludes that philosophy itself had committed a grievous error in its embrace of representation, one that reflected its hegemonic intent

> of allowing representation to conquer the obscure; of allowing it to include the vanishing of difference which is too small and the dismemberment of difference which is too large; of allowing it to capture the power of giddiness, intoxication, and cruelty, and even of death. In short, it is a question of causing a little of Dionysus's blood to flow in the organic veins of Apollo. (ibid.)

Or in more formal terms, the "*alternative between finite and infinite applies very badly to difference*" (ibid., p. 264; emphasis in original), because that division reflects only the antimony of representationalism, the mode of one particular (and limited) form of cognition. Thus, all those mental mechanisms that reduce complex phenomena and experience to a set category, a representation of being, must fail to discern the deeper reality of the object. Deleuze succinctly concludes that "representation is the site of transcendental illusion" (ibid., p. 263), which he defines as the distortion of an image, the subordination of difference to resemblance, the inability to affirm difference through the dominance of what he calls "negativity," and finally, the fourth illusion relegates difference to the analogy of judgment.[5]

In *The Logic of Sense*, Deleuze (1990) extends these principles to begin his philosophical construction of the psyche, which he discerns by contrasting two modalities, a "surface" discourse associated with Freud, and a contrasting "deep" stratum associated with schizophrenia. The latter is, of course, the domain of the undifferentiated unconscious, and to probe those depths, Deleuze constructs a new metaphysics of meaning. Having discovered the "vital body" in the language of the schizophrenic, in *Anti-Oedipus*, the thrust of his assessment attains its full expression. There, Deleuze and Guattari embark on an ambitious, multipronged critique of capitalist society, and no matter how their thesis is received, their collaboration represents the most significant politico-theoretical revisionary interpretation of psychoanalysis since the critiques of Brown (1959) and Marcuse (1955) written a generation before (Tauber 2012a).

IV

Many of the key postmodern themes appear in *Anti-Oedipus* and its sequel, *A Thousand Plateaus*, which together compose *Capitalism and Schizophrenia*: Oppressive power is so pervasive that desire itself becomes self-repressing and therefore diverted, if not perverted, from its own purposes, and thus self-identity is formed only through the *coercive* unification of the fragmented body. And following an antipsychiatry theme prominent in the 1960s (Szasz 1961; Laing 1967; Foucault 2003, 2006), psychoanalysis, in the employ of oppression, creates as well as enforces an ideology that institutionalizes the Oedipal-dominating structure of bourgeois society. Picking out the Lacanian theme, they maintained that Freudianism reduces the richness and vitality of the unconscious to restricted interpretations. They are held within a limited theoretical structure, which limits the expression and fulfillment of desire through intellectual reductions and repressive attempts to place fulfillment within narrow, socially defined confines. To reestablish the creative passion of human life, Deleuze and Guattari proposed a new theory, *schizoanalysis*, as the means to return to the imaginary through a dual approach: (1) They would reformulate Freudian psychology and thereby redefine personhood, and (2) through a concomitant radical reinterpretation of society, they offered a program to change the social contract that would confirm individual freedom.[6]

Schizoanalysis holds to several precepts that merge psychological and social domains by asserting that "every [psychological] investment is social, and in any case bears upon the sociohistorical field" (Deleuze and Guattari 1977, p. 342). Thus, all libidinal investments are not regarded solely as individual vectors of desire but are fundamentally social and played out in a sociohistorical field. In this view, the libido need not be desexualized or sublimated, for it is enacted directly in social intercourse of all kinds. Herein lies a cardinal deviation from Freud's general orientation that would displace sublimation with erotic fulfillment.[7] Moving from the exclusive disruptive character of desire in the Freudian construct, for Deleuze and Guattari, desire becomes a Nietzschean will to power over a spectrum stretching from individual pleasure seeking to the most mundane of social acts.

> We maintain that the social field is immediately invested by desire, that it is the historically determined product of desire, and that libido has no need of any mediation or sublimation, any psychic operation, any

transformation, in order to invade and invest the productive force and the relations of production. *There is only desire and the social, and nothing else.* (ibid., p. 29; emphasis in original)

Leaving genitalized sexuality as only one form of libidinal expression, they see libidinal investment everywhere (ibid., p. 293), even to the extent of being repressive to itself (pp. 352–53).

Foucault's notion of social power as exercised through sexualization has been expanded here to include the libido's expression of desire in all of its forms, productive and destructive, self-serving and not. For these *désirants*, "desire is in itself not a desire to love, but a force to love, a virtue that gives and produces, that engineers" (Deleuze and Guattari 1977, p. 333). From this origin, many contested points with Freudian psychoanalysis (helpfully listed as dipoles; ibid., pp. 381–82) arise, but basically Deleuze and Guattari take Freud to task for limiting sexuality, and desire more broadly, to a biomedical model that instantiates the repression psychoanalytic therapy is designed to understand (pp. 351–52). The offensive against Freudian psychoanalysis is total: dynamically, the reversal of the unconscious as the site of unfulfilled desire to a Nietzschean celebration of its vitality and fullest expression; structurally, the dismissal of the superego and the rational basis of normal ego function for a "schizo" reconstruction; morally, the deconstruction of modern identities, Enlightened modernist subjects in particular. Deleuze and Guattari present a radical program to establish nothing less than

> new postmodern desiring subjects. Where psychoanalysis neuroticizes, producing subjects who conform to authority and law and are repressed in their desire, schizoanalysis schizophrenicizes, opening up the lines of movement of desire away from hierarchical and socially imposed forms. For Deleuze and Guattari, the paradigm of the revolutionary is . . . the schizo-subject, the one who rejects the capitalist axiom, rejects Oedipus, unscrambles the social codes, and breaks the walls of the capitalist order. (Best and Kellner 1991, pp. 92–93)

In this psychosocial scenario, the borders between self and other are dynamic and open, and thus the Kantian ideal ego is part of what must be dismantled, specifically the rational, autonomous persona depicted by Kant as "mature" (Kant 1996) and by Freud as successfully sublimated (Gay 1992).

Deleuze and Guattari build their psychology on foundations established by Lacan, most directly his emphasis on the imaginary phase of development (the stage before the acquisition of language and concept formation) and his theory of desire. For Lacan, whose revisionist theory is further developed in *Anti-Oedipus*, the transition into the symbolic is a loss (in the translation to a form that bastardizes the unconscious), and the transition toward adult socialization is a further forfeiture in that repression assumes its control of creativity and imagination. The schizophrenic is then regarded, building on Deleuze's early work, as celebrating the freedom of an untethered unconsciousness, whose desire may be expressed and exercised without the distortions imposed from without in a language that breaks the conventions of normal discourse. The cost, according to schizoanalysis, is the damage of losing a deeper, truer communication. Children, the primitive, the mad have not been Oedipalized, and thus the schizophrenic (who is championed) remains free of the Oedipal restraints that form the basis of social control.

This deconstruction swept away any notion of the normative, the autonomous, and the coherent (as defined by external cultural standards). Instead, the schizophrenic, whose fragmentation may be more obvious, is not different in kind from the fragmentation of the so-called normal individual. In this respect, *Capitalism and Schizophrenia* breathes the same ether saturating the work of Lacan and Foucault, as well as other French postmodernists, namely, the process by which society permeates the individual—forms and controls her—constitutes a tragic consequence of the pervasive power of modern society. And psychoanalysis, in its traditional elaboration and practice, enslaves by identifying neurosis as maladjustment, as opposed to attacking the oppressive structures of society itself. And Freudianism does so with a theory of the psyche that resonates powerfully with venerable Western identity politics:

> There is no need to tell all over how psychoanalysis culminates in a theory of culture that takes up again the age-old task of the ascetic ideal, Nirvana, the cultural extract, judging life, belittling life, measuring life against death, and only retaining from life what the death of life wants very much to leave us with—a sublime resignation. (Deleuze and Guattari 1977, p. 332)[8]

Freud himself, from the beginning of his theorizing in *Studies on Hysteria*, recognized the scenario Deleuze depicts, but unlike the *désirants*, Freud laconically accepts the political status quo and advocates adjustment:

> I have often been faced by this objection: "Why, you tell me yourself that my illness is probably connected with my circumstances and the events of my life. You cannot alter these in any way. How do you propose to help me, then?" And I have been able to make this reply: "No doubt fate would find it easier than I do to relieve you of your illness. But you will be able to convince yourself that much will be gained if we succeed in transforming your hysterical misery into common unhappiness. With a mental life that has been restored to health you will be better armed against that unhappiness." (Freud and Breuer 1895, p. 305)

Anti-Oedipus directly responds to this oft-quoted admission:

> Psychoanalysis becomes the training ground for a new kind of priest, the director of bad conscience: bad conscience has made us sick. . . . [So although] Freud made the most profound discovery of the abstract subjective essence of desire—Libido . . . he realienated this essence, reinvesting it in a subjective system of representation of the ego . . . on the residual territoriality of Oedipus . . . the despotic signifier of castration, [and consequently] he could no longer conceive the essence of life except in a form turned back upon itself, in the form of death itself. (Deleuze and Guattari 1977, pp. 332–33)

And then the bold agenda of schizoanalysis is revealed: "You weren't born Oedipus, you caused it to grow in yourself" (ibid., p. 334). Here, the postmodern comes full circle as so many have commented before: Assuming responsibility for self requires individual freedom and autonomy. This moral imperative is the watchword of the Enlightenment, and *Anti-Oedipus* declares the mantra again, albeit in a different voice, but in the same self-critical philosophical manner marking modernist thought. The key difference is that the metanarrative, the foundation as it were, has been dispelled, leaving instead a Nietzschean exploration, one resting on a reassessment of values and all that entails overcoming an agency confined by values instilling conformity to a repressive social order.

The strategy drives toward elucidating the unconscious on its own terms, by responding to desire instead of reforming the means of adjustment (which for Deleuze and Guattari is another mode of repression):

> In the unconscious it is not the lines of pressure that matter, but on the contrary the means of escape. The unconscious does not apply pressure to consciousness; rather, consciousness applies pressures and strait-jackets [to] the unconscious, to prevent its escape. . . . [Schizoanalysis reveals] how the unconscious productions and formations were not merely repelled by an agency of psychic repression . . . [but] imposed on it causations, comprehensions, and expressions that no longer have anything to do with the real functioning. (Deleuze and Guattari 1977, pp. 338–39)

In other words, psychoanalysis itself is a means of repression. The Oedipus complex, the death instinct, the "perverse reterritorializations" (ibid.)—the entire analytic scenario—represent and reconfigure the unconscious so that it no longer exists in any form reflecting its own reality.

> It is the very form of interpretation that shows itself to be incapable of attaining the unconscious, since it gives rise to the inevitable

illusions . . . by means of which the conscious makes of the unconscious an image consonant with its wishes: we are still pious, psychoanalysis remains in the precritical age. (ibid., p. 339)

Schizoanalysis, as claimed by its authors, "follows the lines of escape" to undo the blockages imposed by repression and thereby transform "the apparent opposition of repulsion into a condition of real functioning" (ibid.).

In summation, Deleuze and Guattari offer an explanation of how capitalist societies co-opt desire for commodification and the various ways in which psychoanalysis itself serves the bourgeois mentality chained to that socioeconomic system. With that insight they advocate *escape*, which follows two steps: First, they assume an Enlightenment-inspired approach inasmuch as they presuppose that their schizoanalysis offers a crucial insight that liberates. And second, they propose an exchange in which personal desire is articulated and then pursued. In short, Lacan's basic motto has been reiterated in a grand social critique: Be true to one's desire.

By placing the fulfillment of desire front and center of their critique, they have prioritized the libido and attempted to show that the destructive aspects of the psychoanalytic portrait of Westerners is the result of a historical process in which a paranoid (or fascist) political persona has dominated capitalist society. Their effort, broadly speaking, would offer the basis by which personal freedom might be more fully exercised. Note that even the emancipatory methods of psychoanalytic insight surreptitiously enslave the subject further within the confines of an autocratic Oedipal social structure, and thus Deleuze and Guattari discredit what they perceive as a critical arm of the current regime. As revolutionaries, they would revise the entire psychoanalytic enterprise to conform to Lacan's orientation, namely, the identification of desire and then its enablement. If sympathetically received, they have provided a more fully developed philosophical scaffold for the program elaborated by Lacan and provided a liberation politics in the bargain:

How odd the psychoanalytic venture is. Psychoanalysis ought to be a song of life, or else worth nothing at all. It ought, *practically*, to teach us to sing life. And see how the most defeated, sad song of death emanates from it: *eiapopeia* [lullaby baby]. From the start, and because of his stubborn dualism of the drives [also elaborated by Brown 1959], Freud never stopped trying to limit the discovery of a subjective or vital essence of desire as libido. But when the dualism passed into a death instinct against Eros, this was no longer a simple limitation, it was liquidation of the libido. . . . [T]he product of analysis should be a free and joyous person, a carrier of life flows, capable of carrying them all the way into the desert and decoding them. (Deleuze and Guattari 1977, p. 331)

But one must ask, Is this serious political theory or a neoromantic ode of a "free man" who has little but poetic fancy supporting his Zarathustra-inspired celebration? They write,

[S]uch a man produces himself as a free man, irresponsible, solitary, and joyous, finally able to say and do something simple in his own name, without asking permission; a desire lacking nothing, a flux that overcomes barriers and codes, a name that no longer designates any ego whatever. He has simply ceased being afraid of becoming mad. (ibid., p.131)

Beyond celebrating antipsychiatry, what can one make of such a song to madness? Is this simply an adolescent fantasy, a poetic excursion à la Nietzsche to drive a rhetorical point? Or, less sympathetically, has the radical vortex sucked Deleuze and Guattari into a hole from which they cannot escape? Has their conception of desire devolved into a metaphysical concept, as some posit (Best and Kellner 1991, pp. 106–9), which has little traction in realpolitik? By their own account, Deleuze and Guattari step back from the precipice of actuality and concede that they have no political program.[9] And *A Thousand Plateaus* (1987) also fails to offer an expository program for a new politics. Others would build from their work, but conceptually, the Lacanian turn has been sufficiently developed, so now we consider the loyal opposition.

V

Habermas (1984, 1987) proved the most formidable opponent of the *désirants* by arguing for the power and sustainability of a self-critical reason that is forged in the intercommunications of persons in dialogue. Instead of advocating the liberation of libidinal drives and thus emancipating repressed humans from the discontents of civilization by dismantling excessive social constraints and recalibrating the performance principle (Tauber 2012a), Habermas directed the thrust of his critique to reintegrate social life as adjudicated by the norms of "communicative reason." From deliberative, open, and reasoned "testing," putatively intelligent decisions emerge, truth is found, and objectivity and neutrality rule (Rawls 1971; Fisch and Benbaji 2011). On such a view, society holds to its rational foundations and postmodernism becomes only the logical progression of modernism's own self-evaluation, which appropriately arises from the very precepts that govern modernity. Thus, the basic differentiating point between Lyotard and Habermas (and between modernists and postmodernists, more generally) concerns the role of reason in the quest for personal freedom. For Habermas, freedom is achieved through rational exchange, while for Lyotard, reason imprisons desire and restricts individual expression, because for him reason is a means of dominance and an expression of cultural power (a theme developed extensively by Foucault); on the other hand, for Habermas, only through reasoned exchange might individuals attain the potentials promised by modernity.

Habermas easily claims the title Protector of Reason, as he has staunchly defended more traditional notions of rationality, objectivity, autonomy, and truth against various postmodernists, most prominently Foucault, Bataille, and Derrida (d'Entrèves and Benhabib 1997; Thomassen 2006). *The Philosophical Discourse of Modernity* most clearly presents Habermas's arguments for going beyond what he calls "a philosophy of subjectivity" (1987, p. 23) in order to vindicate the rational potential of modernity. By confronting "modernity on its own terms, rather than escaping into a nostalgia for pre-modern traditions, or enthusiastically embracing a technocratic vision of postmodernity, or invoking an anti-modern conception of the 'other' of reason," Habermas would redeem the *unfulfilled* promises of modernity by asserting the responsibility to act (d'Entrèves 1997, p. 4; emphasis in original). What *action* means constitutes the main body of Habermas's philosophy.

According to Habermas, the *Dialectic of Enlightenment* (Horkheimer and Adorno 1993) confused "instrumental reason" and reason as such and concluded that modernity is still an unfinished project, one dependent on present praxis as opposed to some intrinsic fault or weakness of reason (R. Bernstein 2006, pp. 78–79). The issue then is not reason per se but rather a particular form of thought (instrumental rationality) that is driven by an efficiency of a means-end structure. Instead, Habermas would substitute a social form of reason, where, by mutual agreement (or inference or understanding), participants engage in free dialogue guided by shared interests and structured by underlying standards of discourse. Because there are certain, mostly implicit, assumptions in social action and language use, he argued that a "quasi-transcendental" structure framed deliberation and thus was constitutive to it. In other words, language and implicit modes of social exchange, configured by historical and cultural practice firmly lodged within language, carried an ordering function, which is called "reason." So on the basis of "communicative action," oriented toward some mutual interest or end, Habermas maintains that even if rational consensus is not reached, its possibility is presupposed, and on that basis, exchange is grounded in the communal notion of logic and commonly held values governing social practices. More broadly, reason plays its normative role in the pursuit of the Enlightenment's ultimate goal of social emancipation.

Looking at reason as the basis of social exchange, Habermas sought a rational reconstruction of the normative content of social activities and the institutions that support them. And to do so, he conceived of Critical Theory as a mediator of different kinds of knowledge. In his scheme, Critical Theory serves as the third leg of epistemology—natural and social sciences constituting the other partners. Part of his reconstructive effort included a consideration of psychoanalysis, which Habermas regarded as a case example of Critical Theory at work, by interjecting its critical perspective upon natural and social scientific methods: Because psychoanalysis enfolds subjective values, the object of inquiry—the analysand—cannot be objectively disengaged from the analyst. To understand the meaning of another's actions or thoughts requires a negotiation between the different frames of reference occupied by analyst and analysand. After all, values, experience, and presuppositions, whether theoretical, cultural, or psychological, shape the interpretations offered.[10] And at another level, the hermeneutics cannot depend on the transparency of the communication or the veridical status of the emotional or psychological state being reported. For Habermas, Critical Theory would offer the conceptual apparatus for examining those presuppositions and values, and he based the rationale of his argument on psychoanalytic practice as a model for his philosophical strategy. Accordingly, psychoanalysis bridges the natural world (psychiatric symptoms, emotional dysfunction) and the interpretation of those symptoms. Analysis reveals how an unconscious desire may be obsessive, but with insight, the compulsion may be turned and emotional balance attained. Analogously, dispelling dogmatic prejudices (such as positivism) becomes possible through a similar mode of critical reflection, which casts this mode of assessment into wider arenas.

In confronting the skepticism characterizing postmodernism's denial of the epistemological autonomy Critical Theory requires, Habermas must assert that self-reflection changes the cynical calculus of heteronomy. He affirms that humans are capable of attaining freedom; their agency is not irretrievably embedded within the grip of social forces that frame and determine the parameters of knowledge and the character of the values that support it. In other words, where postmodernists deny epistemological and moral autonomy,

Habermas promotes a self-critical stance that would achieve just that freedom his opponents claim has been rendered impotent by social and political forces conspiring to enforce conformity and compliance. In a utopian spirit then, Critical Theory would offer "a political form of social praxis that makes possible the only kind of domination-free, emancipated society in which genuine knowledge can emerge" (Ingram 2010, p. 45).

Pointing to psychoanalysis, Habermas has a science that reveals false consciousness and a model for a reconceived Critical Theory. So just as the neurotic might understand the origins of his behavior by self-critical analysis, so too might a new science reveal the false social and political consciousness of those enmeshed in mass society and a capitalism that obliterates individual choice by setting the conditions of the consumer's desire. Habermas does not base his utopianism *on* psychoanalysis or, more accurately, on a critique of psychoanalysis as other Freudian-inspired critics have done (e.g., Adorno himself), but rather uses psychoanalysis as a model *of* Critical Theory. Habermas reaches much further back to ground his argument in Kantian precepts, which ties the knot comprising several threads of Freud's notion of reason.

Habermas builds on the basic argument of *Dialectic of Enlightenment* that reason suffers from, and in modernity actually succumbs to, the danger of falling under the spell of its own representations. However, where Adorno saw the historical inevitability of reason's vulnerability and transgression, Habermas envisioned rehabilitation by invoking Kant's dictum: Reason, by its very nature, is a self-critical faculty, and because of its own self-examination it must guard against the authority of itself (at least in principle). Modernity has failed to the extent that this self-critical attitude, one enfolded in Habermas's revision of critical theory, has been compromised. So where Adorno attempted to refashion Kantian Reason, Habermas sought to save it.

While his critics argue that the individual has lost autonomy due to the stultifying forces of consumerism, global capitalism, and mass communication, which impose norms that have little rational basis in Enlightenment ideals of the civic Good, Habermas counters with a description of reawakened democratic practice through communicative action. Rather than simply put forth another interpretive exercise from some supreme (unattainable) Archimedean point, he makes a startling claim that goes well beyond Freud's psychology. What was demonstrated as a fecund mode of analysis of the individual is now applied to knowledge writ large: In *Knowledge and Human Interests* (1971), where Habermas first developed his larger thesis, he argued that genuine knowledge can be realized only as a *communal* project in which distorting social and political effects have been eliminated. In other words, the critic must be emancipated from ideology in order to fulfill the philosophical task assigned by Critical Theory. To achieve such a global analytical view, philosophy would "have to become a practical force for emancipation: a social science that criticizes ideology" (Ingram 2010, p. 44). Discarding positivism's experimental inquiry and causal explanation, Habermas argues for an epistemology clearly aware of its historical and interpretive contexts. This would include a synthetic view of facts and values, one in which a thorough examination of science's own values and social scaffolding must become part of evaluating the acquisition and validation of knowledge (Tauber 2009c). Also, by the inclusion of self-examination of ideological prejudice and presuppositions, an accounting of moral knowledge's norms and values closely follows.

Knowledge and Human Interests proposes nothing less than a grand synthesis of theory and practice, knowledge and its critique, epistemology and ethics. Such a program required an intellectual virtuosity that would attain new perspectives and offer penetrating insight for social leadership. Habermas soon abandoned this project for three reasons (Ingram 2010, pp. 27–28): (1) he rejected its presupposed speculative philosophy of history, (2) he replaced the grounding of Critical Theory in presuppositions underlying knowledge instead of social interaction (and thus committed itself to a subject-object paradigm that fueled the dialectic of Enlightenment), and (3) he considered his strategy as both practically and theoretically untenable (by placing the theorist in an unequal relationship with her fellow citizens that would be rejected). In *The Theory of Communicative Action* (1984), Habermas turned to a more developed pragmatic program, in which social interaction is based on communicative competence and where truth follows "validity claims" based on a correspondence theory of truth. In *Truth and Justification* (2003) he further develops the truth criteria of his program, with a theory of reference that builds on the "linguistic turn" and thereby rejects the consensus theory of truth used in *Knowledge and Human Interests*.

Habermas directed the entire thrust of "communicative action" toward an account of the communicative intelligence that coordinates disparate and conflicting interests toward some common, unified, shared goal that enhances individual attainments. That is a given. The question is to what degree reason is Reason, or in another context, To what degree do individuals exercise the autonomous reason required by Enlightenment standards of moral action and rational discourse? Within parameters of the Freudian construct, reason suffers from its compromise at the hands of unacknowledged unconscious desires, yet at the same time, interpretative analysis proceeds. While Habermas clearly is sympathetic to that position, it could not be sustained, and consequently he reconceived reason as a collective property of the *group*, both in the active practice of social exchange and in the establishment of norms. After discarding the psychoanalytic model for a more pragmatic orientation, he drew from what he regarded as a stronger epistemological base— a social intelligence using "communicative reason"—that followed his acknowledgment that the subject-object thinking embedded in psychoanalysis could not withstand the assault of poststructuralist theory. Considering that Habermas was primarily concerned with establishing a philosophical basis for social democracy and countering the postmodern political theory, which seemed to accept as given the limit of choice and diluted freedom commanded by mass society, the thrust of his theoretical efforts clearly falls within the modernist project. The basic philosophical scaffold of this work rests on a concept of reason firmly embedded in the social interaction of communicative skills developed to arrive at social cohesion and advancement of collective goals. And echoing Kant, reason is conceived as a "power" to represent the world in an ordered fashion and conditioned events.[11]

The representations of the subject go beyond her self-legislating *participatory* role in democracy, for the other side of the communicative equation requires a balancing of collective decision making with the individual's need to achieve her own legitimation, justification, assent, and agreement (O'Neill 1989). So a normative component must be registered to connect the epistemological and political identities of the autonomous subject. To achieve that equipoise, the philosophical subject moves from a thing in the world to something close to Kant's original formulation, that is, the subject becomes a function, specifically a faculty by which the world is represented. And here we arrive at the full import of a contemporary Kantian construction of mind that leads to a political philosophy of freedom, which Habermas hopes to strengthen against postmodern critics.

Because the world is represented, an unyielding *separation* between appearances and things in themselves requires (within the very structure of the epistemology) a subjective domain of knowledge and representations. Furthermore, because the conditions of representation reside in the domain of knowledge, not in the world itself, the subject constructs the world according to innate (evolutionarily derived) cognitive faculties. That construction, as a construction, allows for the knowing agent to imagine what is not given (albeit tested against the reality of the world). This is the epistemological freedom by which the world is known—from the mundane construction of everyday life to the sophistication of contemporary science. The world, then, is *"reason's* own world" (Colebrook 2005,

p. 31; emphasis in original), which means that the world as experienced and ordered presupposes a transcendental logical form—a logic that defines the very form of experience. In short, knowledge is obtained and freedom exercised in a world structured by reason's transcendental logic, and thereby each is grounded in the self-grounding of reason itself, a self-critical, autonomous utility.

Habermas resurrects Kantian Reason under the rubric of a "post-metaphysical" theory (Habermas 1992), where, through communal exchange, a universal validation of reason may be attained. Consensus is not given in fact but serves as a *regulative* ideal in the procedures of open communication. The social philosophy required to achieve a modernist revival of democracy depends on free deliberation, and this in turn requires that reason serve its role independent of constricting forces. Indeed, the imperative of freedom drives the Kantian program, and it resides in law derived from rational deliberation, which must be independent of outside authority, including itself. Accordingly, reason continues in the Habermasean scheme to be characterized as a self-legislating, self-regulating, and self-representing function. Note that reason serves an instrumental function in its representing capacity, so there is a critical distinction between the self, who represents, and the self as a representation. In the first instance, reason is an instrument of the self, independent and free to follow its own logic, and in the second case, reason represents the self as some object or function that can be represented to itself. Upon this foundation, Kant's moral component is added to the epistemological:

> Autonomy follows from the subject's capacity—as a subject—to imagine or represent what is not given. It is the self-separation through representation that obliges subjects to decide in relation to their being and to be placed in the responsible position of autonomous judgment. (Colebrook 2005, pp. 8–9)

Thus, individual autonomy is based on reason's self-representing ability, which allows for humans to legislate themselves independent of God or nature. Habermas retrieves this ideal of reason in his social theory of communicative action, where reason resides less within the individual and appears as an emergent property of the process of open deliberation of equals.

Interestingly, the ego has receded from the arena. The individual in this scheme is configured within the social matrix, and thus, Habermas has left his notion of agency susceptible to the postmodern attack, which identifies the social as guided by a logic not necessarily rational as enlightened dictates would promote. Or as Marx remarked, "[R]eason has always existed, but not always in a rational form" (1997, p. 213). Nevertheless, Habermas insists that the separation allowing for knowledge acquisition must include autonomous judgments (an epistemological requirement), and, in parallel, the same autonomy of reason underpins the very notion of freedom (the moral consequence of the subject's self-representation). In other words, the human being is a *representational relation* constituted by the autonomy of reason, which confers both the epistemological and the moral basis of personal identity. And upon this platform, modernity's social philosophy might stand.[12]

Habermas moves reason from its placement in the autonomous ego to its workings in the social collective in open and pragmatic exchange. He thereby leaves the circle of discerning individual psychodynamics that forms the basis of Freud's own social philosophy and essentially discounts Foucault's account of power (Foucault 2001). The Freudian analysis plays no active role in Habermas's mature writings, so he fails to extend psychoanalytic theory as a platform of social philosophy. Instead, he sheds the metaphysics and pushes reason toward its pragmatic applications. In sum, while Habermas begins with a deep respect for modernity's agenda, he ends far from Kant's transcendental formulation and leaves us with what Rorty (1999) will call "solidarity," a pragmatic reliance on some group normative standard and the end point of pragmatic trial and error. Indeed, pragmatism seems to be the one philosophical position that works and that he endorses.

And to what extent has Habermas been successful in defending reason and thereby reestablishing the original philosophical grounding of autonomous individuals as the basic elements of democracy? No doubt individual freedom is profoundly compromised in Western societies, so the issue is whether the Habermasean prescription, based on the promise of Enlightenment ideals of reason and objectivity, still serves as a suitable theoretical framework for liberalism, or whether his humanism must be discarded in light of the postmodern critique. Poststructuralists argue that the logic upon which Kant built his system is "logocentric" (Derrida 1978) and thereby restricted to particular structural assumptions. This highly contested and complex matter has no ready answer, but a tentative way of thinking about these issues has been offered by R. J. Bernstein (2006) and Rorty (2006), who see the respective efforts of Habermas and Derrida (a suitable representative of the postmodern targets of Habermas's critique) as complementary. The antagonists operate in different spheres, inasmuch as Heidegger, Derrida, and the entire cast of those Habermas identified as philosophers of *subjectivity* do not deal with the social domain as a focus of their interests. To the extent Heidegger and Derrida are relevant to the quest for social justice, they are so by critiquing subjectivity directly and thereby attempting to establish new discourses for a discarded modernist notion of selfhood (Heidegger) and the deconstruction of "logocentrism" (Derrida). Theirs is a "private affair" concerned with the persistent role of a certain kind of metaphysics (albeit they would like to discard metaphysics altogether), and they lack any interest in either the empirical study of social interactions or the basis of reason in some communicative context. Accordingly, Derrida is not establishing a theory of "the nature of language" and thus slips past Habermas's own concerns (Rorty 2006, pp. 51–52). In other words, whether through Dasein or deconstruction of language, their effort is tangential to the goals Habermas established for himself as a *social* philosopher. So, where Habermas is creating a philosophy of intersubjectivity (Rorty 2006, p. 48), he finds no traction in debate with them. Simply, their concerns are not his. Indeed, considering that psychodynamics as such do not participate in Habermas's program, despite being the preeminent spokesman for the modernist ideal and thus Freud's best ally, Habermas has wandered past the borders of this study, which is also a statement of sorts.

In moving the discussion from the individual to the social level, Habermas abdicates comment on subjectivity. That he chooses this strategy suggests, perhaps, that the Freudian modernist ego ideal cannot be rescued. Certainly, the Heideggerian-Lacanian-Deleuze attack displaces autonomy as originally conceived. Habermas concedes as much, and in consequence, the metaphysics of personal identity has assumed different contours, one in which the individual is, ironically perhaps, subjected to the collective in its normative rationality. This is, of course, only a partial characterization, but telling nevertheless.

Our narrative might end here. Having presented the two major post-Freudian disputing camps, we discern scant basis for some kind of reconciliation or melding of their respective points of view. However, the story remains incomplete, for another tack rejects the terms of their engagement altogether in the philosophy of psychology developed by Wittgenstein. The next chapter highlights his formulation of agency in a way that neither attempts to revive the modernist ego (Adorno, Habermas) or displace it with another kind of agency (Heidegger-Lacan-Deleuze). Instead, Wittgenstein dismisses both efforts and thereby offers a novel philosophical understanding of the voice we call the self.

7   Wittgenstein and the Quandary of Private Language

Do not try to analyze your own inner experience.

—LUDWIG WITTGENSTEIN, *Philosophical Investigations*

Freud offered a new genre of autobiography, one based on an inquiring agent. Most generally, a strategy of narration structures the psychoanalytic encounter with the past, and in that retelling, identity shifts (Tauber 2010, pp. 197–204). The ignorant becomes enlightened; the oppressed, liberated; the neurotic, healthier, and so on. Stories find their legitimacy in a complex exchange between the narrator and the reality in which the story is placed. In fiction, the author establishes the context; in autobiography, the facts of one's life find their place within the personal domain of a specified social reality in which relationships were enacted and behaviors performed. Each of the critics so far discussed places an agent at the center of his respective delineation of the subject, whether identified as an excessive subject, Dasein, or the schizophrenic. But how would such subjectivity appear if the metaphysics of selfhood abandoned the ego, if the I had no referent?

We have traced the evolution of post-Freudian subject-object thinking and in the process studied the reformulation of the ego in various degrees of its deconstruction. Now we consider why Wittgenstein, referring to the self as "deeply mysterious" (1979, p. 80e), presented the most radical understanding of agency based upon a critique of language and predicate thinking.[1] And in the context of how we might better understand the psychoanalytic project, Wittgenstein's attempts to dismantle the hold of representational depictions of the mind and thus unsettle Freud's project at its very foundations complete our survey of those who would reconfigure the ego and thereby radically change our understanding of subjectivity.

Wittgenstein's philosophy of psychology reduces to a philosophy of language. For him, asking how language captures reality is symptomatic of muddled metaphysics. Language is reality, and the assumed posture of a subject standing apart from the world and finding ways of relating to that world rest on a faulty subject-object structure of experience. So, in place of some correspondence that attempts to meld the subject-object divide, Wittgenstein, like Heidegger, would place the speaker in the world. His inquiry begins with the "innocent" wonder that thought functions smoothly as humans live in the world, but upon reflection, thinking beguiles and escapes explanation:

> "This queer thing, thought"— . . . Thought does not strike us as mysterious while we are thinking, but only when we say, as it were retrospectively: "How is that possible?" How was it possible for thought to deal with the object itself? We feel as if by means of it we had caught reality in our net. (Wittgenstein 1968, § 428, p. 127)

Of course, he goes to great pains to show that such confidence of capturing the real is misplaced. The real is already present, not hidden, obscured, or separate from human being. However, embedded in predicate thinking, the subject easily employs an epistemology about *things* and applies that same mental strategy to various other domains, including one's own subjectivity. These are what Wittgenstein called errors of grammar. Common language obscures the metaphysics assumed by the subject, and that "obscurity *obviously* resides in the question: what does the logical identity of sign and thing signified really consist in?" (Wittgenstein 1979, p. 3e; emphasis in original). Closely following that posit, he asks, "[I]s language: the *only* language?" (ibid., p. 52e; emphasis in original). What do words as representations (the modality by which correspondence had been traditionally understood) misrepresent or omit, and how might language be conceived otherwise?

Wittgenstein appreciated that there is "something which cannot be expressed by a *proposition*. . . . In that case this could not be expressed by means of *language*; and it is also impossible for us to *ask* about it" (1979, p. 51e; emphasis in original). In other words, language is inescapable and it therefore cannot be characterized except by another language logically equivalent to it. Simply, there is no Archimedean point from which a subject might ask such a question about language and its relation to reality. Following a convoluted path in pursuit of redefining the character of language and the metaphysics of the speaking subject, Wittgenstein offered no precise answers, and consequently, his writings and lectures have been a source of seemingly endless controversy. Indeed, it seems fair to conclude that "the most striking characteristics of the secondary literature on Wittgenstein is the over-whelming lack of agreement about what he believed and why" (Braver 2012, p. 4). Nevertheless, the constellation of his diverse and nonsystematic remarks concerning philosophy of language—the logical relationship of word and object, the inability to stand outside language in order to characterize it, the rejection of predicate thinking as applied to mental states, the antipsychologism, the steadfast rejection of metaphysical statements—would revamp the subject-object metaphysics characterizing modernity, and more specifically, notions of self-knowing and the character of agency. He would not deny the experience of inner thought and the common sense of self-identification, but he would demand an understanding of precisely what might be asserted, when one ascribes beliefs or articulates conscious thought: "*Certainly* all these things [states of consciousness] happen to you.—And now all

I ask is to understand the expression we use.—The picture is there. And I am not disputing its validity in any particular case.—Only I also want to understand the application of the picture" (Wittgenstein 1968, § 423, p. 126e). In short, he sought clarity, and in so doing he would expose the "nonsense" of much that passes for truth.

I

In *Tractatus Logico-Philosophicus* (published in 1922), Wittgenstein's "picture" theory of language allowed for the legitimacy of certain propositions based on their facticity, and for the rest— ethics, metaphysics, aesthetics—he advised that we must remain "silent." What that silence means, and what "nonsense" means in disallowing metaphysics, has been subject to intense debate. The traditional reading asserts that the *Tractatus* explores the connection of the world and language, in which

> the form of language and the form of the world reflect each other. The world is made up of simple objects which can combine into facts, and language is made up of names which can combine into propositions. These two types of combination mirror each other, and the fact that they do is what ensures that propositions have meaning. The meaning of a name . . . is determined by an act which ties it to a particular simple object. (Crary 2000, p. 2)

So, simple objects have a logical form that allows their combination with other objects, and names derive their logical forms as mirrors of the world, or in other words, the logical form of a name reflects the logical form of the object it denotes. In Wittgenstein's view, this representational account fails because "*by the very nature of language*, or indeed any system of representation whatsoever, there are things which cannot be stated or described, things of which one cannot speak, but which are in some sense *shown* by language" (Hacker 2000, p. 353; emphasis in original). That interpretation has been the standard reading since the book's appearance (notably the view of Bertrand Russell and Frank Ramsey), which embraces a traditional conception of philosophy: Everything that can be thought can be thought clearly; the task of philosophy is to set limits to itself; philosophy works at establishing logical clarification of thought; metaphysical discussions must have critical purchase on the meaning of what is being said; in short, philosophy is a clarification of thought. Accordingly, one might reasonably ask, "[C]an one whistle what one cannot think, i.e., can one apprehend truths which one cannot even think?" (Hacker 2000, p. 355). No. On that reading, the *Tractatus* argues that "the necessary truths of logic are *senseless*, and that all other putatively necessary truths cannot be said but can only be shown" (ibid., p. 370; emphasis in original).

This Tractarian *truth conditional* theory of meaning (following characteristics of realism) was, according to traditional interpretations, then followed by a post-*Tractarian* period in which Wittgenstein developed an antirealist philosophy, where the meaning of a word is

> fixed not by an act which serves to connect it to particular features of reality but rather by ways in which we use it—by its place in the *language-game* or by its *grammar*. Further, the grammar of a word fixes not only its meaning but also its logical character [i.e., its ability to combine with other words]. (Crary 2000, p. 2; emphasis in original)

So, whether language makes sense is determined by its grammar, by its use, not its correspondence to some feature of reality.

The philosophical problem revolved around the issue of meaning as introduced by Frege, which became a crucial component of the argument about psychologism that so dominated philosophy of this period. Recall that Frege regarded how people happen to reason as irrelevant to logic; logic describes how people ought to think, not how they in fact do, and in his discussion of meaning, he asserted that meaning is not determined by psychological representation. The dictionary meaning of *meaning* is based on some mental construction that corresponds to objects and ideas that are so represented by words. But in asking, What are meanings?, Frege rejected the commonsensical notion that they are objects in the mind that serve as representations. Instead, he argued that meanings must be abstract public objects, which exist in a third realm, neither physical nor psychological.[2] He did not dispute the reality of the "inner realm," but it must be distinguished by two cardinal precepts: The ideas lodged there are neither true nor false—that distinction can be made only by logic (and not by psychology); and ideas are radically private. In *Foundations of Arithmetic*, he prescribed the principles of his antipsychologism: (1) Sharply distinguish the logical from the psychological (i.e., separate the subjective from the objective); (2) meanings can be determined only in the context of a proposition; and (3) always distinguish a concept from an object (Frege 1980, p. x).

> When explaining the second principle . . . Frege notes that failing to keep it forces us to look for meanings of words in the inner realm; we look for "pictures or acts of the individual mind"—ideas. In so doing we fail to keep the first principle, since we fail to separate sharply the psychological from the logical. Failing to separate them sharply, we psychologize logic and meaning. (Jolley 2010, p. 111)

And Wittgenstein's own antipsychologism closely followed Frege's third principle, by which philosophical problems were conceptual problems as distinguished from empirical problems.[3] The latter might be characterized by objective criteria, but on what basis might objectivity be applied to inner states? Simply, inner states could not be investigated as analogous to objects found in the outer realm. While we might impose the same methods of study (i.e., regarding ideas as objects), what is the empirical (objective) basis for investigating ideas?

Wittgenstein extended Frege's distinction to its logical conclusion: Consider that there are no actual meanings, that is, meanings as such (as entities, as representations), but rather language employs words without ostensive (correspondence or representational) meaning. In other words, meanings are not to be found in the inner realm among ideas, but they emerge only in their use. This theory of meaning without stable meanings, a so-called use theory, maintains that words do not possess meanings per se but rather are used to perform certain tasks. "Every sign *by itself* seems dead. What gives it life?—In use it is *alive*. Is life breathed into it there?—Or is the *use* its life?" (Wittgenstein 1968, § 432, p. 128e; emphasis in original). Thus, Wittgenstein would replace the metaphysics of an ego surveying the world, drawing lines of reference from one word to its meanings out in the world with an agent who uses language, which does not *correspond* to anything. Because the subject is contextualized by the world and the discourses with others who share it, the intention of the speaker establishes the instrumental function of words in which the context of the word use determines its meaning. ("I am going to the bank"—for money or to fish?) The correspondence function is thereby displaced by a more direct use function so that meaning emerges in the public sphere of speech exchanges.[4] Thus, Wittgenstein held that the context of use determines truth, and considerations of logic, the nature of reference, or a psychological mechanism could not offer substitute understandings of *practice.*

While Wittgenstein regarded language as a system for solving problems, from another vantage, philosophical problems were characterized as confusions bestowed by language itself, or as he famously noted, "philosophical problems arise when language *goes on holiday*" (1968, § 38, p. 19e; emphasis in original). From that position, he argued against all metaphysical theorizing. The narratives woven around the classic philosophical issues—ethics, aesthetic judgment, personal identity, and so on—are simply misconceived if we expect some kind of analytical formulation. And to direct this discussion to our particular concerns, Wittgenstein sought to comprehend the locks and chains in which language ensnares human dialogue and the philosophical problems that arise from "bad grammar," of which the most glaring is the representation of oneself to oneself as an object, entity, or a circumscribed ego. That theme appears in his early notebook ("The I is not an object. . . . I objectively confront every object. But not the I" [Wittgenstein 1979, p. 80e]), and while his notions of the "I" evolved into a use-based understanding in his last writings (Hagberg 2004), the attack on the Cartesian formulation never abated.

Wittgenstein developed his mature position in the *Philosophical Investigations* (1968), where he disallowed language to serve as a representation of the world, and thus he dispelled any notion that language is governed by a correspondence theory of truth. In other words, the later work corrects or clarifies (depending on one's understanding of this transition and how it fits into Wittgenstein's lifelong project) what is perhaps obscure in the *Tractatus*. Language (coincident with the mind) does not mirror nature; we cannot attain an external point of view of language; we are incapable of devising a metaphysical theory to account for language or thought, but observing our everyday action and expression must suffice for ascertaining meaning.

> [W]hen we envision ourselves occupying an external point of view on language we don't succeed in articulating any thoughts. . . . [S]uch a point of view creates the *illusion* of understanding the sentences we want to utter in philosophy. . . . Wittgenstein distances himself from this or that metaphysical sentence (i.e., for this or that sentence presented as if from an external point of view on language) as indicating—not that he thinks the sentence is false or that it expresses an impermissible thought, but rather—that he thinks it fails to make any claim at all. (Crary 2000, p. 6)

So in the end, Wittgenstein discounted our ability to discern any formal language rules for natural languages, because natural languages do not take form analogously to formal language. For him, actions or behavior defined language and its logical basis in the ordinary sense of daily communication.

By adopting a nonmetaphysical account of language, Wittgenstein proposed that philosophy should concern itself with "therapies," where ordinary descriptions of language would cure attempts at devising metaphysical explanations of language and thought. While the older, standard view holds that Wittgenstein regarded philosophy as failing to find solutions to traditional metaphysical problems because these problems were poorly formed, revisionists argue that it is more in keeping with Wittgenstein's thought that he regarded such issues as "nonsense," by which he meant not realizable in *any* form; plainly put, traditional philosophical questions have been repudiated and a "therapeutic" orientation has been adopted (Crary and Read 2000). Labeled as postmodern (Hacker 2000), their argument hinges on the status of representational thinking in Wittgenstein's account.[5]

The central difference between the nonstandard American view and that of the British traditionalists may be summed up as a dispute over what it means to lose an "external point of view" (Crary 2000, p. 15). Both agree that Wittgenstein rejects the external perch by which to judge how language latches on to the world. However, the British interpretation argues that although Wittgenstein abandoned the idea of an external vantage on language, he still could hold certain epistemic ideals, namely, the agreement between a sign and its object is determined by grammar—words still represent the world. The American revisionists conversely argue that this interpretation mistakes Wittgenstein's intent. They hold that their British disputants, in making the judgment about the unattainability of objectivity, remain committed to a certain epistemic ideal, that is, we can appreciate the existence of features of reality that transcend language and thereby can assert the conclusion about the status of objectivity. In other words, in order to make the judgment about objectivity, the standard interpretation depicts Wittgenstein as holding to forms of knowledge that go beyond language in order to make the judgment *about* language. In contrast, the New Wittgensteinians assert that we are locked, irretrievably, *within* language;

we arrive at pragmatic solutions based on what works but can make no judgment beyond the limits of language itself, which, defines the boundary of thought. Accordingly,

> the *Tractatus* imagines an attempt to think through at the most general level what a conception of sentences as logically interconnected representations of reality requires. . . . [However], on the theory's own apparent telling, there can be no such theory. When we throw away the ladder, we give up the attempts to state what this conception of representation and truth demands of language and the world, give up trying to operate an illusionary level of generality, without however rejecting the conception of truth as agreement with reality. Rather, we understand what this conception comes to, when we appreciate how what can be said can be said clearly, when we appreciate the standard of clarity set up by the general form of sentences. (Ricketts 1996, p. 94)

Wittgenstein is thus understood as introducing a "philosophical method or program for philosophical clarification which consists of making apparent [how] . . . philosophical sentences, which we are inclined to take as making sense, dissolve into nonsense upon closer examination" (Kuusela 2011, p. 125). Thus, there is no external locus from which to survey thought (and language) and therefore no point of view.[6]

The entire matter rests on Wittgenstein's attempt to break the hold of metaphysics, and his target was nothing less than how we construe the knowing agent. Fundamentally, the Cartesian construction places the mind-body duality at the foundation of modern epistemology, and as we have discussed in different contexts, this orientation embraces a particular understanding of selfhood: a singular, personal point of view from which the self serves as a representing faculty from that unique perspective (Edwards 2004). Although different assumptions prevail, both Plato and Descartes are beholden to a metaphysics that attempts to account for how language hooks onto the world, or what is it that makes a cat a cat? For Plato, the answer is some idealized form of cat-ness, which, when applied universally, accounts for the being, the identity, the significance, of any cat. For modern philosophy, the established correspondence of the word *cat* bridges the identification of the individual cat to a learned language that so identifies the object. In short, a representation (a word) designates (and identifies/defines) the cat in question. But the question remains, What is the universal, which grants determinant identity and sense to the ordinary and imperfect? Several candidates have dominated Western thought since Plato: for example, the divine creator, who wrote the book of nature and instructed Adam to name all that he saw; the Cartesian ego mediating the world through its insular, indubitable authority; the Kantian autonomous mind. Each offers a variation of a metaphysical theme that responds to the intuition that

> the sense of things is always and only explicable in terms of what lies "beyond" or "before" or "above" or "beneath" them. The source of Being is always *hidden*, always mysterious, always operating behind the scenes to give meaning and structure to the world we ordinarily confront and seek to manage. Western philosophy, then, is at bottom always *metaphysics*; it always is searching for something "beyond" the "physical," something that articulates the physical into its determinant entities and that gives cosmic and enduring pattern to what would otherwise be senseless flux. Philosophy is metaphysics, and metaphysics is Platonism. (Edwards 2004, p. 128)

Wittgenstein would revamp philosophy by rejecting the *hidden*, by discarding metaphysics altogether.

According to Wittgenstein there is nothing "beyond" and certainly no order or explanation that might be posited as accounting for what humans know. He argued that instead of seeking Hidden Reality that gives order to the world, philosophy should discern how language functions to present the world, and in this sense, language is reality (Rorty 1989a, 1991d, 2001). So for Wittgenstein, the role of philosophy is to clarify problems bestowed by metaphysical confusions through an examination of language itself, which must suffice to present reality to us. "Philosophy simply puts everything before us, and neither explains nor deduces anything.—Since everything lies open to view there is nothing to explain. For what is hidden, for example, is of no interest to us" (Wittgenstein 1968, § 126, p. 55). And Freud, the paramount metaphysician, attempted to discover the hidden mystery of the unconscious, so to accept Wittgenstein's position is to dismiss Freud's entire corpus as metaphysics, and for that matter all the philosophy in which we might situate him is similarly discarded as misdirected and incoherent.

Wittgenstein's opposition to Freud, while focused on making an accusation that psychoanalysis suffers a category error by offering causes for what were in fact reasons or interpretations (see Tauber 2010, pp. 69–73, 238–40), is actually but the edge of the philosophical chasm that separates them. We begin with the most specific of Wittgenstein's views about Freud and then explore deeper strata of philosophical confrontation.[7]

II

Wittgenstein's comments on Freud extend from a general indictment (Freud's "whole way of thinking wants combating" [Rhees 1966, p. 50]) to more specific criticism of psychoanalytic logic, in which Freud's "abominable mess" arose from confusing reasons with causes (Moore 1993, pp. 107–8). Wittgenstein believed that psychoanalysis offered something important;[8] however, the theory exemplified "philosophical mistakes" (ibid., p. 107). The most telling problem concerned the lack of clarity of distinguishing a fact from a hypothesis, which came down to the difference between establishing causes and offering reasons to explain psychic phenomena. For Wittgenstein, knowledge—scientific knowledge (as opposed to interpretation)—requires hypotheses that might be tested and, if true, effective in predicting phenomena. From such studies, rules (laws) might be derived. Psychoanalysis, however, possessed no such rules, none even analogous "to the rules which will tell you what are the causes of stomachache" (ibid.). How would the "correctness" of interpretation, either that of the analysand or the analyst, be determined? The "right" analysis "does not seem to be a matter of evidence" (Wittgenstein 1958, p. 42), nor for that matter, do interpretations of dreams as wish fulfillments fulfill the criteria of proof. Establishment of cause simply does not apply to the psychoanalytic discovery.[9]

Thus, for Wittgenstein psychoanalysis is *speculation* (1958, pp. 43, 44), and while giving up one way of thinking and adopting another may be beneficial, he asks, Does that process reveal the *workings* of the mind? "Can we say we have laid bare the essential nature of mind?" (ibid., p. 45). The Freudian evidence (at best) attests only to the effectiveness of the analyst to help reconfigure the analysand's life story, to create a new "myth" (ibid., p. 51). Accordingly, psychoanalysis is a "language game," a game that has its own rules whose correspondents understand, having learned an entire grammar of speaking.[10] Beyond the lexicon, the grammar includes an array of assumptions, conventions, and history that offers a coherent system of meaning for those committed to its enterprise. As such, Freudianism is first and foremost a cultural *practice*, and that practice cannot masquerade as a science. For Wittgenstein, the game of cause is one defined by scientific practice that fulfills the criterion of some regularity, a cause-effect relationship that is typically characterized by a law or at least a rule. Once a cause is established, ceteris paribus, an expected effect results. Wittgenstein insisted that Freud could not twist reasons into causes by claiming a scientific analysis, simply because no interpretation of the sort provided by psychoanalysis conforms to the kind of objectivity and verification characterizing investigations in the natural sciences.

Instead of providing a positive science of motivation, Wittgenstein regarded psychoanalysis as offering a hermeneutics, closely akin to an aesthetic interpretation, both as procedure and as experience (1980a, pp. 68e–69e). Such an "aesthetic investigation" (Moore 1993, p. 107) does not necessarily invalidate psychoanalysis; the "inspiration," as Wittgenstein called it, remains a crucial personal experience, but it does not qualify as something holding a scientific status, and thus a form of epistemic knowledge. The validity of the interpretation must stand on its own ground and make its own distinctive truth claims as an "aesthetic" procedure, which must be assessed on its own merits. How to judge an interpretation of psychic phenomena then corresponds to an adjudication that must occur as an interpretation undertaken with its own rules. Wittgenstein drew these conclusions directly from his philosophy of mind, and his ideas about language structured his approach.

III

Freud was a great metaphysician; Wittgenstein, an antiphilosopher. The bedrock of their very different conceptions of mental life, and, of course, the more specific issue of sorting out the philosophical intransigence of discerning the mind, resides in the problem of "private language." Wittgenstein's description of the character of private language utterly rejects Freud's own version of accessing the unconscious. Indeed, Wittgenstein's dismissal of the representational model of the mind presents a radically different understanding of the psyche. That issue leads to revamped notions of moral agency and subjectivity, which we will discuss in due course.

Wittgenstein posed a fundamental question concerning consciousness, or more specifically, self-consciousness: On what basis does language capture inner states? What does it mean to say, "I'm in pain" or "I'm feeling depressed"? What status or validity do such expressions signify? Given the previous discussion, it is clear that language holds our experience, but then what are the limits of both public and private language? What, indeed, is private language, the putative métier of thought? This issue has provoked controversy as commentators have contested what exactly Wittgenstein meant by private language as being incapable of being shared and taught, *in principle* (Wittgenstein 1968, §§ 243–315, pp. 88e–104e). The standard thesis holds that because private language does not allow for rule following, no standard of correctness can be established and, consequently, signs are meaningless (Malcolm 1954).

More recent interpretations maintain that Wittgenstein dispenses with enunciating a philosophical truth about language altogether, and he promotes instead an "open" view, where language has no necessary conditions for meaningfulness: "Wittgenstein looked for nonsense, not error. . . . A philosophy of argument—thesis and counter-thesis—is itself a specimen of nonsense he condemns" (Edwards 1982, p. 192). This latter view more severely delimits the analytic approach to discerning the mind through a Cartesian structure, and this orientation will be followed here. The revision-ist account dismantles a commitment to a particular conception of language, and as a result of its analysis of the inner voice, the very character of selfhood also shifts from a Cartesian formulation to something else. It is this something else we wish to understand.

Consider the famous example Wittgenstein presents in the *Philo-sophical Investigations* concerning a beetle in a box:

> Suppose everyone had a box with something in it: we call it a "beetle." No one can look into anyone else's box, and everyone says he knows what a beetle is only by looking at *his* beetle.—Here it would be quite possible for everyone to have something different in his box. One might even imagine such a thing constantly changing.—But suppose the word "beetle" had a use in these people's language.—If so it would not be used as the name of a thing. The thing in the box has no place in the language-game at all; not even as a *something*, for the box might even be empty.—No, one can "divide through" by the thing in the box, it cancels out, whatever it is.
>
> That is to say: if we construe the grammar of the expression of sen-sation on the model of "object and designation" the object drops out of consideration as irrelevant. (Wittgenstein 1968, § 293, p. 100e)

In other words, there is nothing by which John might determine whether his beetle is the same object as the one in Betty's box, or, more specifically in terms of language use, whether the word *beetle* has the same meaning for both speakers.

Wittgenstein constructs this case as an attack on the Cartesian "object and designation" schema, where he shows that sensations are not objects, and thus he rejects "the grammar which tries to force itself on us" (1968, § 304, p. 102e):

> Precisely because the beetle is wholly dissociated from the use of the word "beetle," what is beetle or isn't is irrelevant to the use: It "drops out of consideration" . . . [for] the beetle can be anything or nothing without affecting the use of the word; but this is just a way of saying that it is irrelevant to the meaning of "beetle." What this shows is that it cannot be correct to construe the "beetle" language game on the model of "object and designation." On this model, the object is crucial to the use of the designating expression; it makes a difference to the use. So where the putative object makes no difference to the use of the term, it makes no sense to insist that the grammar of the term is that of a designator. (Williams 1999, p. 32)

If meaning cannot be determined, then the misconstrued object drops out altogether, and "the reason is not that the private object is unknowable, but that it is semantically irrelevant" (Glock 1996, p. 313). That verdict may be a bit overstated, so let us settle with a more circumspect conclusion: In everyday speech, the name of the mental object serves as a placeholder for "normal" exchanges, but the standing of that placeholder remains enigmatic or, at least, unsettled. The question then becomes the value of that description and the utility it might serve as we seek the bridge back to the pragmatics of language with which Wittgenstein was most concerned.

For "public" words the beetle problem vanishes: John points to a beetle, and Betty learns the word; John is building a shed and says, "hammer," and Betty hands him a hammer. "At the bottom of the [so-called] language-game—at the bottom of human life—is not seeing, but doing; not representation, but action" (Edwards 1982, p. 117). And as for private experience, the commonly held notion is that John and Betty eventually learn what *beetle* signifies by, as it were, extracurricular means. In comparing their notions of beetle-ness, John explains in some descriptive fashion what his beetle looked like or how it behaved. Then Betty could compare his account to her experience. Learning the word *beetle* would thus occur through their exchange, that is, their respective conception of *beetle* would be modified until a consensus was achieved so that *beetle* has a meaning shared by the speakers. So if John's beetle was a red ball and Betty's was a blue cube, *red* would be defined through different contexts and Betty would learn that blue was not red, so that another word designated blueness. And the same process would be repeated for the words *ball* and *cube*. Eventually, through public dialogue and demonstration, a common language is derived. Yet even with this nod to the instrumental use of language, the inscrutable problem of reference, especially for inner psychic states, has not been solved.

Given the fundamental privacy of beetle-ness, at what point might John and Betty ascribe *beetle* to the same mental image (for instance, a dream state) or inner experience? They cannot.[11] And as for the speaker, does his memory serve as some kind of infallible resource so he can state categorically that the sensation he felt in the past is the same as the one he experiences now? He is no better able to judge the validity of his report than his interlocutor is, for

> there are no ways of checking subsequent employments of "S" [his sensation] by reference to it, since nothing determines identity or difference between sample and described item. There is no established method for comparing sensations in the way in which there is a method for comparing the lengths of objects by reference to measurements by a ruler. Moreover, one cannot preserve a sensation for future use as a sample. (Glock 1996, p. 313)

According to this view, language does not have the same capacity to capture (represent) bodily experiences, emotions, and private thoughts as it does for public discourse. Betty pricks her finger and says, "Ouch!" John says, "That must have been painful." And in that triangulation of meanings, as described previously, an inner experience we call pain becomes the common property for describing certain feelings of distress. But exactly how that pain is experienced—what it is—remains unshared. Only Betty has the pain, and in that having, no claim to knowledge can be made: For inner states there can be no public adjudication as performed for an object of the world, that is, a hammer or red ball. So in this view, the report of private experience (for example, pain, fear, fatigue, exhilaration, and so on) remains beyond language—indefinable either in speech or in a private language.

And to the larger metaphysical issue, in having that experience, the subject-object relationship of Betty having the pain experience is already a distortion of the singularity of her pain. Betty, after all, has no immediate disjunction between herself and the pain; only by having a reflection, a report, a search for cause and explanation, does the self-knowing faculty trigger a separation of Betty from her experience. The subject-object division arises after the fact as the experience is translated into a speech act and then becomes something else. In sum, because there are no identity criteria for private mental states, sensations cannot be understood as private entities. Simply put, sensations (and by extension all kinds of inner states) have no language—a reliable discursive communicative faculty—despite the routine extrapolations made from everyday public speech to the private domain: No signifier or grammar can speak of inner states in a normative sense. The grammar of communal language is a pattern imposed on inner life, and neither the subject nor his public employs language about mental states as construed in social intercourse about external objects. "In fact the private object is one about which neither he who has it nor he who hasn't got it can say anything to others or to *himself*" (Wittgenstein 1993, p. 451; emphasis added).[12] Indeed, one knows another's mental state better than one's own, precisely because of the public character of knowledge:

> I can know what someone else is thinking, not what I am thinking. It is correct to say "I know what you are thinking," and wrong to say "I

know what I am thinking." (A whole cloud of philosophy condensed in a drop of grammar.) (Wittgenstein 1968, § 458, p. 222e)

Wittgenstein saw the language of inner states as an exemplar of profound philosophical "nonsense" reaching to the very core of Western metaphysics. James Edwards calls this extrapolation from outer, public language to inner, private states "rationality-as-representation," by which he highlights the Cartesian commitment to see all our thoughts as representations and thus in need of justification. Locked into a mind-body dualism, rationality-as-representation is the true root of private language that "forces us to construe all such complaints [pain] as *reports, descriptions, representations*; thus it is that conception which fertilizes the ground for the seed of the object/name picture" (Edwards 1982, p. 188). And *that* metaphysics, with its conception of rationality reaching into the mind and treating it as an it, as an object, is the target of Wittgenstein's attack. His philosophical antidote makes "a radical break with the idea that language always functions in one way, always serves the same purpose: to convey thoughts— which may be about houses, pains, good and evil, or anything else you please" (Wittgenstein 1968, § 304, p. 102e).[13] An "in-use" alternative is offered instead.

Wittgenstein replaces a mental object with mental events, which are manifest; they are literally presented, not re-presented (Edwards 1982, p. 197), and

> since language-thought is always re-presentation, sensation language must be talk *about* sensations, reports on the inner landscape. But . . . language can present as well as re-present, and sensation language can be seen as a way to present to others the reality of one's pain. The verbal expression is learned as a substitute for instinctive ones like groans. . . . [I]t is the thing itself, embodied. (ibid., pp. 192–93)

Accordingly, to cry, "Ouch!" is indeed a true expression of a private language, because the exclamation does not follow the language structure of name and object but rather becomes a manifestation of pain itself by dispensing with the attendant Cartesian subject-object conceptions of thought, language, person, and reality. All those linguistic habits and implicit metaphysical patterns that conspire to make inner states an object distort the experience by imposing a subject-object structure to experience, which in fact is unitary. Indeed, to describe firsthand experience, what he calls phenomenology, Wittgenstein would dispense with the ego altogether as construed as an object.[14] He does not assert that a self does not exist but rather that the self as an entity misconstrues its character (Hagberg 2008, pp. 116–17). What is purchased with this orientation?

IV

The metaphysics that Wittgenstein sought to overturn follows many routes toward diverse targets, but in the context of Freudianism the key issue is the abandonment of *explanation* and the substitution of *description*. Wittgenstein proposed a different way of looking at the world, at ourselves within that world, and at the inner life in which we recurrently take notice:

> A main source of our failure to understand is that we do not command a clear view of the use of words.—Our grammar is lacking in this sort of perspicuity. A perspicuous presentation produces just this understanding which consists in "seeing connections." (1968, § 122, p. 49e)

And those connections constitute a different way of discernment that begins with a startling surmise, namely, our world is not hidden (as Western metaphysics assumes), but rather our reality is presented to us, directly (a view remarkably close to Heidegger's ethos of Dasein[15]), and more, knowledge is public.

> Nothing is hidden here; and if I were to assume that there is something hidden the knowledge of this hidden thing would be of no interest. But I can hide my thoughts from someone by hiding my diary. And in this case I'm hiding something that might interest him. (Wittgenstein 1990, § 974, p. 126e)

Wittgenstein regarded the notion of a hidden reality as arising from a metaphysical confusion, which he tracked back to a misapplication of language, or what he referred to as a false application of grammar: "A philosophical problem has the form: 'I don't know my way about'" (ibid., § 123, p. 49e), and for Wittgenstein the correct method of finding our path is not "to *penetrate* phenomena" (§ 90, p. 42e) of language and meaning but to better arrange "what we have always known" (§109, p. 52e). Instead of seeking some hidden bedrock of the psyche, a Wittgensteinian formulation would present inner psychic phenomena in perspicuous arrangement. In short, Wittgenstein would seek "*Clarity* instead of *Truth* (Edwards 1982, p. 132; emphasis in original). Thus, a Wittgensteinian-inspired psychoanalysis would offer insight through "perspicuous presentations," whereby interpretations would not be confused as establishing some kind of (scientific) causes of unconscious forces but rather insight into the reasons psychic events appear as they do and the influence antecedents might have on behavior and affect. Accordingly, those reasons will become more accessible and thereby enrich interpretations by allowing them to speak for themselves to become manifest. And here we arrive, via a very different pathway, to a similar position assumed by Lacan and the *désirants*: Allow the emotions to speak for themselves; do not impose an intellectualization upon them; do not constrict their meaning with an imposition of language dragging along its attendant subject-object grammar. The unconscious *is* the affective life, and the challenge remains how to allow that emotional domain to utter its own voice. Wittgenstein does not delve into this territory directly, and we would distort his position by drawing unwarranted parallels, but the general attitude that dismisses an authoritative, self-conscious ego draws these obviously very different philosophies into an unexpected alliance.

So, if inner states cannot have the same object status as public phenomena, what is the status of a language that endeavors to describe the unconscious? For Wittgenstein, because language and thought were inseparable, much of experience would remain inarticulate. This ethos draws from the romantic tradition, where "a wordless or incommunicable vision" becomes distorted when transferred into a linguistic medium (Halliwell 1999, p. 21). Self-consciousness, and even the language in which such awareness might be expressed, is a bastardization of the primary experience or intuition. In other words, "a fundamental discrepancy always prevents the observer with coinciding fully with the consciousness he is observing" (de Man 1993, p. 12), even if the observer is oneself![16]

> The same discrepancy exists in everyday language, in the impossibility of making the actual expression coincide with what has to be expressed, or making the actual sign coincide with what it signifies. It is the distinctive privilege of language to be able to conceal meaning behind a misleading sign, as when we hide rage or hatred behind a smile. (ibid.)

In short, no sign can represent anything ontologically prior to experience, and there are no unmediated meanings outside the realm of signification, nor, for that matter, some transcendental consciousness of experience lodged in self-consciousness or any other faculty.

If science regards the world from "nowhere," holding an Archimedean point of reference from which neutrality and objectivity govern, then a romantic view of the world valorizes precisely the perspective of the individual and the primacy of personal experience (Tauber 2001, 2009c, pp. 80–85, 175–86, 2012c),[17] and the status of inner thought (most pertinently, nonlinguistic thought) becomes an acute issue. For example, Coleridge identified the complex dialectic of the self as self-consciousness and its turning that self-awareness into an object of scrutiny:

> [O]bject and subject, being and knowing, are identical, each involving and supposing the other. In other words, it is a subject which becomes a subject by the act of constructing itself objectively to itself; but which never is an object except for itself, and only so far as by the very same act it becomes a subject. It may be described therefore as a perpetual

self-duplication of one and the same power into object and subject, which presuppose each other, and can exist only as antitheses. (1983, 1:273)

But what is that subjectivity, or better, how is it expressed or known? For Coleridge, "self-consciousness is the fixt point. . . . [It] is not a kind of being, but a kind of knowing, [and while the] objective is assumed as the first, we yet can never pass beyond the principle of self-consciousness" (ibid., p. 285). Thus, the self-consciousness *of* self-consciousness, what Kierkegaard later described as the endless regress of a self reflecting upon itself, articulates a post-Cartesian conception of subjectivity (Tauber 2006). Wittgenstein's own inquiry originates in what became *the* romantic quandary: On what foundation does the self stand? Descartes's posit of an autonomous cogito had been dislodged, and consequently, the epistemological scaffold tottered. So when the romantics asked, What is the voice of self-consciousness, or in another parlance, How is *my-ness* spoken?, they reconceived personal identity resting on a bedrock of certainty to become the *problem* of finding a basis for self-identification.

In a most commonsensical way, one generally thinks of the ego in terms of conscious awareness—feelings, thoughts, choices, actions, relations, emotions—all of which are ultimately subsumed under the designation of selfhood, a person who assumes identity and responsibility and experience and memory as a self. Whether assessed as conscious awareness of bodily actions or as an agent engaged in rational decision making, the conscious self serves as a would-be judge of itself—both in terms of actions directed at the outer world and in regard to inner deliberative thought processes. And in contrast, the Other comprises all those outside the personal domain—those who confront, complement, dialogue, and exchange that which one is not.[18] However, given the philosophical structure presented by Wittgenstein, the ego's language (its story, if you will) constitutes a contrivance of a scrutinizing faculty that is an artifact of the mind looking in upon itself. Simply, a grammatical error has been committed.[19]

As discussed, for Wittgenstein, while experience must belong to someone, that someone has a grammatical pronominal position, whose predicates of consciousness remain constant whether reference is made to an I, he, she, or you (Strawson 1959; Frank 1997). Consciousness then becomes a state of affairs that finds linguistic expression in a proposition (Tugendhat 1986; Frank 1997), and the I cannot be characterized from an external or perceptual perspective:

> The knowledge in question is radically different from perceptual knowledge. The reason one is not presented to oneself "as an object" in self-awareness is that self-awareness is not perceptual awareness, i.e., is not the sort of awareness in which objects are presented. It is awareness of facts unmediated by awareness of objects. But it is worth noting that if one were aware of oneself as an object in such cases (as one is in fact aware of oneself as an object when one sees oneself in a mirror), this would not help to explain one's self-knowledge. For awareness that the presented object was φ [psychic experience or states] would not tell one that one was oneself φ, unless one had identified the object as oneself; and one could not do this unless one already had some self-knowledge, namely the knowledge that one is the unique possessor of whatever set of properties of the presented object one took to show it to be oneself. Perceptual self-knowledge presupposes non-perceptual self-knowledge, so not all self-knowledge can be perceptual. Recognition of these facts should help us to dispel the notion that the nature of self-knowledge supports the Cartesian view that the self is a peculiar sort of object, or the Humean view that it is no sort of object at all. (Shoemaker 1984, p. 105)

Freud failed to recognize this philosophical insight.

Because Freud proceeded as a scientist, he devised a grammar that had to be representational, for science re-presents the world and, as psychology, the mind. But the mind in its fundamental function engages the world, not itself. Neuroscientists study the mind as brain states, physically; psychologists study the mind by deciphering cognitive mechanisms; psychoanalysts study the mind with a theory based on inferences; but people *live*, and when healthy, their minds function within the world—coordinated seamlessly between themselves and their otherness. When the moods, sentiments, emotions—the affects—demand attention, then consciousness does what it always does as its evolutionary function: Facing a problem, it scrutinizes, analyzes, judges. Usually the target is the world, but in our culture, it also includes the self-conscious mind itself.[20]

The question remains, Of what value is the psychoanalytic narration if its truth claims are undermined by inferences conceived in fantasy, whose plot lines hold to some mythic construction, and the ego who tells the story is herself an artifact of a discarded metaphysics? Wittgenstein's telling critique did not argue that those autobiographies were wrong, but they could not be true in any formal or final sense. Placing one's emotion in a representational mode must, as the romantics had noted a century before, make the experience into something else. Not so much a distortion as simply another representation, an entity unto itself within a frame of reference irredeemably different from the original. If we look at the issue this way, much of twentieth-century philosophy has been a refashioning of the romantic insight about the limits of language. And more broadly, Wittgenstein, like Heidegger, would place humans more firmly within their world as opposed to their viewing it as detached observers. They would thus diffuse the subject-object distinction. With that move, a reenchantment of nature and human life becomes a cardinal aspect of their respective formulations of thinking and being. So the effort of both Heidegger and Wittgenstein to eliminate any external point of view codifies a multifold meeting of diverse forms of criticism that meet at the same juncture: the self *in* the world. The metaphysics of this nonsituated position have percolated into all of the human sciences with immeasurable effects. Although we cannot begin to track how their respective philosophies have influenced later understandings of personal identity, our concluding remarks comprise a few general observations in regard to this question.

Conclusion: Reason and Its Discontents

In a Northern German city a robber was sentenced to death on the wheel, but the local authorities gave him a chance to save himself. It was shortly before the "Walpurgisnacht," the night in which the devil and the witches are said to have their meeting on the Brocken mountain. The delinquent would have been released with a pension if he ascended the Brocken mountain during "Walpurgisnacht" and reported afterwards what he had seen. The robber rejected the offer. He preferred the extremely terrible death on the wheel (people often lived up to nine days after the execution) to the possibility (or certainty in his eyes) that he would meet the devil and fall into eternal damnation after death.

—ERNEST BLOCH, quoted by Raffael Scheck, "Did the Children's Crusade of 1212 Really Consist of Children?"

Freud's own misgivings about the rationalizations of interpretation and the ever-receding limits of self-understanding joined a tide that would radically alter notions of personal identity in the post-Freudian period. With autonomy compromised, freedom restricted, reason imperiled, Freud himself provided a portrait of agency in which the ego's ambivalent standing proved a vulnerable site for attack. His critics argued, employing psychoanalysis as their own instrument, that (1) the Cartesian ego is an artifice;

(2) a representational model of the mind (the exercise of such an agent) falsifies experience, especially of inner states (i.e., self-consciousness); and thus (3) predicate thinking based on a subject-object dichotomy misshapes our understanding of thought. In short, the commitment to a psychology organizing psychic life dependent on such a representing subject fails to account for mental life—at least according to Freud's most adamant disputants. In their view, the ego, the key architectonic element in the Freudian edifice, arose from diverse social sources that included a politico-judicial notion of citizenship, an epistemological construction to certify scientific objectivity, and moral theories to account for individual responsibility. In short, diverse cultural and historical demands have coalesced around the construction of the self, which fails to fulfill a transcendental ideal (Taylor 1989; Seigel 2005).[1]

The repercussions of this revised understanding have percolated throughout Western culture. With the Freudian contribution to the collapse of the cogito as the foundation of agency, the multiperspectival program advanced. This parallax view of reality, with the loss of an objective "view from nowhere," bequeathed epistemological pluralism and moral relativism, inasmuch as no vantage is necessarily privileged over another. Each drew from the metaphysics of the destabilized post-Freudian ego, which suffered from insecure self-knowledge and its accompanying unsteady compass that oriented self-responsibility. Some of the inflection points of this massive shift in how we conceive personhood have been reviewed, and now an accounting is due.

I

Many have observed that both modernism and postmodernism pivot on the "question of the self," and in terms of defining autonomy (and responsibility), the character of identity is framed by determining the degree to which reason may be marshaled for insight and personal liberation from repressive influences. Reason, of course, must be distinguished from selfhood, but to the extent that the cogito was conceived as a self-conscious *rational* faculty, the overlap of selfhood and the rationality it employs draw the two domains together, at least in the Kantian understanding. So with the postmodernist abdication of Enlightenment ideals, the rational pretensions of the modernist ego became a key target.

Adhering to a rationality that would forever present itself to the tribunal of self-criticism, Kant (and Freud) offered a philosophy that fulfilled the human quest for true knowledge and ethical conduct. This formulation of reason drew upon a nonsubjectivist account of reason, whereby reason is "a force not only in the individual mind but also in the objective world— in relations among human beings and between social classes, in social institutions, and in nature and its manifestations" (Horkheimer 2004, p. 4). Resonating with our earlier discussion of psychologism, this objective theory of reason resides beyond the subjective as a Logos, and because of its universality, the proper function of objective reason is to place humans in harmony within the totality of their social and natural universes by mediating some "reasonable" relationship with the world. In contrast, subjective reason is a partial or limited expression of such a universal rationality and serves an instrumental function enabling (or finding) the means for achieving individual needs (ibid.). In the postmodern context, objectivity has been redefined (Tauber 2009c), and in that recalibration, subjective reason has attained new authority. Indeed, Kant's response to Hume's challenge by enthroning reason as the final arbiter of the real has become highly problematic, to say the least. This Humean triumph, which vanquishes the pretensions of rationality residing in its own autonomous realm, has far-reaching philosophical and political consequences as these two competing visions of reason— autonomous and self-regulating versus emotional and interest driven—have vied for dominance with heterogeneous effects in every realm of human industry.

Adorno and Horkheimer saw the balance between subjective and objective forms of reason throughout history shifting, but in late capitalist societies, the "eclipse of reason" resulted in the loss of faith in social structures and relationships that hitherto had been subjected to standards of some universal conception of rational discourse and deliberation. For them, "reason has displayed a tendency to dissolve its own objective content" (Horkheimer 2004, p. 9), and more polemically,

> the philosophers of the Enlightenment attacked religion in the name of reason; in the end what they killed was not the church but metaphysics and the objective concept of reason itself, the source of the power of their own efforts. Reason as an organ for perceiving the true nature of reality and determining the guiding principles of our lives has come to be regarded as obsolete. Speculation is synonymous with metaphysics, and metaphysics with mythology and superstition. We might say that the history of reason or enlightenment from its beginnings in Greece down to the present has led to a state of affairs in which even the word reason is suspected of connoting some mythological entity. Reason has liquidated itself as an agency of ethical, moral, and religious insight. (ibid., pp. 12–13)

However, reason's uncertain standing goes well beyond contemporary moral and religious discourse. While reason still holds dominion in the sciences (despite the ideological attempts to dislodge its authority), the applications of scientific findings often provokes contentious disputes, for the standards of objectivity and rational methods practiced in the natural sciences are not easily extended to the human sciences, the courts, governmental agencies and schools (Tauber 2009c). Indeed, in the domains of social policy and assessment of human purpose, the conception of objective reason holding some universal status has suffered from postmodernist assaults.

A prominent cause of reason's demise rests on Freud's couch, for how might one assess true reason and cause given the inscrutable character of human drives? Wherein lies objectivity? What is truth in the matrix of competing social values and needs? And at the base of the insecurity of truth claims lurks the insecurity of self-knowledge. By dismissing reason's august standing, the modernist understanding of selfhood changes. The suspicions of presumed rational motivation and deliberate calculation, coupled with the shaken confidence of the individual perspective assumed in exercising choice and drawing conclusions, lead to a recalibration of personal autonomy. Such circumspection about the authority of reasoned thought (self-conscious or not) extends to a reassessment of the self altogether. Here, psychology meets philosophy.

Some have seen the eclipse of reason as marking the crisis of Western civilization. For instance, on the eve of the Second World War, Husserl lamented,

> The "crisis of European existence" . . . was born out of ideas of reason, i.e., out of the spirit of philosophy. The "crisis" could then be distinguishable as the apparent failure of rationalism. The reason for the failure of a rational culture . . . lies not in the essence of rationalism itself but solely in its being rendered superficial, in its entanglement in "naturalism" and "objectivism." There are only two escapes from the crisis of European existence: the downfall of Europe in its estrangement from its own rational sense of life . . . or the rebirth of Europe from the spirit of philosophy through a heroism of reason that overcomes naturalism once and for all. (Husserl 1970, p. 297)

To pose the crisis in terms of heroism points to the desperate straits in which Husserl saw the demise of communal rationality, and he would regard the betrayal of those, such as his protégé Heidegger, as retreating from an entire constellation of values that must support civilization, or at least as Husserl conceived it. Freud shared this basic sentiment; however, given the cataclysmic movement of twentieth-century technology, culture, geopolitical changes, and the intellectual characterizations accompanying these shifts, the structure of identity politics cannot be the same or even fall into the same orbit as the one in which Husserl presented his philosophical version of the cogito and Freud conceived his psychology. After all, as the epigraph to this chapter dramatically illustrates, the conception of reason reflects the entire panoply of cultural beliefs and modes of normative behaviors. Obviously, the world of today has dramatically changed from that of a century ago, and accordingly, reason's character (and ultimate authority) reflects those changes. So the issue is perhaps not the eclipse of reason but the current understanding of its place in various discourses. The question presses, for more than an epistemological issue, reason also informs ethics, and here the profound repercussions of the postmodern mind appear most evident.

Having discharged Freud's own humanist commitments based on the autonomy of the moral agent, the postmodernist subject has been portrayed as the product of various modes of social power to nullify individuality, deceived by the conceit of reason, and placed within a value structure that only feeds the insatiable appetite of mass culture. And with this deconstruction, How might *moral* structure of agency be conceived and directed? Beyond some pragmatic, utilitarian, and self-gratifying optimization, what guides social and individual perfection? Given the ether of relativism in which we live, does perfectionism reek of a discarded nineteenth-century idiom (S. Cavell 1990)? Have we really evolved to a "post-humanism" of homogenized consuming cyborgs (Hayles 1999; Lanier 2010; Wolfe 2010)? Is social transformation a vain hope as each of us is paralyzed by the paroxysms of power that jostle us like so many leaves in a windy storm (Foucault 2001)? To what degree has the latitude for social liberation been curtailed by shifting and unstable signifiers that leave meaning an evanescent property of human discourse (Derrida 1978)? Has the linguistic turn truly locked us within language, and reality then becomes a product of the discourses in which we are imprisoned (Sarup 1993)? If these questions are answered in the affirmative, then we are left only with what Rorty (1999) describes as a political ideal of "solidarity," where we group together to coalesce around pragmatic solutions of shared needs. Of course, without foundations those needs are themselves contentious, and the question of what constitutes the "glue" of the communal remains nebulous (Putnam 2004).

Instead of some idealized rationality that had served the Enlightenment ethos, pluralism now reigns with diverse values informing deliberation. Reason, from the postmodern perspective, is a derivative of a complex calculus of language, social interests, historical contingencies, and cultural parameters operative in local communities. So with the general dismissal of metanarratives, deaccessioning the urtext in which Reason was written became a key goal of the postmodern agenda. And with dethroning the Logos that might serve as a foundation of communal choice, insecurity raises its hoary head: On what basis, beyond self-interest and parochial beliefs, adjudicate competing concerns? Power? If so, the jeopardy of human rights subordinated to the greater good counters much of democratic history and its ideals founded on notions of personal autonomy. Without philosophical foundations, we have good cause for apprehension if the certainty of reason has been replaced with a pervasive skepticism.

Sitting in the midst of these deeply seeded shifts, we struggle to comprehend the import of recent criticism. Postmodernity no longer appears as a novel cultural phenomenon. It commanded headlines for a generation, but the dust has settled, and a significant shift in cultural, artistic, and philosophical self-identifications seems fulfilled. This is not to suggest that modernity has been eclipsed. Indeed, some regard postmodernity as the logical and inevitable outcome of modernism's own program, or perhaps, as Bruno Latour quips, "No one has ever been modern. Modernity has never begun. There has never been a modern world" (1993, p. 47). The self-criticism of relentless inquiry has shown that the structures that had been erected to formulate language, human nature, social order, historical evolution, and so on were fundamentally untenable.

Post-modernism signals the death of such "metanarratives" whose secretly terroristic function was to ground and legitimate the illusion of a "universal" human history. We are now in the process of wakening from the nightmare of modernity, with its manipulative reason and fetish of the totality, into the laid-back pluralism of the post-modern, that heterogeneous range of life-styles and language games which has renounced the nostalgic urge to totalize and legitimate itself. (Terry Eagleton, quoted by Harvey 1990, p. 9)

So modernity, in one dimension, claims to find some commonality of experience over history and in the diversity of human cultures, yet this unity is also

a paradoxical unity, a unity of disunity: it pours us all into a maelstrom of perpetual disintegration and renewal, of struggle and contradiction, of ambiguity and anguish. To be modern is to be part of a universe in which, as Marx said, "all that is solid melts into air." (M. Berman 1982, p. 15)

If postmodernity indeed has arrived, a nagging question persists: How truly radical are the changes under the new banner? Modernism, in establishing the terms of discourse, has set the debate upon its own framework, and thus the critiques are embedded in the conceptual structure already provided.

[I]t is just because the "modernity" which modernism prophesied has finally arrived that the forms of representation it originally gave rise to are now unreadable. . . . The intervening (and interminable) holocaust was modernization. Modernism is unintelligible now because it had truck with modernity not yet fully in place. Postmodernism mistakes the ruins of those previous representations, or the fact that from where we stand they seem ruinous, for the ruin of modernity itself—not seeing that what we are living through is modernity's triumph. (T. Clark 1999, p. 3)

Accordingly, modernity and postmodernity may be regarded as a single coin with two sides. Perhaps we are now living the "flip side."

Yet metaphysics evolve, and in following the Freudian theme, a Promethean challenge has been set before us as we continue to unravel the puzzles Freud so cogently presented and that have provoked such rigorous dissension. Indeed, the rich philosophical comment stimulated by psychoanalysis may be regarded as an expression of a great awakening. After all, an anthem, heard from the romantics to the postmodernists of our own era, cries for other forms of knowing to fracture the imperialistic grip of one kind of thinking in exchange for expanded ways of understanding. Freud holds a central place in this intellectual drama, for his theory, with one foot in the Enlightenment, also contributed to the evolving zeitgeist that emerged in postmodernism. He thus straddles "the Continental Divide" (Gordon 2010).

II

In a profound sense, we are following the Freudian paradigm and must glean that which remains from what has been discarded. To understand Freud's enterprise and its importance, we must distinguish both his error and his achievement. Following the recount offered here, the error begins with the psychoanalytic depiction of the ego. Despite recognizing the ego's destabilization by unconscious elements and the resulting compromise of autonomy and self-direction, Freud held on to the claims of the rational agent to engage that unruly intrapsychic presence.[2] This interpreting (representing) ego is the same epistemological subject who scrutinizes the world; however, in the psychoanalytic scenario, that faculty is problematically turned inward. Many have accused psychoanalysis of failing to fulfill its own standards of objective practice, because subjective mental states do not have the same epistemological standing as those objects found in the external world. Freud himself intuited the "arrogance of consciousness" (1910a, p. 39), which he understood as the mistaken construal of the conscious ego's own assumed dominance of the unconscious mind. He argued for the power of rationalization employed as a psychodynamic mechanism of defense, which contributed to the broader appreciation of the compromised standing of normative reason that arose from diverse philosophical criticisms and psychological studies. His interlocutors extended the charge of arrogance to Freud himself!, a philosophical arrogance in the misapplication of the scientistic faculty to inner psychic life. They argued that the subject-object dichotomy (i.e., the ego's autonomous representing function) simply does not hold. The dispute is not about the vulnerability of the ego that must rely on its own rationality, for all recognized the limits of deliberative thought about the subjective, but rather the disputants held divergent views regarding the standing of reason itself: Freud followed a strategy of analysis and ultimate mastery; many of his critics dismissed the attempt as misguided.

From the perspective of later philosophical criticism, Freud's error may be summarized as the "mistake of modernity," namely, the faulty application of an epistemology effectively designed to investigate the external world but misapplied to inner (mental) states. Further, to characterize subjectivity and its associated domains (ethics, metaphysics, aesthetics), which are governed by values, meaning, and affects, with the same forms of reason applied to objectifying the public space (i.e., nature) conflates two ways of knowing. The distinction is crucial, and Freud committed the "sin of scientism" as he sought a "new science of the mind," when he, in fact, devised a new hermeneutics, whose claims of objectivity received little support outside the psychoanalytic community. We might well regard his commitment to science as an overriding ideology that would establish the very basis of reality, for as a positivist he believed that "scientific work is the only road which can lead us to a knowledge of reality outside ourselves" (Freud 1927, p. 31). Such a depiction of the world is, of course, only one picture, but more to the point, his inquiry was directed inward. Ridding Freud of his scientistic straitjacket reconfigures psychoanalysis as a humanistic exploration of personal identity that provides the means to address the discourse swirling around nihilism, meaning, personal identity, and such (Tauber 2010). And in regard to understanding personal identity, an account of emotional life requires another modality to serve as a direct conduit to the passions on their own affective terms. And from this position, we begin to perceive that Freudianism demands a philosophy better suited to address its humanist quest.

Freud's confrontation with those who would deconstruct even his modified version of the modern cogito has sparked continued debate (e.g., Elliott and Spezzano 2000; Chessick 2007; Schwab 2007), and it would be premature to hail the victor, for despite the various assaults on psychoanalysis, he tapped into some shared intuition about the emotional life of Westerners, which has had broad appeal and influence. How to present those insights in a form that makes sense, after his contributions have been so thoroughly debated and so much history has passed, remains an outstanding task. According to the critiques we have considered, a different way of thinking presents different notions of subjectivity. Reason in Freud's positivist modality has brought us only partway, as the critics of psychoanalysis have so clearly demonstrated. Consequently we must ask, If the scientific offering has become suspect, is there another formulation that better suits the widely shared appreciation of the relevance of the psychoanalytic quest?

A distinction between a revised notion of subjectivity and the discarding of the ego altogether must begin this discussion. First, while the *self* no longer can be regarded as some entity, as a "thinking thing," a "self-ness" still serves as the operative *function* of placing ourselves in the world. Despite Heidegger's efforts to enfranchise Dasein, the self is irreducible as the "I" relates to places, objects, times, and other people. Indexicals—here, there, that, this, now, tomorrow, you—make the human world the relationship of an agent configured by space, time, and others (Davidson 2001b). And from intersubjectivity, objectivity, the best approximation of knowledge (whether finally true or not) is gleaned from the comparison of inner beliefs and experience (Tauber 2009c). That inner sense of the reality in which we live then confers an identity function, where "I" exists in the world and navigates it.

Coupled to this essential (irreplaceable) epistemological configuration, a moral dimension emerges: That which is mine (or identified as "me") in relationship to the world in which an "I" lives
also commands various degrees of responsibility. And as I assume
authorship or possession, the adjectival construction of "mine"
moves beyond the Cartesian noun of a "thing" or entity to an identity function. No longer the indubitable Cartesian cogito, selfhood
thus shifts its grammatical alliances and leaves the parameters
of selfhood to a possessive adjective, and as an agent engaged in
actions, to a verb. So while the postmodern self has been decentered
(and/or disenfranchised) from its modernist conceit, a functional
definition of *me* or *I*, for which I take responsibility, remains intact.

In sum, a subject fulfills three criteria: (1) someone who recognizes herself as an "I," as having her own peculiar perspective; (2)
an agent who is able to be self-reflective; and (3) one who assumes
responsibility for herself (M. Cavell 2006, p. 1).[3] This orientation
does not gainsay the critique of individuality as a product of both
manipulative social power (Foucault), unconscious opportunism
(Freud), or distorted subject-object relations (Heidegger). It makes
only a modest claim: The "me" (or "I") serves as the variable linguistic label of a possessive identity *function*, which in the translation of Freud's *das Ich* has been forever called (inaccurately [Bettel-
heim 1982]) "the ego." Simply, "me" is not an ego or a self. Those
are philosophical or psychological creatures of intellectual disciplines that seek definitions, foundations, borders, and so on. "I"
defies such reductions. The fact that Freud does not use the word
Selbst (self) perhaps reflects his own dismissal of the question (Tauber 2010, p. 266).

III

Even though the Freudian enterprise has proven incapable of
achieving the epistemological standing he sought, the major tenets
of personal identity refracted by psychoanalysis firmly grip a

common sensibility. That attachment rests snugly within the modernist metaphysics of the subject, and despite the influential critiques considered here, it is hardly obvious that the ego (despite the insecurity of its older Cartesian posture) has been dislodged. Why? The "modern error" notwithstanding, Freud's major accomplishment rests on his recalibration of subjectivity by providing a new form of mythologizing human experience. Desire, locked within the unconscious and stymied in a self-contained universe of its own being, leads to the pessimism of Freudianism, according to which all life is unhappiness, because of the inevitability (and insatiability) of unrequited wish. In the original psychoanalytic construct, unfulfilled desire remains humankind's destiny, and thus man's place in the human cosmos is irretrievably tragic (Dienstag 2006, pp. 84–117; Tauber 2010, pp. 152–61). Nevertheless, like the mythic heroes whose stories he loved so well, Freud depicted the psychological roots of human struggle, and both the metaphysical basis and ethical obligation for that struggle. This psychoanalytic vision offered the newest version of humankind's Western self-portrayal.

The Freudian narrative has proven a fecund method of rewriting personal identity, not necessarily on the same plot line Freud suggested (i.e., the mechanistic schemata of psychoanalytic theory), but rather because the very claim that one might rewrite one's life history according to a reconstruction of hidden elements and forces has broad appeal. The point is not that psychoanalysis provides the only mode of self-understanding but that the very process of redescribing a life through a hermeneutics that depicts hitherto hidden dimensions and forgotten events directly taps into the creative reservoir of fantasy life to reveal *a* truth (Whitebook 1995). Westerners are still adjusting to Freud's re-presentation of an ancient myth, the myth that one's identity is not, in fact, that identity at all. In other words, he suggested ways in which we live a fantasy, the fantasy lodged between unrequited desire and the realities of social interchanges with others. Fantasy as invented, constructed, imagined, not in the sense of unreal or pretended but rather as vital and creative; as compensated and negotiated; building from, and holding on to, the excessive place from which subjectivity draws from its own psychic resources to reach into the world.

The second credit for Freudianism's powerful hold on the contemporary imagination, despite the force of posthumanist criticism, derives from the psychoanalytic commitment to personal freedom. Here we witness the slide of the knowing agent into her moral context. Freud's theory ends in a paradox: On the one hand, psychoanalysis depends on finding a causative sequence to reconstruct unconscious states and follow their obscure pathways that become manifest in overt behavior or experienced emotion. This formulation, one steeped in the scientific metaphysics of cause and effect, and originating in Freud's materialism upon which his science rested, has the unconscious exhibiting demands that will not (cannot) be denied by "the proud superstructure of the mind" (Freud 1919, p. 260). This deterministic formulation became the central tenet of Freudianism, and wherever in his writings Freud discusses free will, he admonishes readers who assert their belief in such freedom as harboring a deep illusion (Tauber 2010, pp. 139ff.).[4]

On the other hand, choice is constitutive to human self-consciousness, and self-appraisal remains its linchpin. So in the Freudian context, analysis yields insight from which the analysand might achieve various degrees of freedom from unconscious trauma and desire. Thus, a tension resides at the base of psychoanalytic theory: In the province of consciousness—where recognition, reflection, reason, and resolve all reside—choice seemingly has the potential of being exercised. This is the realm of free will, which is derived from Freud's humanism and functions within a second metaphysics, one that Kant called autonomy (Tauber 2010, pp. 125ff.).Why else become an analysand if potential freedom from the tyranny of the unconscious did not exist? After all, the very promise of psychoanalysis builds upon the ability of reason, albeit with emotional reconciliation, to reveal the secrets of unconscious drives and thereby better to live with them: "Analysis does not set out to make pathological reactions impossible, but to give the patient's ego the *freedom* to decide one way or the other" (Freud 1923a, p. 50; emphasis in original). And herein lies the inescapable paradox of Freud's theory: We are determined, yet we are free.

How might we balance these competing positions? Freud, like Spinoza, regarded the ability to recognize the emotional shackles of human bondage as comprising the only freedom humans possess (Tauber 2010, pp. 217–19). And like Spinoza, Freud drew upon reason to understand and thus free the individual of ignorance:

> A neurosis would seem to be the result of a kind of ignorance—a not knowing about mental events that one ought to know of. . . . Knowledge is not always the same as knowledge: there are different sorts of knowledge, which are far from equivalent psychologically . . . [and] there is more than one kind of ignorance. (Freud 1916, pp. 280–81)

Accordingly, psychoanalysis exposes how our lives are determined by past experience and the needs of unconscious desire, and in that process the analysis also reveals that we are strangers to ourselves; thus, the process of self-discovery is endless. In that recognition, hope is derived: Whatever understanding might be achieved will translate into a better psychic functional state. This is a progressive vision. But more, through an interpretive self-inquiry, responsibility for one's actions is assumed. In this sense, psychoanalysis becomes an ethical venture, one that gives psychoanalysis its broadest cultural warrant (Reeder 2002; Egginton 2007; Tauber 2010).

If we assess Freud as a moral philosopher, the lasting influence of his work rests squarely on the meliorism derived from the effort to achieve insight, explanation, and a new emotional equilibrium. Whether the results are true in any final sense misses the import of the analytic process, for psychoanalysis seeks meaning, whose subjective parameters may not conform to standards of truth in the public sphere. While some consistent logic and integrated theory are required for its discourse, given the limits of that analytic structure, one must respond only to the challenge of achieving self-knowledge and deriving significance that fulfills the therapeutic mandate. Accordingly, "meaning is wider in scope as well as more precious in value than is truth" (Dewey 1927, p. 2). From this perspective, psychoanalysis then becomes a modality of self-identification, which shifts Freudianism from a clinical discipline to a type of moral inquiry (Tauber 2010). "Moral" in this context refers to all those components that contribute to formulating the needs, values, and normative basis of behavior and emotional well-being. Accordingly, the larger project of exercising self-knowledge in the pursuit of personal freedom and the possibilities of self-determination (ironically placed within the context of psychic determinism) makes Freud's tragic vision our own. This new myth has wide appeal, inasmuch as it taps into the very foundations of Western personhood.

In short, although the ego has been defrocked of certain conceits, Freud portrayed humans as capable of struggling against their Oedipal fate—not necessarily the primal family drama but rather the mythic labor against the determinism of undisclosed social and psychological forces. This heroic toil still has a powerful hold on Western notions of personal identity, and psychoanalysis has been enlisted in strengthening efforts to achieve greater personal liberation (not a final escape from one's fate determined by personality and past experiences). Thus, the Freudian vision celebrates the sense of freedom achieved in the effort to recognize one's fortune. In this view, freedom becomes an achievement of understanding as one pursues self-knowledge in the face of psychic determinism. And, while Freud held that belief in free will was illusory, that faith was necessary.

This Spinozan vision is not readily mortgaged, much less, forsaken. Indeed, despite efforts to displace the modernist metaphysics of the Western mind, the basic precept of human autonomy is not easily dislodged. Accordingly, Freud's error serves a larger agenda, namely, to fortify a subjective commitment to individualized self-fulfillment, on the one hand, and personal responsibility, on the other hand. Rights and obligations are held hand in hand. Assuming a moral posture in the face of contradictions hardly constitutes a unique case in which putative objective knowledge supports an ideological, religious, or social belief (e.g., Tauber 2009c, pp. 25ff.). Strict conceptual coherence may be forfeited for a mosaic of philosophical positions, each addressing a different agenda or need. Perhaps both acknowledging and accepting that fragmentation is the key characteristic of our age.

Nietzsche had set the stage for this moral and intellectual scenario, for each of our principal actors, including Freud, were caught in a Nietzschean zeitgeist that sought to salvage emotional and moral strength in a world in which meaning could be derived only from freely exercised choice and volition, and where reliance on reason faltered to leave a gaping hole in human self-confidence. In the shared reconstruction of human aspirations in the face of such looming insecurities, a utopian circle may be drawn around our protagonists. To the extent the options offered by psychoanalytic theorizing gain purchase, it must be in ways that such formulations of personhood allow for the creativity and choice of moral freedom in an ever-oppressive postindustrial society. Yes, we must acknowledge the limits of human self-consciousness and self-control and guard against the undermining of individuality by the insidious effects of mass culture, yet Freud held out a modest hope that the individual might "raise himself above them [group identifications] to the extent of having a scrap of originality and independence" (1921, p. 129). So while recognizing the limits of psychoanalysis (Freud 1937a), Freud's circumspect views still reflect the redemptive character of Western consciousness. It builds on conceptions of identity structured upon a humanist infrastructure, which I believe still must serve as the foundation of a philosophical architectonics to erect a *post*-postmodernist conception of the individual.

To conclude, in important respects, the post-Freudian epistemological arguments satisfied the criteria of a new philosophical orientation, which then posed a different set of problems for moral philosophy. Indeed, with the displacement of a human-centered epistemology, the moral calculus also changed, and thus humanistic notions of human agency assumed a different character in this new philosophical climate, one not necessarily adequate to respond to the demands of our era. While we might sympathetically consider the weaknesses of Freud's philosophy exposed by later epistemological critiques, we also must balance those criticisms with a lingering, unanswered challenge: If the humanism Freud espoused, and upon which he built his ethics, is repudiated, how successful are the quandaries of identity politics addressed by posthumanist moral philosophies? This book has offered no prescriptions, nor have predictions been offered. So any answer to the question posed about the future character of moral agency awaits a later assessment. However, we have the opportunity, perhaps even the privilege, of *living* our own response to the challenge of post-Freudian identity politics and thus participating in the inevitable evolution of notions of personal identity. Whether our answer to this challenge will evoke an elegy or an epithalamion awaits future comment.

Notes

Introduction

1. The representational model of the mind considered here (proposed by Kant, developed by Freud, and critiqued by interwar philosophers) deliberately omits discussion of contemporary debate regarding the representational character of the mind, which has largely been informed by the influential writings of Jerry Fodor (1987) and Fred Dretske (1988). Their attempt to provide a naturalistic theory of mental content is directed at creating a theory of the physical or biological properties of brain states that suffice to make these states representations of the world: "[C]ognition is *mental representation*: the mind is thought to operate by manipulating symbols that represent features of the world or represent the world as being a certain way" (Varela, Thompson, and Rosch 1991, p. 8; emphasis in original). Opposing positions (e.g., Dennett 1981, 1991b) argue that "the Dretske-Fodor view is mistaken because it does not take seriously the special properties of human interpretive practices; interpretation is not just an attempt to lay out the hidden structure of a complex machine" (Godfrey-Smith 2004, p. 150). Alternatives to representationalism range from "connectionism," which emphasizes the global characteristics of a system characterized by elements in distributed operations (as opposed to localized, symbolic processing) to an "enactive" model in which cognition is described as an "enactment" of the world through "embodied" cognition in which (1) the character of perceptive faculties determines reality; (2) cognition may be explained independent of computational processes or representations; and (3) the body plays a constitutive role in cognitive processing, and thus cognition emerges from dynamic interactions among the brain, body, and world (Shapiro 2011). Although hardly resolved, some variant of representationalism clearly dominates thinking in the broad

arena of cognitive science, while those opposing current representational theory as unable to account for folk belief and complex interpretations have dominated the debate among philosophers (Dennett 1991a; Rey 1997; Clapin 2002; Frankish 2004; Godfrey-Smith 2004; Ramsey 2007; for review, see Stich and Warfield 1994; Adams and Dietrich 2004).

2. In Freud's last model (1923a), the ego is depicted as having both conscious and unconscious domains, thus leaving the original ego boundaries with ill-defined borders.

3. The philosophies discussed here complement a parallel critique of representationalism embedded in psychological-cognitive science models of the mind. In these cybernetic-inspired theories, representations are phrased in terms of a defined code—symbolic and static—that comprises a vocabulary governed by syntax. However, this code translates from a contingent reality that is not intrinsically significant. In seeing the main thrust of twentieth-century philosophy offering an antirepresentational philosophy of mind, I align myself with those psychologists who have attacked the "representational-computational view of mind" (RCVM) (Shanon 1993, p. 2) by building on a Wittgensteinian-inspired conception of a more dynamic, context-dependent understanding of cognition and mental life. To replace a computer-based reductionist notion of code composed of fixed representations, the alternative view offers a "presentational" formulation rooted in ordinary-language philosophy and phenomenology, where mind is lodged firmly in body, action, and culture in dynamic interplay. This view rests on the impossibility of fixing meaning, and only in the plasticity of language (i.e., context) might signification be determined. In this view, language is effective to the extent that words cannot be reduced to necessary and sufficient semantic features, for meaning shifts with circumstances and applications that cannot be fulfilled with fixed meanings of a code. Simply, language is incomplete, and polysemy allows language the plasticity to present the world and thought dynamically.

Inasmuch as RCVM creates the problem of reference for itself, the solution lies in the integration of knower and known: "Given that the world which is perceived cannot be defined independently of the agent who perceives it, there is no gap to be breached. Furthermore, since the world is structured by the activities of the perceiving agent, all the information that makes for perception is in the world itself. In J. J. Gibson's terms, rather than being detected and encoded, the information is picked up. Consequently, no mediation by representations is needed. Perception is, in other words, direct" (Shanon 1993, p. 122). This orientation is indebted to the ecological perception psychology of Gibson, who maintained that what is perceived is not raw, senseless sensory data but meaningful, species-specific information (ibid.). In other words, the world cannot be described independent of the agent who perceives it, and thus the epistemological gap of RCVM vanishes as a metaphysical artifice of the Cartesian divide. This general orientation will frame our discussion as we explore the philosophical critique of Freud's representational model of the mind and consider revisions suggested by this criticism.

4. While Bergson opposed orthodox representative conceptuality, he was unable to free himself entirely of the representational modality. He saw metaphysics working best not so much when it dispenses with concepts as when it "frees itself of the inflexible and ready-made concepts and creates others very different from those we usually handle, I mean flexible, mobile, almost fluid representations" (Bergson [*Creative Mind*], quoted by Mullarkey 2000, pp. 153–54). These might be metaphors, similes, comparisons, or some intermediate Bergson labeled an *image* in the introduction to *Matter and Memory*: "[B]y *image* we mean a certain existence which is more than that which the idealist calls a *representation*, but less than that which the realist calls a *thing*—an existence placed halfway between the *thing* and the *representation*" (quoted by Lacey 1989, p. 89). In seeking a compromise between realism and idealism, Bergson's influence had largely expired by World War II and had virtually no influence on psychoanalytic thinking. Indeed, little scholarship has been directed at identifying resonances between Bergson and Freud (Guerlac 2006, pp. 23, 110), and even Deleuze, when comparing Freud and Bergson, refers to how differently Bergson conceives the unconscious—to denote a nonpsychological reality (Deleuze 1988, p. 56).

5. Dewey's point was that "mind" and "reality," like "stimulus" and "response," name nonexistent entities: They are abstractions from a single, indivisible process. It therefore makes as little sense to talk about a split that needs to be overcome between the mind and the world as it does to talk about a split between the hand and the environment, or the fork

and the soup. For Dewey, things are what they are experienced as, and thus knowledge is not a copy of something that exists independently of its being known; *"it is an instrument or organ of successful action"* ([Dewey 1908], quoted by Menand 2001, p. 361).

6. The historical reconstruction of the self's genealogy within the Freudian context has been reviewed elsewhere (Tauber 2010), and suffice it to note here that given the intractable difficulty of defining such an entity as "the self" (Tauber 1994) by various postromantic philosophical, biological, and psychological formulations of selfhood, none has established hegemony over competing constructs.

Chapter 1

1. Self-consciousness, and conscious will in particular, is postulated as arising as an evolutionary mechanism to appreciate and remember experience and, furthermore, to consider future action (Wegner 2002). If one becomes self-aware of options and choices, then action follows a kind of primitive reason or "cognitive feeling" (Clore 1992, p. 133), and thus reason moves from its Kantian transcendental status to a product of a naturalist mind.

2. Any theory of the mind or of human nature carries with it philosophical commitments—knowingly or not—and these direct the kinds of conclusions their authors draw. Freud, of course, held strongly to positivism, naturalism, and materialism, but he nevertheless *worked* as a dualist, because he acknowledged the impossibility of drawing a causative chain from physical brain states to mental states. Despite the advances of contemporary neurosciences that have increasingly localized brain functions, traced metabolic pathways, drawn correlations between biochemical mediators and behavior, the mind-brain dichotomy remains. The temptation to extrapolate postulated mechanisms derived from brain studies to postulated modules of thinking (e.g., Bechtel 2008) may provide increasingly sophisticated maps of mental functions, but when extended to descriptions that might account for consciousness, I find no convincing models, leaving the mental–brain states divide intractably separate.

3. Whether assessed through cognitive science studying perception or through psychology assessing motivation, unconscious mentation has been conclusively demonstrated (e.g., T. Wilson 2002; Sio and Ormerod

2009; Tauber 2013). But whether there is *the Unconscious* (a separate entity) and how it may function in Freudian depictions is another matter altogether. Today, the particulars of Freud's early mechanistic descriptions and later metapsychological constructions are highly problematic even for the psychoanalytic community, and Freud himself regarded his theory as only a preamble to future models of the mind.

4. Freud employed inferential interpretation to travel the "royal road" to the unconscious (1900, p. 608). "Inference to the best explanation" (Lipton 1991) provides not a syllogistic proof but rather an interpretive venture with a particular *telos*, i.e., the analyst reconstructs the intention of the speaker (Freud 1937b; Rubovits-Seitz 1998). Of course, the entire interpretation must hang together as a whole; one piece supports the others, so a hermeneutic circle is established. Note that an inference is a mode of reasoning from a premise to a conclusion; however, the logical structure of Freud's argument shows that he drew his inference from a premise that already contains the conclusion. What he hoped to derive along a causal chain of reasoning from empirical data is in fact an inference drawn directly from his *definitions* of the mental (constituted by conscious and unconscious activities), which he did not establish. Thus, his reasoning is circular, and the entire argument for the unconscious collapses as an exercise in deductive logic, which does not gainsay other interpretive strategies (see Tauber 2010, pp. 63–66). The scientific battle (the ground where Freud himself chose to wage his campaign), in my view, has been decisively won by the skeptics and, absent convincing controlled studies of efficacy, defenders of Freud's therapeutic endeavor have been hard-pressed to secure his original claims (Grünbaum 1984; Webster 1995; Macmillan 1997).

5. Criticisms of Freud's theory typically focus on the scientific standing of his claims and the basis for the inferences that serve as the basic scaffolding of psychoanalytic theorizing. In a famous exchange, Freud reminded Einstein that in the end all science rested on some untestable metaphysical foundations and noted that "does not every science come in the end to a kind of mythology like this? Cannot the same be said to-day of your Physics?" (1932, p. 211), by which he referred not only to the provisional character of scientific theory but also to a metaphysical boundary, a domain beyond human understanding, which Freud believed

underlies all human knowledge. But that observation hardly validates the philosophical assumptions of psychoanalytic theory! In any case, Freud at times admitted the tenuous claim to scientific validity. For instance, when he posited a metaphorical censor, "the watchman," to preside over a gateway that determined which psychic contents pass from the large unconscious "entrance hall" to the smaller "drawing-room" in which consciousness resides, he observed, "I know you will say that these ideas are both crude and fantastic and quite impermissible in a scientific account. I know that they are crude: and, more than that, I know that they are incorrect. . . . They are preliminary working hypotheses" (1916, p. 296). Admitting that his science was still inadequate to explore the unconscious directly (and presuming that new scientific methods would alter his theory), he nevertheless proceeded as if his method and theory had scientific credibility (Tauber 2010, pp. 57–58) on the basis that his constructions were required to help establish psychic *laws* (Freud 1940, p. 158). Moreover, he maintained that such theorizing followed the same basic procedures employed by natural scientists, who used similar approximations to link their findings into some coherent model useful to order phenomena otherwise uncoordinated (ibid., p. 159).

6. Others have observed that Freud took "representations" as the basic element with which the psychic apparatus operates from the first generation of scientific psychologists, e.g., Johann Herbart (1776–1841) (De Kesel 2009, p. 295). Herbart posited that "all mental phenomena result from the actions and interactions of 'ideas' (presentations [representations]); that ideas are of different kinds, stronger and weaker; that arrested (inhibited) ideas are obscured and disappear from consciousness, leaving the field to others; that such inhibited, unconscious ideas constitute a mass and continue to exert their pressure against those in consciousness; and that there is a continual conflict between conscious and unconscious ideas at the threshold of consciousness" (Whyte 1978, p. 143). Thus, Herbart, who assumed Kant's Königsberg philosophy chair in 1809, was heavily influenced by Kant's representationalism. Herbart's associationistic psychology had an important influence on Freud's early theorizing, but he is best known for his attempts to mathematize psychic forces according to a physics model, which deeply influenced Gustav Fechner (1801–87), whose theorizing directly influenced Freud's own

Newtonian psychodynamic postulates (Ellenberger 1970, pp. 478–79, 489). However, as explained later, Freud's own understanding of Kant's representational model of the mind served as the *philosophical* foundation upon which psychoanalysis was built, and associationism offered Freud a strategy to probe unconsciousness.

7. Kant's functional characterization makes the ego an object like any other, and while "intimate," the operative modalities of knowing remain the same as for objects in nature with the net erasure of the Cartesian "thinking thing." This same approach, when applied to introspective analysis, offers a way to scrutinize the human mind with the same faculties employed for phenomenal cognition. Thus, the *noumenal* self (which in principle could not be known, just as "the-thing-in-itself" could not be known because for Kant, the *noumenon* exists independent of cognitive faculties and therefore exists prior to the categorization imposed by the mind) was formulated as a "transcendental apperception of the ego" (Tauber 2010, pp. 148–51). "Transcendental" refers to those required conditions for knowing, which ultimately provided the means to navigate both the natural and moral universes. In effect, Kant turned reflexivity back into the world, essentially acknowledging the limitation of self-consciousness (a summation undoubtedly oversimplified and disputed [Keller 1998]).

8. This notion of self-consciousness being a special case of objective consciousness is untenable from various points of view, but most simply, the first consciousness (in the position of the object) requires a second consciousness (in the position of the subject), which, being itself unconscious, requires yet another consciousness, and so on in a regressive cycle. While some have defended "self-conscious" = "consciousness of the I" (e.g., Kant, Fichte, neo-Kantians, Husserl), others, in order to break the recursive circle, have sought to characterize consciousness without mediation by representation with so-called nonegological theories of self-consciousness (e.g., Brentano, James, Sartre, Lacan) (Frank 1997, p. 13).

9. To the extent Freud considered the nature of consciousness as a neuroscientist, he followed Helmholtz's theories of perception (Makari 1994), which drew from Kant's representational model of cognition (Tauber 2010, pp. 99–100).

10. As I have described previously (Tauber 2010, pp. 117–21), Freud mused on parallels between his own conception of the mind

and Kant's transcendental idealism (Binswanger 1957; Bergo 2004). In 1910, Binswanger reports that Freud entertained that his version of the unconscious was close to Kant's *noumenon*, which suggests that Freud identified the difficulties he faced in studying the unconscious as a case example of the same general philosophical issue Kant faced in deciphering the mind's engagement with nature. References to Kant's *Critique of Pure Reason* are sprinkled throughout Freud's writings. Indeed, Freud knew Kant well enough to dispute certain basic Kantian precepts (Freud 1920, p. 28) and Kantian arguments (1990, pp. 110–11) or to draw on detailed Kantian insights (1905, p. 12). (The English *Standard Edition* lists nineteen instances where Freud invoked Kant [Guttman 1984].)

11. In his clinical investigations, Freud remained unhesitant in pursuing the unconscious as a *natural* biological entity (Tauber 2010, pp. 162–64). Clues provided by dreams, slips of the tongue, jokes, neurotic behaviors, etc., then serve psychoanalysis as "perceived" objects, which assume their meaning through psychoanalytic techniques. If we put aside the irreconcilable differences between an experimental system and the psychoanalytic couch, the impossibility of controlling the boundary conditions of an analysis, and the vastly different interpretive criteria, the striking character of Freud's epistemology is the persistence of applying his notion of a Kantian *noumenon* to the problems of deciphering unconsciousness. Of course, he made that linkage with the intent of legitimating psychoanalytic methods as a form of science. However, Freud denied any affinity with philosophy, and despite the parallels drawn here, we must note the vast chasm separating Freud's commitment to empiricism and positivism and any form of philosophical idealism, Kant's included. (See Tauber 2010, pp. 144–45.)

12. Whether Freud's new epistemology may be regarded as structured as a language is a matter of dispute. Michel Henry, in his critique of Freud's representationalism, rejects Lacan's own version of the unconscious structured as a language: "On the one hand, a linguistic formation is substituted for the dream proper, for a pure imaginary that as such has nothing to do with language. All the categories that concern language are then invested in a given that is incompatible with them. What is merely a metaphor, the dream as the 'text' of the analysis, as its object,

is taken literally, as an intrinsic determination of that object's essence. The contamination or denaturation of psychoanalysis by linguistics and the whole of the disciplines associated with it is now possible. In all seriousness, people can now say that the unconscious is structured like language [Lacan]. In Freud himself, the consideration of words all too often vitiates the delimitation of the real phenomena and the research into their actual determinants" (1993, p. 292).

13. Freud studied the unconscious in a fashion he considered analogous to the epistemology of physical phenomena, by putatively following the scientific logic drawn from physics (e.g., electric effects) and from biology (e.g., variation within species), i.e., phenomena are witnessed and then accounted for by measuring forces—electromagnetism and natural selection, respectively. Indeed, Freud explicitly drew parallels between psychoanalysis and physics, since he regarded each discipline as following the same basic scientific strategy. Perceptive abilities are constantly improved; sense perceptions permit connections and new dependent relations to be established, which are "somehow reliably reproduced or reflected in our internal" thought; "understanding" follows, which in turn permits prediction and control (Freud 1940, pp. 196–97). And of course, by tracing back observations to their underlying causes, Freud attempted to establish the dynamics of psychic determinism, which became the arch-principle of his project.

14. Kantian knowledge derives from "pure reason," whose categories in which we think—substance, causality, etc.—determine the "is-ness" of our perceptions (*phenomenon*) rather than the thing in itself (*noumenon*). Kant's antirealism did not deny that there is an *an sich* (in itself), only that we have no direct (unmediated) knowledge of it. Thus, humans are restricted to know the world by their cognitive faculties, whose structure permits only a particular refraction. "What the things may be in themselves I do not know, and also do not need to know" (Kant 1998 [B333], p. 375). Accordingly, the manner of perceiving the world and acting in it depends on the particular character (viz. biology) of the human mind and that the world exists for us (i.e., can be known) as defined by those faculties of knowing. Thus, the picture created is neither final nor absolute. Indeed, reality itself is only what human cognition knows or might know. However, the argument is not about reality but rather about

how we know and whether the mode of knowing determines what *is* (Tauber 2009c, pp. 60, 100–102).

15. Johan Eriksson tracks the Kantian influence on Freud from the very inception of psychoanalysis as an investigation of mental states: "By abandoning his theory of seduction Freud hence lost, in an etiological perspective, and in his own words, '[t]he firm ground of reality' [Freud 1914b, p. 17]. And thus his theoretical focus . . . [shifted] from the external in the direction of the internal, from the material reality in the direction of the psychic reality, from the interpersonal in the direction of the intra-psychical" (Eriksson 2012, p. 19). And with this shift, "psychoanalysis was created as a science of subjectivity, [which] . . . is much more closely related to transcendental philosophy" and by extension, phenomenology (ibid., p. 22).

I have placed Freud in a philosophical context that does not speak to a phenomenological orientation (Tauber 2010), whereby Freud transforms "a shift of attention from the experienced *world* to the *experienced* world" (Eriksson 2010, p. 144). "The domain for psychoanalytical research—the psychic in its Freudian sense—is thus equivalent to what we may call *our lived experience*. Or, psychoanalysis is a science of subjectivity. In this, Freudian psychoanalysis adheres, at least in its principal traits, to transcendental philosophy as it was first created by Kant through his 'Copernican turn' and then developed by phenomenologists like Husserl and Heidegger" (Eriksson 2012, p. 19). See Askay and Farquhar (2006) for a comprehensive phenomenologically oriented interpretation of Freud's theory.

16. A normative ether pervades Freudian psychology, which then drives his metaphysics: A *healthy* construction of reality—that which controls and potentially gratifies desire—provides the mature, healthy target of cathexis, so in the healthy state, the self seeks its "other" outside its own agency in love and work. In the narcissistic setting, where the self becomes the object of desire, a cascade of emotional events leads to ever-deepening neurosis as the original exterior object of desire remains unfulfilled and an *unhealthy* reality is then operative. The psychoanalytic trick, as it were, is to direct and even teach the id to follow the ego's lead as it probes the world for fulfillment of desire. This clinical scaffolding represents a second layer to the deeper metaphysical structure of Freud's theory of reality described previously.

17. Freud clearly knew the first *Critique*, and he followed Kant closely in drawing epistemological parallels between the *noumenon* and the unconscious (albeit with glaring errors). In that construction, a subject-object relationship is established by an ego that serves as a faculty to represent the mind to itself (see Tauber 2010, pp. 179ff.). However, Freud apparently did not know or appreciate Kant's third *Critique*, *The Critique of Judgment* (1983). There, Kant attempted to establish how scientific thinking, as objective knowledge, might be reconciled with subjective ways of knowing. In some sense, Kant heralded the romantic recognition of the inner tensions between these two modes of knowledge, and while they by and large altogether rejected the objectification of nature and self, Kant sought the appropriate place for both forms of knowing to function authentically. Kant tried to mend the division he invented, i.e., the separation of reason into two modalities, one to deal with the natural world (pure, or theoretical reason) and the other to navigate the moral (practical reason) (Tauber 2010, pp. 125ff.). Although dealing with different domains, reason still functioned as a whole, and he recognized that certain human experiences simply did not reduce to the knowable as defined by objective standards. To address this failing of his system, Kant posited a synthetic function, which was carried out with a third faculty, *judgment* (*Urteil*), which brought unity to thought. Judgment coordinates with different cognitive faculties so that reason still functions as a whole to achieve unity to thought, and by drawing that synthesis, Kant (1987) provided a rationale—and outlined the ability—for individuals to connect the theoretical (i.e., natural) and practical (i.e., moral) aspects of human reason with what we would describe as the emotional or human-originating experience. The "sublime" was such an example, namely, a category of the human confrontation with that beyond comprehension and understanding. "Wonder," while not definable in analytic terms, was nevertheless *real*, and very much of human experience. Indeed, in some respects, facing the sublime signifies a supreme human fulfillment. So judgment not only serves to bridge the other forms of reason in Kant's system but also addresses that domain of experience that requires its own modality— the cultural, social, and aesthetic dimensions of human life as specified cases of the judgment faculty at work.

18. For a cogent critique of this basic assumption, see Searle (1992, pp. 151–73).

19. This discussion remains focused on this particular aspect of Freud's theory and makes no attempt to assess the place of representationalism in contemporary psychoanalysis, which is thoroughly reviewed by Perlow (1995; see especially the discussion of Joseph Sandler's writings, pp. 74ff., and subsequent theorizing, pp. 121ff.; Sandler et al. 1997).

20. Unconscious deliberative *thinking* has been demonstrated, and it follows a normative strategy (Dijksterhuis and Nordgren 2006; Sio and Ormerod 2009; Tauber 2013). If the concept of active repression is discarded in this scenario, then the intermediary position held by preconsciousness—a psychic locale in which unconscious thinking, later available to consciousness, occurs—has been verified and Freud's original tripartite structure of the mind seems credible: an unconscious, whose materials are forever lost or hidden; conscious thought, accessible to immediate reflection; and a preconsciousness, which serves as a latent reservoir of thinking available to consciousness as required. In this view, two basic depictions of the unconscious seem plausible. The first simply ascribes lost memory to unconsciousness, which may, under some complex emotional and cognitive calculus, influence mental life. A second formulation is more direct and requires reconceiving the unconscious altogether, i.e., a domain of mental life that is ontologically prior to thinking, namely, the more primordial emotional realm, in which drives dwell and desires form. Here, a repressive mechanism may be the mechanism of psychic control.

21. Freud's *Project for a Scientific Psychology* (1895) posited the ebb and flow of the incessant processing of neurophysiological events in a hierarchy of neurons (D. Smith 1999a, 1999b, 2004). In such a schema, simple processors are arranged in an interconnected network, which Freud postulated as three integrated functional systems: (1) perceptual input, (2) cognitive processing, and (3) consciousness generating. See Greenberg (1997, pp. 165ff.) for a full discussion of Freud's prepsychoanalytic writings on the relationship of neurology and psychology, and more particularly, the development of his philosophy of mind based on Kantian representationalism.

22. "The idea, or concept, of the object is itself another complex of associations composed of the most varied visual, auditory, tactile,

kinaesthetic and other impressions. According to philosophical teaching, the idea of the object contains nothing else; the appearance of the 'thing,' the 'properties' of which are conveyed to our senses, originates only from the fact that in enumerating the sensory impressions perceived from an object, we allow for the possibility of a large series of new impressions being added to the chain of associations (J. S. Mill). This is why the idea of the object does not appear to us as closed, and indeed hardly as closable, while the word concept appears to us as something that is closed though capable of extension" (Freud 1953, pp. 77–78). Note that Freud's use of the term *Vorstellung* (presentation) rests on Mill's philosophical construction, which in turn relies on Kant, that "a Sensation is to be carefully distinguished from the object which causes the sensation" (J. S. Mill, *A System of Logic* [1873, p. 34], quoted by Greenberg 1997, p. 165).

23. Strachey's translation of this passage from Freud's *On Aphasia* (originally published in 1891), which appears as prefatory remarks to appendix C of "The Unconscious" (Freud 1915b, p. 209), refers to a disruption of the "word-presentation" and the "object-presentation" (ibid., p. 214). He explains, "[T]here is an important and perhaps confusing difference between the terminology Freud uses here [*On Aphasia*] and in 'The Unconscious.' What he here calls the 'object-presentation' is what in 'The Unconscious' he calls the 'thing-presentation'; while what in 'The Unconscious' he calls the 'object-presentation' denotes a complex made up of the combined 'thing-presentation' and 'word-presentation'—a complex which has no name given to it in the *Aphasia* passage. The translation has been made specially for this occasion, since, for terminological reasons, the published one was not entirely adapted to the present purpose. As in the last section of 'The Unconscious,' we have here always used the word 'presentation' to render the German '*Vorstellung*,' while 'image' stands for the German '*Bild*'" (ibid., p. 209). The history of Freud's use of the word *Vorstellung* is a complex one, but crucial to understanding his philosophical construction. In *On Aphasia*, Freud omits *Vorstellung* in a diagram of his psychological model of a word-presentation, but Strachey adds "Word-[presentations]" in the *Standard Edition* (Freud 1915a, appendix C, p. 214). How Freud built the conceptual infrastructure of the *Project for a Scientific Psychology* (1895) on this conceptual template is discussed by Greenberg (1997, pp. 172–73).

24. The problematic relationship between an "idea" and its unconscious association was recognized at the beginning of psychoanalytic theorizing and was commented upon by Josef Breuer in the jointly authored *Studies on Hysteria*: "The objections that are raised against 'unconscious ideas' existing and being operative seem for the most part to be juggling with words. No doubt 'idea' is a word belonging to the terminology of conscious thinking, and 'unconscious idea' is therefore a self-contradictory expression. But the physical process that underlies an idea is the same in content and form (though not in quantity) whether the idea rises above the threshold of consciousness or remains beneath it. It would only be necessary to construct some such term as 'ideational substratum' in order to avoid the contradiction and to counter the objection" (Freud and Breuer 1895, p. 223). Note that Breuer directly links the mental state to the physical brain state to justify his nomenclature, and in that easy translation of categories, he echoed Freud's own efforts (in the *Project for a Scientific Psychology* [Freud 1895]) to correlate a hypothetical neurological system with the psychology they were describing at the same time.

25. In James's account, presented in his chapter "The Emotions" of his magisterial *Principles of Psychology* (published in 1890), emotions are "nothing but the feeling of a bodily state, and [have] a purely bodily cause" (1983, p. 1074). In other words, emotions are reduced to physiology, whose manifestations are interpreted at higher cognitive levels as feelings—fear, love, anger, etc. He reversed the commonsensical notion that the emotion causes a bodily change that expresses it. Instead, James insisted that a person who sees a charging lion runs, and the running, with its associated bodily changes, is experienced as fear: "*[B]odily changes follow directly the perception of the exciting fact,*" and the resulting feeling of those changes is the emotion (ibid., p. 1065; emphasis in original).

26. While contemporary cognitive science embraces the "iceberg-model of knowledge" (De Mey 1992, p. 19) and thereby affirms basic Freudian precepts (i.e., [1] certain cognitive processes are not only hidden but cannot be brought into consciousness; and [2] the self is fundamentally nonunified and because of its fragmentation, self-awareness represents only a small segment of cognitive processes [Varela, Thompson, and Rosch 1991, pp. 47–51]), the epistemological privilege asserted by Freud

is dismissed out of hand. The contemporary cognitivist turn asserts a far more circumscribed view of ego function, and while Freud acknowledged "the arrogance of consciousness" (1910b, p. 39), he still assigns the ego an authority that seems ill placed: "Confusion arises from the Cartesian dualism which still pervades many basic concepts in psychology . . . such as *I* and *self* are considered entities to which we—somehow—have direct access by means of some privileged observation channel called 'introspection.' . . . In the cognitive view however, it is hard to see how any basic distinction between two forms of observation like introspection and extrospection could be justified. There is no *direct perception, neither* of parts of the *world nor* of the *self* in any of its aspects. The cognitive view holds that *all* perception is mediated by models. Our concept of an 'outside world' and an 'inside self' are conceptual models used to filter sensations of the same kind. Nothing justifies a special cognitive status for a notion such as 'self'" (De Mey 1992, p. 26; emphasis in original).

27. It is difficult to judge Freud's considered opinion about the character of consciousness from this comment, although speculation abounds (e.g., Natsoulas 1984, 1985). On balance, I think he took the ego's representing function as given, and similarly, he understood consciousness as requiring no further examination and summarily dismissed any requirement for a definition: "There is no need to discuss what is to be called conscious: it is removed from all doubt" (Freud 1933, p. 70). So for Freud, consciousness per se does not appear as an issue to explore or even define (Meissner 2003, p. 75), and with that wave of the hand, he pursued his project without further ado. Of course the philosophical status of consciousness is closely linked to the problem of representation we are considering, so it is noteworthy that Freud failed to deal explicitly with the status of conscious thought given his circumspect view of the ego's autonomy.

28. We find this refrain sprinkled across Nietzsche's notebooks (e.g., "We place a word at the point where our ignorance begins—where we can't see any further" [Nietzsche 2003, p. 106]; and "Parmenides said: 'One does not think that which is not'—we are at the other extreme and say: 'What can be thought must certainly be a fiction.' Thinking has no grip on the real" [ibid., p. 261]).

29. While Nietzsche and Freud most evidently separate on the role of reason (Tauber 2010, pp. 161–73), this configuration too starkly

differentiates them, for they both recognized the centrality of the affects as the basis of psychic life. For Freud, reason, as an analytic tool, serves a particular instrumental function in identifying the putative causes of anxiety arising from repression and accompanying guilt. Thus, the analysis is focused on the pursuit of better-balanced emotional dynamics through reasoned self-knowledge. Such insight putatively modulates (even resolves) guilt and ultimately relieves the analysand from dysfunctional behaviors. In other words, reason serves to awaken an emotional awareness and recognition, namely, release from the tyranny of the traumatic past.

30. For example, one might describe pain and find language incapable of capturing the experience, and analogously, the phobia of Little Hans has no conceptual intermediaries for the child (Freud 1909).

31. Many have commented on how a subjective, emotional resistance can interfere with the therapeutic potential of transference (e.g., the case of Dora [Bernheimer and Kahane 1990]), and the converse, where Freud's receptivity to the emotional torment of his patient exemplifies how empathy serves the analytic project. Jonathan Lear (1990) calls the analyst's accepting attitude a kind of love, and it sits in stark contrast to the "scientific Freud," who sought objectivity much as a surgeon might regard a lesion for extraction (Stepansky 1999). For example, in the case of the Rat Man (Freud 1909), Freud exhibits an empathy that served to discharge the patient's contempt for himself by placing the responsibility for the aberrant behavior in a past in which the patient had no control. With Freud at his side, the patient was enjoined to confidently battle his inner adversary and find a means for self-forgiveness. Empathy is more than mere emotionalism—it is also a substrate for thought with at least three distinct domains at play in the clinical setting: (1) a cognitive orientation, where the physician enters into the patient's experience yet maintains a clinical perspective; (2) an emotional focus where emotions resonate between doctor and patient; and (3) an action component, where dialogue establishes enhanced communication and understanding. So empathy may be regarded as a form of "emotional reasoning" (Halpern 2001). After all, much of the evaluation of the world and others is colored by subjectivity, and, indeed, emotions are evaluative, not in the same way as logical precision commands but as lenses by which perceptions are refracted by mood, personal experience, and temperament (Nussbaum 2001; Tauber 2001). (Note that empathy is not sympathy;

physicians may be empathetic even when they cannot be sympathetic [Wispe 1986; Tauber 2005, p. 199].)

Chapter 2

1. Written in 1944, published in Amsterdam in 1947, republished in Germany in 1969, and finally translated into English in 1972, *Dialectic of Enlightenment* has remained the pivotal text of the Frankfurt School's theorizing.

2. "Once reason accepts *itself* as self-legislating and self-representing, it needs to avoid any representation *of* reason. At the very least, any representation must be recognized *as* representation (and not as an image or norm to which reason ought to submit). If modern societies risk falling into an indiscriminate economism, where the quantifiable comes to govern life, then this can only be overcome through the retrieval [self-conscious awareness] of representation: all those external systems, orders and reified structures must be seen as human representations and reunited with the domain of responsible and intentional constitution. This is where the political demand for democratic representation intersects with the epistemological demand for enlightenment. Subjects have the power to represent themselves as free individuals because they are rational; but rationality is also the responsibility of recognizing man as a representational animal. His order and law is not imposed from without but is represented through the law-giving power of reason. . . . It is this separation of the representing self from the self that is represented that leads to autonomy as an unavoidable duty. Autonomy follows from the subject's capacity—as a subject—to imagine or represent what is not given" (Colebrook 2005, pp. 7–8; emphasis in original).

3. Expressing an elitist disdain for the masses (Freud 1927, p. 7) and doubt that education would change matters for them, Freud lodged his hopes in the psychoanalytically enlightened, who chose to be civilized and presumably would lead the "majority" (ibid., p. 9) with enlightened "kindness" (p. 8). Even that somewhat muted hope underwent a darker expression three years later, when Freud shifted to a minor key and left his readers with an agnostic prognostication (1930, p. 145).

4. Freud's musings on the social closely followed the development of his clinical theory. In the early development of psychoanalysis, coincident

with his preoccupation with human sexuality, he criticized bourgeois sexual repression (Freud 1898, 1908); in response to Jung's concoction of a collective unconscious, Freud (1913) offered his own version of primal murder and subsequent organization of paternal society; and after World War I, following the metapsychology he had developed, a more complex formulation appeared. The revision of the original libidinal instinctual theory maintained its dualistic character, but now as a struggle between Eros and the death instinct (Freud 1920). In these late writings, where social theorizing appears most clearly, Freud suggested that the complex interplay of the Eros-death instinct required a healthy dialectic for individual and social health. Indeed, finding that equipoise suggested *social* therapeutic possibilities. The acceptance and integration of the death instinct then becomes both an ethical and existential task, which if denied (in Freudian terms), putatively leads not only to a thwarted life but neurosis (Drassinower 2003; reviewed in Tauber 2012a). "To tolerate life remains, after all, the first duty of all living beings. Illusion becomes valueless if it makes this harder for us" (Freud 1915, p. 299), and thus he considered it "a scientific duty, to apply the research methods of psychoanalysis, in regions far remote from its native soil, to the various mental sciences" (Freud 1919, p. 260). So beyond the direct elucidation of psychic disease, Freud's theory of culture became an inquiry into the viability of the human species.

5. Two general readings arise from Freud's swings between an austere realism and modestly hopeful assessments: On the one hand, he may be interpreted as deeply pessimistic about the effective control of the instincts (in particular, destructive Thanatos) and thus ultimately despairing of psychoanalytic redemption (Thompson 1991; Dienstag 2006). On this fatalistic account, basic psychic structural dynamics doom humankind. This "melancholic" or "negative" state describes "an enduring past that misshapes and deforms the present, which, in turn, presents the future with a steadily increasing burden" (Moss 2005, p. 379). Although a despondent Freud vividly appears in his works, an alternative voice may also be discerned, i.e., the cautious optimism of psychoanalytic therapy, which would extend the lessons learned from individual therapy to society at large. With a general perfectionist vision orienting his thought, strategies might be devised to better integrate erotic and death instincts to

form an enriched psychic dialectic (e.g., Brown 1959; Drassinower 2003). On this view, instead of destructive conflict, Freud sought a means of achieving improved psychic harmony, which he hoped would offer an alternative mode of acculturation.

This latter romantic interpretation describes contrasts with a classic view: The classic motif finds the meeting of inner nature and outer reality as unavoidably painful, whereas romantic views see it as potentially harmonious (Strenger 1997). Critics have noted the dangers of such utopian thinking on interpreting psychoanalysis proper (Eckstein and Caruth 1965) or outlining the hidden effects of a utopian orientation on the analysand herself (E. Berman 2000; Werbart 2007). As Donald Moss observes, the utopian orientation follows from Freud's basic analytic method, which is "implicitly utopian . . . an impossible ideal whose achievement would mark the end of mind as we know it; that is, the end of repression—psychoanalytic utopia. . . . Each successful treatment goes further than anyone could have been imagined. In spite of being burdened with the weight of Zeno-like paradoxes, the accumulated history of these private transgressions has the potential to move us all incrementally in a utopian direction. This potential for excess is the necessary ingredient for effective clinical work. The potential reveals a utopian presence, an idea protected from the policing forces of the norm" (2005, p. 379).

6. "Freud is the author who most challenged what could be called modernity's narcissism, that is, an omnipotent belief in reason. . . . [He also] recognized the particularly postmodern insight that there is an 'other' to reason that defines what reason is—even communicative reason. Unlike the postmodern critic, however, for Freud the acknowledgement of the unconscious is the starting point of an eminently rational (and modernist) endeavor: psychoanalysis" (Steuerman 2000, p. 15).

7. Freud showed no interest in discerning the biological or philosophical character of consciousness (1933, p. 70), and similarly, the philosophical understanding of reason eclipsed his interests. Given the centrality of reason in Freud's theory and its bifurcation between a scientific discourse and a narrative one (Goldberg 1988), one might ask why the philosophical standing of reason has not been more interesting to Freud's commentators, especially considering the problematic status of rationality as revealed by psychological studies over the past three decades. Concerns

about the status of rationality were not of apparent interest to Freud. He never delved into the biological basis of reason, nor did he comment on its philosophical foundations, and he did not experimentally probe the psychology of decision making, memory, analysis, or any of the other cognitive functions grouped under "reason."

8. Adorno's relationship to Freudian theory has been subject to general discussion (e.g., Buck-Morss 1977; Alford 1988; Benjamin 1988, 1998; Dews 1995; Schmidt 1998; Chessick 2007), and for a (sympathetic) rebuttal of Adorno's understanding of rationality as critiqued by Habermas, see Cook (2004). However, only Joel Whitebook (1995, pp. 132ff., 2004) and Yevonne Sherratt (2002) explore (in English) the depths of this relation in regard to how Adorno appropriates aspects of psychoanalytic theory for his own social criticism. Both Whitebook and Sherratt portray a utopian Adorno resisting postmodernisms, but with different strategies and interpretations. Whitebook sees Freud as anticipating certain postmodern themes but draws the distinction of how the decentered, split subject emerges: Instead of enlisting in the reduction of the ego to the dominant unconscious, power, or *la langue*, he traces the deconstruction of the self to Piaget's (1929) genetic theory of development. While Whitebook emphasizes Adorno's "negative" dialectic, Serratt regards Adorno as a utopian thinker employing a "positive" dialectic and takes greater pains to distance him from postmodern discourse. My presentation closely follows her interpretation.

9. For Freud, the superego, an internalized authority and policeman, which employs guilt to enforce conformity, serves as the most powerful tool civilization deploys against the destructive instincts. In *Civilization and Its Discontents*, he dissected the internal and external causes of the guilt complex, of which a significant portion concerns fear of external authority, as well as the anxiety generated from the internalized power of the superego. Guilt can hardly serve the pleasure needs of the individual, and in an unrelieved regression, he saw guilt leading to further repression and (following his "hydraulic thinking") increasing frustration of the id-instincts with their eventual violent expression in direct relation to their suppression (Freud 1930, p. 132). Freud pondered the likelihood that the dynamics he described might be redirected to avoid the apparent inevitability of cultural barbarity and self-destruction

and left a noncommittal opinion about the prospects for psychological reform.

10. "Where nature confronted men as mythic power, Adorno called for the control of that nature by reason; but where rational control of nature took the form of domination, Adorno exposed such instrumental reason as a new mythology. The fluctuating meanings of Adorno's concepts, their purposeful ambivalence, are a major source of the difficulty of interpreting his works. But it was precisely his intent to frustrate the categorizing, defining mentality which by the twentieth century had itself become 'second nature'" (Buck-Morss 1977, pp. 58–59).

11. Odysseus must deny his own identity in order to escape the Cyclops and thus ironically allows the Cyclops to achieve its own end (Horkheimer and Adorno 1993, pp. 60, 65–68).

12. "What appears to be the triumph of subjective rationality, the subjection of all reality to logical formalism, is paid for by the obedient subjection of reason to what is directly given. What is abandoned is the whole claim and approach to knowledge: to comprehend the given as such. . . . The task of cognition does not consist in mere apprehension, classification, and calculation, but in the determinate negation of each im-mediacy" (Horkheimer and Adorno 1993, p. 26–27).

13. The stratagem sought to uncover (1) non-identity of the concept with the object: superfluous aspect of the concept (subjective fantasy), and (2) non-identity of the object with the concept: the objectivity that lies beyond the concept (Sherratt 2002, pp. 132–33). Adorno presented "the process of thinking through a series of unavoidable contradictions, pursuing this idea not dynamically under the sign of some preordained progress, but by inscribing it emphatically within the conflictual network of a 'negative dialectic.' If we say A, we must also say B, but there is no longer any C in which both terms could successfully be 'sublated' (*aufgehoben*). A and B continue to stand over against one another" (Früchtl 2008, p. 142).

14. Rothenberg's construction (discussed later) builds upon Adorno's non-identity principle, which she not only explicitly develops as a philosophical construction of the subject; she has also added an important social contextual element largely undeveloped in Adorno's reconfigured Marxism, or what Buck-Morss calls his "Marx minus the proletariat" theorizing (1977, pp. 44ff.).

15. The construction continues a debate dating to Hegel's own discursion about the relationship of reason and reality. (In Hegel's preface to *Philosophy of Right* he famously writes, "What is rational is real; and what is real is rational" [2001, p. 18] and "To apprehend what *is* is the task of philosophy, because what *is* is reason" [2001, p. 19]; for discussion of interpretations and alternate translations, see Tauber 2009, pp. 197–98.) Where Hegel conceived synthesis and unity in the dialectical construction, Adorno's negative dialectic found no such resolution in principle, for only nonreconciliatory thinking portrayed the reality of contradictory sociohistorical conditions. Thus, the substituted negative dialectic would distinguish "the real" from "reason" altogether, and more radically, because the real is not "the rational," another epistemology must capture that which identity thinking lost.

Chapter 3

1. When Adorno assumes his Marxist stance, the control comes from social context and the demands of economic performance, where "thinking submits to the social checks on its performance. . . . Thought, having lost its autonomy, no longer trusts itself to comprehend reality, in freedom, for its own sake" (Adorno 2005, #126, p. 196).

2. Ample evidence from cognitive science studies has demonstrated how Asians and North American Caucasians perceive scenes or presentations differently (Nisbett 2003).

3. The following description is based on Mary Anne Rothenberg's (2010) exposition of the term "excess," which she principally employs as a means of defining the social agent, and is particularly concerned with how to apply various poststructuralist theories to issues of democratic citizenship and political theory in answer to conflicting theories of social identity and social causation. This model of the subject is relevant to exploring the nexus created by the convergence of psychoanalytic theory, critical theory, and Kantianism.

4. This formulation builds from Lacan's notion that the subject is a signifier for another, which implicitly suggests that the subject cannot control its own message; and because the message cannot be "stabilized," a dialectic of messages and meanings must transmit what, from the Hegelian perspective, is the ongoing self/other dialectic, where "my"

identity emerges as a product of becoming a "you" for another, where every "subject begins its social life as an extimate subject—its fundament is already a function of otherness" (Rothenberg 2010, p. 202).

5. Lacan introduced the Möbius image (constructed by taking a rectangular paper, twisting it 180 degrees, and gluing the two ends together) to discuss desire and to offer an image that graphically depicts how "internal" and "external" may be regarded as sliding into one another (Lacan 1978, p. 156). This topographical construct represents an unbounded yet finite spatial object, a so-called nonorientable object, which characteristically has a distinct surface, such as an inside, that transforms into an outside surface without crossing a discontinuity (an edge or hole). "Every subject is an 'excessive' subject. For convenience, I refer to this excessive subject—the subject born of and bearing excess—as the 'Möbius subject' because the topology of the Möbius band (with its apparently impossible configuration of two sides that turn out to be the same) provides a convenient model for understanding how, at every point in the social field, an irreducible excess attends social relations" (Rothenberg 2010, p. 10).

6. "Lacan coined the term 'extimacy' to describe the form of causality peculiar to the subject of the unconscious. He was the first to see how the extimate causality, the concept necessary to explain the advent of the subject, also recalibrates the investigation of social relations, a topic he took up most vigorously in Seminar 17 . . . *The Other Side of Psychoanalysis*" (Rothenberg 2010, p. 11). Accordingly, "extimate causality" names the "operation that generates subjects in their social dimension—that is, the operation generates identities, properties, and relationships. . . . [and] also leaves a remainder or indeterminacy, so that every subject bears some unspecifiable excess within the social field" (ibid., p. 10). For Rothenberg, cause is either "exceptional" (external) to a social field (e.g., Marxist theory of capital and market forces) or "imminent" (internal) to the field (Foucault's depiction of power subsisting within the field in question). In the latter case, subjects can never stand in a position counter to a system, determined as they are by it, and in the former case, how to relate the field of effects to underlying cause (economic base) is never clear. Dissatisfied with the restrictions of either orientation, Rothenberg has attempted to find a means for accounting for

each in a synthesis. So if the two forms of causation are combined, their complementary relationship generates a melded external/internal causal structure—"extimate" cause—which potentially offers a means both to keep cause and effect distinct (overcoming Foucauldian restrictions) and still provide a way of linking cause and effect in the social field of effects (correcting the Marxist weakness) (Rothenberg 2010, pp. 6–10).

7. Aura's history reflects the evolution of the aesthetic, which in primitive life was incorporated seamlessly into everyday experience; the next stage placed the aesthetic into the religious realm, where it was associated with ritual, and then in the modern period the aesthetic was further marginalized into an autonomous sphere, where it was divided between high and low forms. For Benjamin, in the present era, art has lost all forms of aura in the reproductive expressions of mass culture, since it vacates the ritual significance and uniqueness art possessed when associated with religious practice. Indeed, the distance separating the subject and art object has been eliminated, and with that shrinkage, the association of the sublime (i.e., the experience of indeterminacy, a comprehension well beyond us) has been replaced with the trivial and displaced the aura that makes art, art (Adorno 1997, pp. 274–75, 310; Krakauer 1998, pp. 42–57).

8. How the aesthetic becomes socially integrated remains a vexed problem in Adorno's program: "Art can only retain its utopian promise in virtue of its autonomy, but it is just this autonomy that preserves art from any entanglement with the real business of existence" (Ryle and Soper 2002, p. 52). The issue has stimulated extensive commentary (e.g., Zuidervaart 1991; Huhn 1999; Ryle and Soper 2002; Kaufman 2004) and goes to the heart of the Benjamin-Adorno-Lukács debate about the place of art in bourgeois society and the capitalism that supports it (Adorno et al. 1977; Eagleton 1990).

9. "The self no longer tries to be *better*, but to be *otherwise*. To reach this level human beings must be able to transcend and relinquish two great stages, that of the ought and that of the will, if they are to arrive at the stage of the (affirmation of) being [Nietzsche]: 'Higher than 'Thou shouldst' stands: 'I wish' (the heroes); higher than 'I wish' stands: 'I am' (the Gods of the Greeks)" (Früchtl 2008, p. 152).

10. Adorno goes on to explain the basis of his rejection of sublimation: "[E]ach successful expression of the subject, one might say, is a small

victory over the play of forces of its own psychology. The pathos of art is bound up with the fact that precisely by withdrawing into imagination, it renders the superior power of reality its due, and yet does not resign itself to adaptation, does not prolong external violence in internal deformation. Those who accomplish this, have without exception to pay dearly for it as individuals, left helplessly behind by their expression, which has outstripped their psychology. . . . No work of art, within the organization of society, can escape its involvement in culture, but there is none, if it is more than mere handicraft, which does not make culture a dismissive gesture: that of having become a work of art. Art is inimical to 'art' as are artists. In renouncing the goal of instinct they remain faithful to it, and unmask the socially desirable activity naively glorified by Freud as sublimation—which probably does not exist" (2005, #136, p. 214).

For a sustained critique of Adorno's position and a defense of sublimation as a specific rejoinder to Adorno's criticism, see Whitebook (1988, 1995, 2004), whose argument is reviewed elsewhere (Tauber 2012a).

11. "Moreover, psycho-analysis itself is castrated by its conventionalization: sexual motives, partly disavowed and partly approved, are made totally harmless, but also totally insignificant. With the fear they instill vanishes the joy they might procure. Thus psycho-analysis falls victim to the very replacement of the appropriate super-ego by a stubbornly adopted, unrelated, external one, that it taught itself to understand. The last grandly-conceived theorem of bourgeois self-criticism has become a means of making bourgeois self-alienation, in its final phase, absolute, and rendering ineffectual the lingering awareness of the ancient wound, in which lies hope of a better future" (Adorno 2005, #40, p. 66).

12. In a preamble to Foucault's conception of power and control of individuals, Freud observes, "This replacement of the power of the individual by the power of the community constitutes the decisive step of civilization" (1930, p. 95). Then two power vectors must be computed: (1) the restrictions on individual freedom imposed by the strictures of society, and (2) the successful deployment of sublimation, which not only redirects libidinal energies for individual satisfaction but becomes the crucial element in forging the collective into a cohesive social whole. Simply, sublimation and its accompanying work ethic push individual interests

into synchrony with the group's own interests (Gay 1992). However, Freud did not develop a theory of sublimation, and consequently this aspect of his social criticism remains nebulous.

13. "Terror before the abyss of the self [*Ich*: I, ego, self] is removed by the consciousness of being concerned with nothing so very different from arthritis or 'sinus troubles' [in English in original]. Thus conflicts lose their menace. They are accepted, but by no means cured, but merely fitted as an unavoidable component into the surface of standardized life. At the same time they are absorbed, as a general evil, by the mechanism directly identifying the individual with social authority, which has long since encompassed all supposedly normal modes of behaviour. Catharsis, unsure of success in any case, is supplanted by pleasure [*Lustgewinn*] at being, in one's own weakness, a specimen of the majority; and rather than gaining, like inmates of a sanatorium in former days, the prestige of an interesting pathological case, one proves on the strength of one's very defects that one belongs, thereby transferring to oneself the power and vastness of the collective" (Adorno 2005, #40, p. 65). The indictment offers no respite.

14. The freed ego rests upon a humanistic conception of the individual, where personal autonomy and freedom of thought are assumed and only because of repressive forces remain subordinated to social authority. Perhaps the exemplar of this position is Erich Fromm (1955, 1969, 1973), who, like Freud, tacitly accepted a self-knowing, independent rational agent. With proper guidance, such an autonomous agent might achieve freedom from a repressive and domineering society. Arguing from a humanist perspective, Fromm believed that such an ego, strengthened by psychoanalytic insight, was capable of asserting her own liberation and thus counter the alienation characteristic of those living in modern mass society. Espousing a human-centered social philosophy, Fromm's views radically differ from conceptions offered by other members of the Frankfurt School of the same period. Adorno attacked the very foundations of agency bestowed by the Enlightenment, namely, the belief that our knowledge can fully capture reality and that rational understanding can be determinant. Accordingly, reason must be strengthened; otherwise, impoverished rationality ends in both its collapse and dismantlement of the notion of the ego's autonomy upon which the entire edifice rests. In

this sense, Fromm and Adorno were cut from the same cloth, or at least aspired to like-minded goals, but radically differed in their understanding of the ego and the character of Enlightenment reason.

15. The relationship between Heidegger and Adorno, while subject to scholarly comment (e.g., Dallmayr 1989; Macdonald and Ziarek 2008a), has been limited by Heidegger's refusal to respond to Adorno's criticism (Adorno 1973a), which stretches from what constitutes authenticity to the very character of philosophizing: "Thinking that renounces argument— Heidegger—switches into pure irrationalism" (Adorno and Horkheimer 2011, p. 72). Nevertheless, they shared essentially the same attitude about positivism, technology, mass contemporary culture, and the problem of establishing an ethics responsive to these challenges. These common concerns were then framed by a deep commitment to a conception of philosophy that should serve history and experience (Macdonald and Ziarek 2008b, p. 2). In this regard they shared the view that with modernity, humans submitted to "the calculating and rationalizing process of objectification, and thus the on-going process of manipulation and control" (Früchtl, 2008, p. 151). And most important, they inherited the same romantic tradition of practicing a "life philosophy" that made "appeal to the aesthetic dimension as the appropriate *model* for thinking . . . to rethink metaphysics under specifically modern conditions, or to put it differently . . . to reconcile modernity once again with metaphysics" (ibid., p. 154). Despite their obvious differences, one might say that Adorno and Heidegger swam in the same waters, albeit taking very different directions.

Chapter 4

1. Heidegger's (1997) argument was published shortly thereafter as *Kant and the Problem of Metaphysics*; see Friedman (2000) and Gordon (2010) for philosophical comment and a full description of the historical context of the Heidegger-Cassirer debate.

2. "The Cartesian *cogito ergo sum* is a piece of anthropomorphic and rationalistic hyperbole. The reverse is the case: 'I am, therefore I think.' Existence is the necessary precedent and enabling condition of thought. There is, certainly in the very sense in which Descartes sought to establish the two terms, existence before thought. Thought is only one of the

articulations of *Dasein*. Platonic-Cartesian cogitation and the Cartesian foundation of the world's reality in human reflection are attempts to 'leap through or across the world' in order to arrive at the noncontingent purity of eternal Ideas . . . and certitudes. But this attempted leap from and to abstraction is radically false to the facticity of the world as we encounter it, as we live it" (Steiner 1978, p. 88).

3. Freud makes no mention of Heidegger in any of his writings, and Heidegger engaged Freud only late in his career at the urging of the psychoanalyst Medard Boss (Boss 1979). The far-ranging comments Heidegger made to Boss in correspondence and in a group of seminars has been collected and serves as the primary source for exploring Heidegger's understanding and interpretation of psychoanalysis (Heidegger 2001; discussed by Dallmayr 1993; Askay and Farquhar 2006). In Boss's (1963) adaptation of a *Daseinsanalyse*, he attempted to translate Heidegger's philosophy to psychiatry by building upon "Heidegger's description of human existence as a clearing or illumination of being. Following Heidegger, Boss acknowledged that humans exist only insofar as they relate to (i.e., disclose and perceive) others, self, and the world. People are world-disclosing in their very being. . . . Hence, each individual's 'world-relations' are one's own ways of being human, of openness to the world as such which includes an immediate and direct understanding of others" (Askay and Farquhar 2006, pp. 308–9). And correspondingly, those who were neurotic and psychotic suffered from a constriction, or blockage, of their world-openness. "Symptoms are not reduced to elements as in the manner of Freud. Rather the quest is after those traits characterizing the being of Da-sein regarding its relation to being in general" (Heidegger 2001, pp. 119–20). Thus, Heidegger dismissed Freud's "ontic" project, where man is objectified and reduced to mechanics, and of course the particulars of Freudian psychoanalysis, e.g., the unconscious, libido theory, repression, transference, etc. (Dallmayr 1993, pp. 238–41; for an extended discussion of key theoretical differences between Freudianism and Daseinsanalysis, see Kockelmans 1979.).

4. Two prominent psychoanalytic appropriations of Heidegger's philosophy, i.e., Boss (1963) and Binswanger (1967), highlight what Needleman refers to as the phenomenological versus existential approaches, respectively. Heidegger clearly endorsed Boss's

phenomenological extrapolations, which criticized Binswanger's existential view that neurosis can be treated as modifications of the essential structure of Dasein. According to the orthodoxy espoused by Boss, as the receiver of objects, Dasein does not reflect; it serves only as a receptacle, and thus no variation of the a priori structure of Dasein is permitted, i.e., the formal structure of Dasein is "invariable" (Needleman 1967, pp. 125–26). Binswanger, in following Sartre (1956), regards the ego, in its exercise of freedom, as having the full capacity to constitute Being and, instead of looking for causes or basic drives as Freudian psychoanalysis does, seeks to uncover why such causes and drives have their effects: "Binswanger's Daseinsanalyse is the effort to ascertain in each individual that which makes his experience and the phenomena of the world possible" (Needleman 1967, p. 139).

5. Jacob Rogozinski argues that Heidegger's attempt to displace the ego as an agent that must, by its very character, drive toward a self-destructive nihilism (1) mistakes Descartes's own understanding of the ego and (2) conflates later nihilistic developments in European thought with the formulation of the Cartesian ego as such. If the self is no longer mine, the resulting erasure of singularity and "egological difference" homogenizes the I with the They, and authenticity thereby is radically compromised, for "only what most strongly resists the influence of the They can free me from my alienation, and this could not be enacted by a [Heideggerian] Self, but only by an ego, the me that I myself am, the ego that is always mine" (Rogozinski 2010, p. 20). Furthermore, Rogozinski maintains that humans do not first experience oneself as a self but rather as an ego, as a me, and from this sense of identity, the me and the demarcation of the other are constituted through the relation to others, and a self-consciousness of both those relationships and the irreducible presence of oneself. In other words, authenticity begins with a sense of oneself as an ego, as an identity distinct and thereby defined in contrast to the other. Heidegger, by asserting Being as the presence of my-ness, robs the subject of all concrete meaning and experience. And in regard to Heidegger's notion of how death authenticates, i.e., that which permits one to face death, carries not only deadly political baggage (Rogozinski 2010, pp. 31ff.; Faye 2012) but a transcendence that obviates the primary experience that constitutes the being of the ego: "Because the 'there' means 'over

there,' or 'on-the-outside-of,' Da-sein must be understood as a *present-being*. The term 'transcendent' does not designate some distant afterworld or objects situated beyond my consciousness but rather the ability to transcend *oneself*, which belongs to a finite existing being" (ibid., p. 39; emphasis in original).

6. The "Letter on Humanism" (Heidegger 1993a), published in 1947, quickly propelled Heidegger to the status of France's "master philosopher" (Rockmore 1995, pp. 81ff.). It was conceived as a rebuttal to Sartre's humanist existentialism: Heideggerian "authenticity does not refer to action as opposed to thought but rather to thought in the light of being that is already action. Human being cannot be understood in itself but only comprehended through being, in a word as existence" (ibid., p. 97).

7. Existential psychologies, derived from Heidegger's conception of Dasein (most prominently, Binswanger 1967), have been omitted from this discussion because they did not contribute a novel critique of representationalism beyond embracing a general antiscientism. A cardinal feature of such an orientation was a rejection of Freud's scientific orientation *en court*: "Heidegger's phenomenological-philosophical analytic of existence is important for psychiatry . . . [for] it does not inquire merely into particular regions of phenomena and facts to be found 'in human beings,' but, rather inquires into the *being of man as a whole*. Such a question is not answerable by scientific methods alone. . . . What is needed is the return to (subjective) transcendence, to the Dasein as being-in-the-world, even while constant attention is being accorded its objective transcendence" (ibid., p. 211). Simply, the holism marking such a psychology maintained that "no 'whole man' can be 'grasped' with the methods of science" (ibid., p. 220), and it was those inaccessible regions of human experience that became prominent in what Binswanger called *Daseinsanalyse*.

8. Although Heidegger steadfastly denied divine connotations to his presentations of Being (e.g., 1993a), his early training and continued interest in theology (Steiner 1978, pp. 73–75) undergird the religious elements of his philosophy (Gordon 2010, p. 165).

9. "Freud's metapsychology is the application of Neo-Kantian philosophy to the human being. On the one hand, he has the natural sciences, and on the other hand, the Kantian theory of objectivity"

(Heidegger 2001, p. 207). Beyond my discussion in Chapter 1, this comment may be followed in several other directions (e.g., Dalton 1999; Brook 2003; Bergo 2004) but most fundamentally concerns the basic Kantian structure of Freud's thought: "Freud's metapsychological theory is to be taken, essentially, as a set of transcendental arguments whose concepts should be taken as formal predicates. . . . The most important difference from Kant is of course that Kant's formal categories pertain to experiences of a theoretical kind, and most notably of a natural scientific kind, while Freud's metapsychological concepts pertain to the specific experiences made in the clinical praxis of psychoanalysis" (Eriksson 2012, p. 25).

10. Frege's understanding of logic as factual has not fared well, but his notion that logic is normative has continued to organize much debate beyond the particular issue he addressed. Some, like Alan Musgrave, thought that "only a few cranks officially subscribe to [psychologism] about the nature of logic. There is progress in philosophy after all!" (1972, p. 606), while others remain far more circumspect about Frege's triumph (Hanna 2006).

11. Later, with the rise of the fascist political disaster, Husserl saw the "problem of reason" moving from the logical domain to reach into the very soul of European culture. Although assuming very different contours taken by his student, Heidegger, Husserl (1970) also lamented the rise of scientism and the objectification of reality as inimical to the path a nonnaturalistic philosophy had historically pursued.

12. Heidegger's doctoral dissertation, *The Doctrine of Judgment in Psychologism* (1914), joined Husserl's attack on psychologism and argued that the "proper logical object is neither the mental process of thinking, nor the reality (whether physical or metaphysical) about which one thinks, but the *Sinn*, understood both as the meaning of a sentence and as the identical content of judgment" (Mohanty 1999, p. 81). In his examination of four kinds of judgment, Heidegger argued that "while each is representative of a different sort of psychologism, all are inapplicable to logic" (Dahlstrom 2001, p. 4). Emphasizing the distinction between the psychic act and the logical content, Heidegger endeavored to find the philosophical grounding of *Sinn*, which had been used to define the domain of logic. (*Sinn* refers to a thought, as distinguished from *the*

act of thinking.) This became part of a program that would replace a naturalistic psychology with one based closer to Husserl's intentional, eidetic, descriptive psychology. From this platform, Heidegger pursued his own agenda of going beyond the provisional distinction of the real and the ideal to ask "how the logical contents or *Sinn* are related to the acts of thinking, and eventually to the thinking being that man is" (Mohanty 1999, p. 82). In what would eventually appear in a radical rereading of the history of philosophy, Heidegger posed a series of questions concerning the philosophy of logic that served as the framework of his mature work:

1. How can we understand the intentional structure of judgment?
2. What is the relation of the "being" of the copula and the "being" of ontology?
3. What is *meaning*, and what is its relevance for the possibility of judgment?
4. What is *truth* related to *judgment*? Is it a property of judgment?
5. Why has philosophy traditionally distinguished propositional and self-evident truth, and what is their relationship? Which truth is primary, theoretical, or practical?
6. How is human thinking related to human existence?
7. What is the metaphysical foundation of logic? (ibid., pp. 87–88)

Heidegger concluded in this early work that the essence of *Sinn* cannot be established by *Vorstellung* but rather in the fact that it *alone* can be either true or false (ibid., p. 90) and thus rejected psychologism for an ontological study of thinking.

13. This revisionist construction begins with Dasein possessing its freedom by facing finitude and thus asserting a "freedom-toward-death"; Lacan follows the death trope as well, by drawing the ego as submitting itself to die, i.e., its own illusory status is revealed in its recognition of its own death (Rogozinski 2010, p. 49), and in this sense, he closely follows Heidegger.

14. Whichever neo-Kantian track is followed (Tauber 2010, pp. 106–14), the adherence to a Kantian approach falls into disarray. Emil Lask clearly understood the consequences of discarding Kant's schematism of the understanding (the removal of space-time as the intermediary between pure intuition and sensation) (Friedman 2000). A gap separates formal

logic—what we might call "pure" logic of necessary truths, objective thoughts, or "propositions in themselves"—from transcendental, material, or epistemological logic. The latter concerns a theory of categories, how a concrete object of experience or knowledge is constituted by thought. What, indeed, is the relationship between them? When Kant's theory of space and time as pure forms of sensibility is discarded in the initial neo-Kantian move, the intermediary between pure forms of thought and unsynthesized sensation is lost. Lask asserted that without a glue to hold the two realms together, the concrete object, already categorized as a real object of experience, is primary. From there, formal logic is *derived* through a process of abstraction in which the unitary categorized object is broken down into form, matter, subject, and predicate, etc. On this view, pure logic becomes an artifact of subjectivity, because material or transcendental logic is not derived or based on formal logic, and Kant's metaphysical deduction of the categories, which is based on the logical forms of judgment, must be disallowed. So while psychologism might have been denied, where does this predicament leave logic?

15. Heidegger traces *analytic* to the ancient usage of *analysis* that meant "unraveling" (in the *Odyssey*, every night Penelope unraveled the woven cloth she wove during the day); it also means "to loosen," i.e., from chains to liberate from captivity (Heidegger 2001, p. 114). So Heidegger interprets the meaning of the analytic in the *Critique of Pure Reason* as a "dissection" of the faculty of understanding.

16. Turning toward this other, "the synthesis of the representations rest on the power of the imagination, but their unity (which is required for judgment) [rests] on the unity of apperception [transcendental apperception of the ego]" (Heidegger 1997, p. 82 [quoting Kant]). As we will discuss later, Lacan takes this basic construction and builds his theory upon it: "Psychoanalysis reveals that every relation of subject and object is triangulated by a third position, the locus of the Other" (Bootby 2001, p. 192), which of course signifies the unknowable unconscious.

17. The argument for reason's autonomy is provided in "[t]he antimony of pure reason" (Kant 1998 [B474–75], pp. 484–87). There Kant attempts to solve the contradiction of comprehending causal (natural) law of the world as something universal by positing that "causality through freedom" lies not in the empirical domain but in the "intelligible character"

of the agent, i.e., freedom is not an empirical concept. (The argument is schematized by Allison 2004, pp. 378, 382; and Watkins 2005, pp. 306, 308.) So the world of appearances and the intelligible world are governed by noncontradicting types of causality, an argument that rests on Kant's fundamental *noumenon*/phenomenon distinction (Kant 1998 [B566–67], pp. 535–36). For different interpretations of how Kant based his construction, see Guyer (1987, pp. 411–12); Allison (2004, pp. 376ff.); and Watkins (2005, pp. 304–16).

18. Heidegger attempted to rectify the impasse by showing the lexical relationship of "reason," "being," and "ground": *Grund* (ground, or in this context, the fundamental principle of reason) is the direct translation of *ratio*, and *Vernuft* (Reason) also serves as a translation of *ratio*. Heidegger comments, "Under hazard of appearing to exaggerate, we may even say that if *ratio* did not speak in modern thinking with the double sense of 'Reason' and 'grounds,' then there would not be Kant's critique of pure Reason as the circumspection of the conditions for the possibility of the object of experience" (1991, p. 98). He then unpacks the Latin *ratio* as functioning within the realm of "producing and coming about" or "cause" (ibid., p. 99), but its more direct meaning pertains to "reckoning," "deliberating," or "calculating" through representation. "In reckoning, something is imputed . . . [and] what is imputed, computed, is that upon which something rests, namely what lies before us, supportive, what is reckoned in a reckoning; *ratio* is therefore the basis, the footing, the ground" (ibid., p. 104). Thus, *reason* and *ground* find their common root. However, the key move is made when Heidegger argues that *ratio*, the root holding reason and being together, is traced to the Greek Logos. At this level, being and reason merge in an undifferentiated unity (ibid., pp. 105–13).

Chapter 5

1. Lacan adopted a far more muted Heideggerian theoretical orientation than either Boss (1963) or Binswanger (1967).

2. Reeder (2012) cites Freud's *Project* (1895) as the cardinal source for understanding *das Ding*. In a progressive development, tension within the newborn child's neuronal apparatus presumably occurs when a current perceptual image does not immediately coincide with a wished-for

memory image. Such a state of lacking identity between two images generates a "wishful state," which causes "pressure" that is relieved by establishing a state of "identity" and thus "appeasement": (1) production of a hallucination that will reduplicate the wished-for image; (2) reliance upon specific acquired patterns of movement to see the object of desire; and (3) pursuit of identity by one or more circuitous paths of associations, i.e., when perception only partially coincides with the wished-for memory image or not at all. In this last case, the aim of achieving immediate identity has been abandoned, and *das Ding* comprises the object of desire as a complex constituted of an impression with constant structure as *a thing* [*Ding*] and a cognized element understood as the activity of memory that can be traced back to information from the subject's own body. In this hypothetical process, the child takes a decisive developmental step (as compared to the wishful state when she or he either hallucinated the desired object or made a movement to get it in view) for the wished-for image, which is now exchanged for a chain of memory images or impressions found within the child's own experience. This step signifies "a capacity for remembering, thinking, imagination and fantasying (besides that of judgment) . . . [and] it is the first time that Freud describes how the subjective world of the infant shifts from the biological to the mental. He not only captures the moment when the psychic universe that henceforth is the theoretical object of psychoanalytic inquiry comes into being, but in so doing also lays the metapsychological foundation for what at the time was the advent of the clinical practice of psychoanalysis" (Reeder 2012, pp. 37–38).

3. "At a time at which the first beginnings of sexual satisfaction are still linked with the taking of nourishment, the sexual [drive] has a sexual object outside the infant's own body in the shape of his mother's breast. It is only later that the [drive] loses that object, just at the time, perhaps, when the child is able to form a total idea of the person to whom the organ that is giving him satisfaction belongs. . . . The finding of an object is in fact a refinding of it" (Freud 1905, p. 222).

4. Freud offered a basic model of the cognitive process in the early *Project*: "Let us suppose that the object which furnishes the perception resembles the subject—a *fellow human-being*. If so, the theoretical interest [taken in it] is also explained by the fact that an object *like this*

was simultaneously the [subject's] first satisfying object and further his first hostile object, as well as his sole helping power. For this reason it is in relation to a fellow human-being that a human-being learns to cognize. Then the perceptual complexes proceeding from this fellow human-being will in part be new and non-comparable—his *features*, for instance, in the visual sphere; but other visual perceptions—e.g. those of the movements of his hands—will coincide in the subject with memories of quite similar visual impressions of his own, of his own body, [memories] which are associated with memories of movements experienced by himself. Other perceptions of the object too—if, for instance, he screams—will awaken the memory of his [the subject's] own screaming and at the same time of his own experiences of pain. Thus the complex of the fellow human-being falls apart into two components, of which one makes an impression by its constant structure and stays together as *a thing*, while the other can be *understood* by the activity of memory—that is, can be traced back to information from [the subject's] own body. This dissection of a perceptual complex is described as *cognizing* it; it involves a *judgement* and when this last aim has been attained it comes to an end" (Freud 1895, p. 331).

5. In Lacan's formulations of the 1930s, "the real" opposed the realm of the image (i.e., situated in the realm of being beyond appearances). In 1953 the real assumed one of three orders by which all psychic phenomena could be described, the other two being the symbolic and imaginary orders. Whereas the symbolic is a set of differentiated signifiers, the real is undifferentiated and outside language, so with the introduction of words (representations) "a cut in the real" occurs in the process of signification (Evans 1996, p. 159). And as this cut occurs, an "excess" remains uncaptured by the representation, which Lacan calls *objet petit a* or just *objet a*—a theoretical innovation that has been called (perhaps) Lacan's most original contribution to psychoanalysis (Boothby 2001, pp. 242ff.): *Objet a* is a spin-off of the representation process, residing as a kind of remainder, a sort of residue that is not assimilated by either the imaginary or symbolic orders. Functionally, *objet a* is "the absent locus around which the drives revolve" and serves as "the incitement of desire . . . a stimulus, an intensive vortex around which the drives rotate" (ibid., p. 244). (*Objet a* is neither subject nor object but suspended between each and carrying aspects of both and is not equivalent to *das Ding* as described earlier.) Lacan coined

the term "extimate" to indicate how the theory must capture "something of the subject's own . . . yet always appears elsewhere, outside the subject and eluding its grasp" (ibid., p. 243). (See above pp. 231–32)

6. Lacan adapted the mirror stage from the findings reported by Henri Wallon in 1932 that "unlike monkeys of the same age . . . the human child is able to recognize itself in the mirror beginning at about six months of age, which helps the child to construct the image of its body. Seizing upon this empirical observation, Lacan raises it to the rank of an 'ontological structure of the human world' and concludes that the child *identifies itself* with its specular image. Lacan sees in this identification the very origin of the ego, 'the symbolic matrix in which the I is precipitated in a primordial form' [Lacan 2006, p. 76]. It is a matter of an originary identification" (Rogozinski 2010, p. 50; emphasis in original). Further discussion of Lacan's appropriation of the mirror phenomenon follows.

7. This stage then is the introduction of the imaginary order, which in the later formulation negotiates the dynamics between the three orders. In fact, Lacan's theoretical construction is more complex, because the ego itself is divided by distinguishing two forms of the ego (which also appear, albeit not so developed, in Freud's writings). The "ideal ego" is a projection of the ego's ideal image upon the world, whereas the "ego-ideal" is the introjection of another external image that has a new (deformative) effect on the psyche. In effect, the ego-ideal provides the subject with a secondary identification, and according to this formulation, the ego is a *necessary* imaginary function of the subject (Lacan 1991).

8. Consider an analogy: A man living alone on an island marks the routes to various sites so that he will not forget important locales: "The man who 'sends' the message is not the same man who 'receives' the message. Were he, there would be no need to construct or sense in constructing the 'language' in the first place" (Neill 2011, p. 18).

9. As discussed previously, for Lacan, the ego's dismemberment results from the fault lines that formed with its very conception, i.e., the mirror metaphor portrays the original misconceived (or mistaken) step in the ego's creation as an enduring illusion. However, Rogozinski makes the cogent point that in the mirror's reflection "I see myself, I recognize *myself* . . . as if I had captured my gaze in it. So that I may identify myself with my reflection and transfer to it the character of being mine,

of being me or ego, I have to be *already* identified with myself. In order to recognize the image of my body in the reflection, I must *have a place of residence* in this body, live it already *as mine*" (2010, p. 56; emphasis in original). On the one hand, we perceive that the ego recognizes itself because it already *is* a self, a subject who possesses a sense of my-ness, and on the other hand, Lacan refuses to recognize the ego's standing, despite its obvious presence and instrumental roles in psychic economy and capacity to initiate imaginary or symbolic identifications.

10. Lacan can hardly claim to have freed psychoanalysis from representationalism, inasmuch as the emphasis he placed on the unconscious as a language (with signifiers adapted from Saussurean linguistics serving as a fulcrum of his theorizing), the articulated truth of one's desire in speech, and the role of language in the analytic exchange each require representation of one kind or another. The schemata he devised to capture the dynamics of psychic structure and function are highly abstracted representations, which became increasingly complex as his theory developed (summarized by Evans 1996, pp. 168–71). These were used, however, in an effort to deconstruct the representationalism of the conscious ego and present a formulation that better captured what representationalism is from the Lacanian perspective. Assuming a global view, Lacan might have constructed a ladder similar to Wittgenstein's, who threw it away after climbing to the platform where he viewed the "nonsense" that he had discarded (Wittgenstein 1981, p. 189). (The ladder metaphor is deeply set in the debate concerning nonsense, which is discussed in Chapter 7.)

11. "The unconscious is the sum of the effects . . . at the level at which the subject constitutes himself out of the effects of the signifier. This makes it clear that, in the term, *subject* . . . I am not designating the living substratum needed by this phenomenon of the subject, nor any sort of substance, nor any being possessing knowledge in his *pathos* . . . nor even some incarnated Logos, but the Cartesian subject, who appears at the moment when doubt is recognized as certainty. . . . This is what the unconscious is" (Lacan 1978, p. 126).

12. "This is why the subject is entirely submitted to this Other that is the cause of it: it exists only as 'subject' of the signifier (in the feudal sense of the term), subjected to it in an alienation without return. If the signifier

represents the subject, it is always for 'another signifier,' because there are signifiers only in a network or chain, taken up as in a structure that puts them in relation to others" (Rogozinski 2010, p. 65; emphasis in original).

13. Commentaries abound, e.g., Turkle 1978; Lee 1990; Borch-Jacobsen 1991; Fink 1995, 1997; Althusser 1996; Evans 1996; Boothby 2001; Rogozinski 2010.

14. The counterargument to Lacan's interpretation builds upon the developmental psychology of the same period in which he first presented the mirror mechanism of ego formation (Piaget 1929; Wallon 1983). The observations of those studies were interpreted as showing that the infant ego builds a body image through movement, exploration, and physical experimentation to identify itself in the world and thereby establish an identity, a subject in active dialogue with its world. Accordingly, the ego is not an imaginary locus or necessary construct for the unconscious but rather is to be regarded as an agent with its own agenda that has emerged from a more primeval mental province to exercise its specialized functions. The immediacy of ego self-awareness, one of its functions in the plethora of its diverse roles and activities, cannot be delegated to some illusory construction of another disguised locus of psychic activity.

15. This translation (offered by Reeder 2012) is superior to that given in the standard work (Lacan 1992, p. 319): "[T]he only thing of which one can be guilty is of having given ground relative to one's desire."

16. Having dethroned the self-determined ego, Lacan complemented Foucault's conception of the ego as a receptacle of diffuse social forces, and thus it lacked autonomy. Indeed, given the various political, historical, and cultural forces that configure enlightened Reason and employ it for larger social requirements, Kant's formulation appeared as a vulnerable site for manipulation by mass forces, which conspired against individual choice and freedom. Foucault (1970) followed this line of criticism by depicting the self as an invention of nineteenth-century human sciences. Since individuals have no essential features, he presented them as mere creations of imminent (internal) social forces (power) to which they were subject (Foucault 2001). Accordingly, individuals can never stand in a position counter to a system inasmuch as they are determined *by* it. Foucault observed about his own project and the potential of psychoanalysis to raise political consciousness, "What I am trying to do

is grasp the implicit systems which determine our most familiar behavior without our knowing it. I am trying to find their origin, to show their formation, the constraint they impose upon us; I am therefore trying to place myself at a distance from them and *to show how one could escape*" (Foucault, quoted by Turkle 1978, p. 78; emphasis in original).

17. Lacan and Althusser (1996) begin with Freud's early works, where they discern a more critical view of self-knowledge and the search for meaning, and they thus dispense with the later metapsychology works, which they see as having different concerns, i.e., the mechanisms of negotiation between ego and social reality at the expense of the earlier commitments. They also dismiss the alliance of psychoanalysis with sociology and anthropology, which in this context became assimilatory vehicles for social power and manipulation.

18. The implications for ethics building from a Lacanian base explicitly contrast with the ethics of responsibility to the other extolled by Levinas and Derrida, as well as utilitarian ethics (see Rothenberg 2010, pp. 194, 205ff.).

19. Rogozinski (2010) argues that Lacan's strategy, directed at freeing the subject-I from alienating identifications with an Other, radically reinterprets the recurrent Freudian theme "Wo Es war, soll Ich werden" (Where id was, there ego shall be; 1933, p. 80) by reversing Freud's original meaning: Freudian psychoanalysis remained committed to strengthening the ego "to make it more independent of the super-ego, to widen its field of perception and enlarge its organization, so that it can appropriate fresh portions of the id" (Freud 1933, p. 80). However, Lacan, in dethroning the ego, requires instead the submission *to* the Other: "[W]here I, me, the ego, was, the Other now comes forth to subject me" (Rogozinski 2010, pp. 78–79). Having first defined the ego as an imaginary illusion and placing the unconscious subject as the signifying language of the psyche, Lacan left the ego in its primordial emergence, forever demoted to being subject to the Other of a deeper subjectivity. Lacan's theory thus vacillates between assigning the subject a universal and neutral function and a singular subjectivity, and in either case, one alienation is continuously exchanged for another in the signifying chain of psychic discourse (ibid.). Rogozinski insists on terminating the sequence of identifications with the Other (in any of its presentations) and then recognizing the basic

epistemological structure that must confer logic to Lacan's schema: "Does not all identification necessarily consist in being identified *with itself* in order then to be able to identify with this other? How can I identify myself with an other if it is not me who recognizes myself in the other, or if I did not already exist prior to any identification?" (ibid., p. 70; emphasis in original).

Lacan fails to address these questions, because the ambiguities and the vortex of schemata he draws of the psyche basically reflect an aporia. Identifications require a something that must identify, and that something is an ego, a faculty that can represent the other, and itself, for that matter. While Lacan's commitment to reconfigure the unconscious in psychoanalytic theory must displace the ego altogether, the *logic* of that move cannot be sustained on Rogozinski's account.

Sartre, who insisted that "human reality must begin with the *cogito*" (1956, p. 84), presented a parallel to this basic argument against Heidegger. If we hold that Heidegger "completely avoided any appeal to consciousness in his description of Dasein" (ibid., p. 85), an insurmountable philosophical impasse arises, for "understanding has meaning only if it is consciousness of understanding. . . . Otherwise the whole system of being and its possibilities will fall back into unconsciousness. . . . Behold, we are thrown back again towards *cogito*. We must make this our point of departure" (ibid.). And regarding consciousness, to avoid a regressive spiral, self-reflection must be preceded by some prereflexive consciousness of self so consciousness does not become its own object, i.e., structured by a subject-object relationship. Simply, for Sartre self-consciousness is not a case of propositional knowledge (Frank 1997, p. 7).

Chapter 6

1. As an American classicist, Norman O. Brown might appear out of place among the French philosophers discussed here, but he joins their intellectual heritage in the shared admiration of Nietzsche, and, as a Marxist, Brown, much akin to these Frenchmen, situated his study of psychoanalysis within a critique of the capitalist setting in which it functions. And like those considered here, he would emancipate desire. Indeed, *Life against Death* (1959) snugly fits into the French psychoanalytic criticism in its central theme: Brown argued that despite

Western civilization's attempts—through "parental discipline, religious denunciation of bodily pleasure, and philosophical exaltation of the life of reason"—to renounce (or at least to effectively repress) the pleasure principle, the unconscious held fast to its own nature and thus, from the inevitable conflict, neurosis results. "Man remains unconvinced because in infancy he tasted the fruit of the tree of life, and knows that it is good, and never forgets" (p. 31). He then embarks on his major thesis that "childhood remains man's indestructible goal" (ibid., p. 32), because we remain pleasure-seeking animals. His analysis and utopian program to free humans from asceticism, like Marcuse's (1955), focuses upon social reform organized to release Westerners from their chains of repression by recapturing the potential first tasted in childhood and then lost. Brown does not fall into the philosophical trajectory organizing our study inasmuch as his analysis builds on what he thought constitutes Freud's basic error—structuring psychoanalytic theory on conflict-ridden dualisms, e.g., hunger-love, love-hate, love-aggression, and Eros–death instincts—and sought a new synthetic dialectic where classic psychoanalytic theory posited drives in opposition (Brown 1959, pp. 79–80; Tauber 2010, pp. 237–38). Among the French postmodernists who soon followed, Brown's treatise had little if any impact. Nevertheless, Brown set an agenda that continues to linger and has been reconsidered in less radical terms (Tauber 2012a).

2. Just as Nietzsche served as a philosophical lodestone for much of postmodernity's orientation, so do those opposing that agenda focus on Nietzsche's antihumanism in their critique of Deleuze and Foucault (e.g., Ferry and Renaut 1990, 1997; Renaut 1997) or Heidegger (e.g., Rockmore 1995; G. Smith 1996).

3. *Libidinal Economy* (1993) has been described as "almost embarrassing. [The writings] read as a naïve, enchanted ode to the body" (Steuerman 2000, p. 13). A general assessment, endorsed by Lyotard himself, concludes that the book came "to a theoretical dead-end, trapping its author in a series of untenable positions" (Best and Kellner 1991, p. 157). Notwithstanding its naïve naturalism, its aporetic style (which Lyotard referred to as a *façon de parler*—a way of speaking [ibid., p. 158]), and the unintelligibility of its philosophical structure, the ideas form a kind of prose poem of how inarticulately desire might be

represented within the strictures of representational knowledge. The value of this work, therefore, is not in what Lyotard advocates but rather in how his intuitions about desire could not be adequately expressed. Precisely in his failure, he conveys his message.

4. In a historical review, Deleuze argued that difference mistakenly had been subordinated in the workings of reason, inasmuch as modern philosophy traditionally employs identity, opposition, and analogy to define its objects of interest. While these serve as powerful tools for scientific study, for Deleuze difference better preserves the character of experience, and in terms of deciphering the psyche, a far superior interpretive method of analysis, inasmuch as it approaches the unconscious on its own terms (1994 p. 96). Through repetition of desire's fulfillment, pleasure is obtained, and then, through successful habit, such repetition also orients the id toward future satisfaction: "[T]he *idea* of pleasure obtained and the *idea* of pleasure to be obtained act . . . to form the two applications, past and future" (ibid., p. 105). The pleasure principle thus evolves as a principle once satisfaction "exceeds its own instantaneity" (ibid.).

Deleuze argues that repetition contrasts with the generalizations sought by science, for in the creation of a repetitive sequence, the unique character of the repetition becomes evident in the particular setting and expression of the process. In obvious correspondence with Freud's own interpretation of the death drive in the repetitions of an obsessive act (Deleuze 1994, p. 104), Deleuze draws the more general inference about the character of identity as forming from an analogous resistance to generality, or stated in the affirmative voice, recognizing the unique character of individual repetitions. In other words, difference is the epistemologically relevant characteristic of experience or identification by valorizing how each repetition is unique in its genesis and fate. In short, Deleuze explained his project as an effort to focus upon difference and repetition as philosophical categories in themselves (ibid., p. xv). And repetition was understood in like terms, i.e., corresponding to the identical, the similar, the equal, or the opposed, so "we treat it as a difference without concept" (ibid.). Deleuze, in raising difference to an independent conceptual status, would then use that concept to challenge the logic of representationalism and the means of identification.

5. "Identity must itself be represented every time in a certain number of determinable concepts. These originary concepts . . . are called categories or genera of being. On the basis of such categories, specific derived concepts can in turn be determined by a method of division—in other words, by the play of contrary predicates within each genus. In this manner, difference is assigned two limits, in the form of two irreducible but complementary figures which indicate precisely its belonging to representation (the Large and the Small): the categories are *a priori* concepts and the empirical concepts; the originary determinable concepts and the derived determined concepts; the analogous and the opposed; *the large genera and the species*. This distribution of difference in a manner entirely dependent upon the requirements of representation essentially belongs within the analogical vision of the world. However, this form of distribution commanded by the categories seemed to us to betray the nature of Being (as a cardinal and collective concept) and the nature of the distributions themselves (as nomadic rather than sedentary and fixed distributions), as well as the nature of difference (as individuating experience)" (Deleuze 1994, p. 269; emphasis in original).

6. Deleuze and Guattari clearly distinguish their political schizoid identity from the clinical schizophrenic: "[W]e do not at all think that the revolutionary is schizophrenic or vice versa. On the contrary, we have consistently distinguished the schizophrenic as an entity from schizophrenia as a process. . . . [W]e have only spoken of a schizoid pole in the libidinal investment of the social field, so as to avoid as much as possible the confusion of the schizophrenic process with the production of the schizophrenic. The schizophrenic process (the schizoid pole) is revolutionary, in the very sense that the paranoiac method is reactionary and fascist" (1977, pp. 379–80). Note that they frame political identities on the social orientations of paranoid or schizophrenic and espouse the united assault of analytical and political forces by the latter against the former, who are painted with a Freudian brush.

7. "There is a hypothesis dear to Freud: the libido does not invest in the social field as such except on condition that it be desexualized and sublimated. If he holds so closely to this hypothesis, it is because he wants above all to keep sexuality in the limited framework of Narcissus and Oedipus, the ego and the family. Consequently, every sexual libidinal

investment having a social dimension seems to him to testify to a pathogenic state, a 'fixation,' in narcissism, or a 'regression' to Oedipus and to the pre-oedipal stages. . . . We have seen on the contrary that what the libido invested through its loves and sexuality, was the social field itself in its economic, political, historical, racial, and cultural determinations: in delirium the libido is continually re-creating History, continents, kingdoms, races, and cultures. . . . [O]ur choices in matters of love are at the crossroads of 'vibrations,' which is to say that they express connections, disjunctions, and conjunctions of flows that cross through a society. . . . [I]t is certainly not, as Freud believed, the libido that must be desexualized and sublimated in order to invest society and its flows; on the contrary, it is love, desire, and their flows that manifest the directly social character of the nonsublimated libido and its sexual investments" (Deleuze and Guattari 1977, pp. 352–53).

8. In *Anti-Oedipus*, death is conceived as part of the desiring-machine, a component of desire much as Brown (1959) conceived, and not a principle as construed by Freud (Deleuze and Guattari 1977, p. 332).

9. Deleuze and Guattari forthrightly admit that "schizoanalysis as such has strictly no political program to propose. It does not take itself for a party or even a group, and does not claim to be speaking for the masses. . . . [It] does not claim to be speaking for anything or anyone, not even—in fact especially not—for psychoanalysis: nothing more than impressions, the impression that things aren't going well in psychoanalysis, and that they haven't since the start" (1977, p. 380). And then they acknowledge their own compromised intellectual (rational) standing: "We are still too competent; we would like to speak in the name of an absolute incompetence" (ibid.). So *what* are they trying to do? Their incompetence is a ruse, a disingenuous plea bargain for not being held too closely to critical review of their own interpretation. Of many diatribes, nothing more than a fanciful soliloquy under a spotlight, consider: "Shit on your whole mortifying, imaginary, and symbolic theater. What does schizoanalysis ask? Nothing more than a bit of a *relation to the outside*, a little real reality. And we claim the right to radical laxity, a radical incompetence—the right to enter the analyst's office and say it smells bad there. It reeks of the great death and the little ego" (ibid., p. 334; emphasis in original).

10. The implications of this general concern about reason's scope and truth claims (Hanly 1992) for psychoanalytic interpretation are self-evident. If we put aside the theoretical orientation adopted (no small matter!), how does the intention of the analysand (and analyst) drive to the derived results? What contextual factors are at play? The emotional valence of each member of the analytic dyad similarly plays a critical role, not to mention his or her respective values, intelligence, cultural backgrounds, etc. To expect some kind of uniformity of interpretation that might fill a scientific standard of objectivity and offer any semblance to predictable outcomes seems far-fetched, something Freud himself acknowledged (1926a, p. 266).

11. Accordingly, Habermas portrayed reason as an operative tool, which developed over history to serve social communicative functions, and it fulfills that role through certain transcendental characteristics. He argues that the three types of knowledge—characterized by distinctive objects of inquiry and unique logics governing their methods—oriented by deeper, nonsubjective values, or "transcendental interests," address different basic human actions (Ingram 2010, pp. 46ff.). Each of these actions is, in turn, oriented by a human interest required for survival. So a naturalistic argument (concerning the evolution of the means to address natural scarcity and social control) is coupled to a transcendental argument about the necessary and universal conditions for knowledge of different kinds. The naturalistic context accounts for the interests of mastering nature and uniting with others to attain common goals. The revised schema follows the three-part mechanism that Habermas originally introduced, where the rationality by which societies have evolved requires (1) instrumental or experimental reason (natural science), (2) communicative action based on mutual interest and understanding (social science), and (3) critical reflection (Critical Theory). Each of these efforts requires common values and norms, all of which are directed to achieving various kinds of freedom. And the corresponding transcendental argument, which shows the necessary and universal characteristics of reason, follows the same tripartite formulation: (1) Instrumental action enables experience of the sensory world of material objects with measurable qualities and causal relations; (2) communicative action permits understanding of a social world composed of others structured by various relationships with

norms, values, meanings, and identities; and (3) reflection, while not constituting a domain of reality as such, mediates some final adjudication of knowledge through various degrees of insight. So Habermas would describe rationality to capture the collective reason of social action within an evolutionary context.

12. "Democracy is not just the collection of self-seeking interests and expressed desires of competing individuals. In representative democracy the will expressed is that of an individual adopting the 'universal standpoint'; this is not what the individual in particular wants, but what the very structure of the individual demands: freedom, self-determination and autonomy. The political ideal of Athenian democracy—a social whole that is representative of its members—can only be fulfilled through an enlightenment conception of the subject, a subject who is nothing other than a capacity for (self) representation" (Colebrook 2005, p. 16).

Chapter 7

1. That story is typically placed historically in dialogue with Frege and Russell (e.g., Coffa 1991; Reck 1997; Cerbone 2000; Conant 2000; Diamond 2000; Hanna 2001), but an older tradition also commands attention, namely, the romantic recognition of the limits of language and the corresponding boundaries of knowledge (discussed later).

2. The public aspect of meaning that Frege proposed has followed a fecund course, but the epistemological quandary of some third realm could not be sustained, for how would any correspondence be achieved (Dummett 1981)? The literature assessing this issue is immense; for a comprehensive anthology of the most influential positions, see Ludlow (1997), and for an overview, see Soames (2003).

3. "Understanding a form of representation, in the terms of the *Tractatus*, is understanding an activity in which human beings represent and measure the world; this will be a logical matter, and so cannot encompass what stands outside of the realm of logic—that is, nonsense" (Reid 1998, p. 131).

4. There can be no description of language in its application; "there can only be translation from one application of language to another logically equivalent one. That is, one demonstrates mastery of a method of representation in applying it, which is a matter of making and evaluating

assertions about the world; the attempt to say anything about the method of representation itself results at best in translations of assertions about the world made using that method of representation into assertions about the world using another, logically equivalent method of representation. Making sense of an assertion is making sense of the demands it makes on the world in terms of its truth or falsity: that is fundamental to language. . . . [U]nderstanding a human being comes to no more than making sense of her assertions" (Reid 1998, pp. 141–42).

5. A revisionist account, offered by so-called New Wittgensteinians, maintains that the *Tractatus* is continuous with the later *Philosophical Investigations*. According to Crary (2000), the genesis of this alternative vision begins with imaginative readings by Stanley Cavell (1962, 1979), John McDowell (1981), and Hilary Putnam (1994), whose general orientation was more fully developed by Cora Diamond (1991) and James Conant (1991). "[E]nthusiastically urging them on, stands the puckish figure of Burton Dreben, a benevolent and humorous *Geist der stets verneint* ["I am the spirit of perpetual negation;" from Goethe's *Faust*, line 1338]" (Hacker 2000, pp. 356–57). The influence of Dreben has yet to be documented. As Quine's editor and philosophical confidante, Dreben mentored generations of Harvard-trained analytic philosophers. Although he published little, he still exerted a pervasive "nihilistic" reading of Wittgenstein and, by extension, of modern philosophy. At least for some, Dreben was the godfather of the New Wittgensteinians.

6. The key text presenting the debate, *The New Wittgenstein* (Crary and Read 2000), has been followed with an update of the various positions (Read and Lavery 2011), which has further focused the issues and discerned different so-called resolute readings. For a stalwart attempt at finding value in the opposing positions, see Oskari Kuusela's contribution (2011), where he writes about how one might accept the new reading about the method employed in the *Tractatus* while still arguing the standard view that Wittgenstein imparted some general views about the logic of language.

7. This discussion is adopted from Tauber (2010, pp. 69–73). Two sources provide the most developed recounts of Wittgenstein's views: (1) summaries of lectures (offered in the early 1930s) reported by his colleague G. E. Moore (1993) concerning Freud's purported conflation of

cause and reason, and (2) informal conversations with Rush Rhees about psychoanalysis (1966). More generally, Wittgenstein regarded philosophy as a therapy, where explicit parallels with psychoanalysis were developed by his confidant, Friedrich Waismann (Baker 2004, pp. 144–222). In addition, we have materials from Wittgenstein's lectures (Wittgenstein 1958); occasional notes written between 1931 and 1948 (1980a); reports on lectures concerning the philosophy of psychology, specifically (1980b, 1980c, 1992); and further casual comments in conversation (e.g., Bouwsma 1986). Despite the apparent cursory character of these observations, much has been written on Wittgenstein's philosophical comments about Freud and psychoanalysis (e.g., MacIntyre 1958; Peterman 1992; Johnston 1993, pp. 225–33; Bouveresse 1995; Cioffi 1998; Baker 2004).

8. Wittgenstein's criticisms of psychoanalysis were made in the context of a deep ambivalence about Freud's achievements (Rhees 1966, pp. 41–52; McGuiness 1982), which ranged from measured admiration (e.g., Rhees 1981, p. 151) to disparagement (e.g., Wittgenstein 1980a, pp. 19, 36, 56, 87). That he took Freud worthy of comment attests to his intrigue with psychoanalysis, which belied his dismissals. Rhees reported that Wittgenstein would speak of himself at times as "a disciple of Freud" and "a follower of Freud" (1966, p. 41). In 1936 Wittgenstein even considered practicing lay analysis but quickly disabused himself of the idea, both because of inhibitions to reveal his own secret life and the danger of analysis producing "infinite harm" (Rhees 1981, p. 151).

9. Later commentators, Donald Davidson most notably, challenged Wittgenstein's categorical separation of cause and reason to argue that reasons could, in many instances, be fairly construed as causes. In a famous paper published in 1963, "Actions, Reasons, and Causes," Davidson argued that an action might be rationalized by a reason and in this sense cause established: "A reason rationalizes an action only if it leads us to see something the agent saw, or thought he saw, in his action—some feature, consequence, or aspect of the action the agent wanted, desired, prized, thought dutiful" (1980a, p. 3). The explanatory role of what Davidson calls a "primary reason" is a rational construct that allows for teleological behaviors. In this sense, primary reasons order both simple and complex actions, and Davidson thus attempted to recapture the commonsense attitude that "the agent performed the action *because* he

had the reason" to do so (ibid., p. 9), or as he wrote elsewhere, "a reason is a rational cause" (1980b, p. 233). Davidson's argument, however, is a bit tangential to Wittgenstein's, inasmuch as the question pertains not to reasons as causes in the sense Davidson allows but rather the question of establishing *a*, or *the*, reason for a given behavior or action, one whose antecedents have no boundaries and whose potential interpretations are myriad. The issue in psychoanalysis is how to establish reasons, validate them, and ultimately define precipitating causes in some ordered pattern of sequential psychic events that has no prescribed (discerned) order. The point is that cause and effect must be directly coordinated to fulfill Wittgenstein's objections, and Freud could not establish psychoanalytic causation by such criteria. A psychoanalytic reason is always one of several candidates, each of which resides in a fluid array of various reasons with diverse effects. In short, according to Wittgenstein, psychoanalytic cause is radically undetermined by diverse reasons and could not be understood in the common fashion that Davidson attempted to capture in an "ordinary language" philosophical approach. For further discussion, see MacIntyre (1958), Hart and Honré (1959), and Sherwood (1969, pp. 146–79).

10. Wittgenstein sourly complained about the game qua game: "My super-ego might say of my ego: 'It is raining, and the ego believes so,' and might go on 'So I shall probably take an umbrella with me.' And now how does this game go on?" (1980b, p. 130e).

11. "There are no mental analogues to the essential features of public ostensive definitions. The logical category of the definiendum needs to have been determined, that is 'S' must be the name of a sensation. However, 'sensation' is a word in our public language which is defined by reference to behavioral criteria. Since the private linguist denies or severs this connection, he must explain the category or 'post' of 'S' afresh. However, simply muttering 'This is S' does not make 'S' the name of a sensation, since it leaves undetermined what 'this' is. Concentrating one's attention cannot establish criteria of identity for subsequent uses of 'S.' Such criteria can be provided only by specifying what kind of thing is at issue through a sortal term. But the private linguist has not established what it is he is concentrating on. He cannot say that it is a certain 'experience' or 'phenomenon,' since he lacks the resources for explaining those terms provided by our public language. He cannot even say that 'S'

refers to something he has, since 'has' and 'something' are likewise terms from our public language with a determinant grammar" (Glock 1996, pp. 312–13 [see Wittgenstein 1968, § 257, p. 92e, §§ 261–63, p. 93e]).

12. See Peter Carruthers's recent study, which, from a cognitivist perspective argues that "our only mode of access to our own thinking is through the same sensory channels that we use when figuring out the mental state of others. Moreover, knowledge of most kinds of thinking (and hence by extension knowledge of our own standing attitudes) is just as interpretive in character as other-knowledge. Our common-sense conception of the transparency of our own minds is illusory . . . and *opaque* to us" (2011, p. xii). The standing of one's own thoughts is further developed by Anthony Brueckner and Gary Ebbs (2012).

13. A potentially important development from cognitive science supports Wittgenstein's antirepresentational approach and sheds an intriguing postulate about the character of private language. Although cognitive scientists have generally embraced the representational paradigm, a line of research promoting a dynamic orientation is moving in a different direction (Ramsey 2007, pp. 188ff.). Without delving into the experimental basis for this position, suffice it to note that the dominant cognitive representational model basically mirrors (and thus extrapolates) common experience to brain functions. For instance, eyes are thought to process images much like a video camera and as in mechanical viewing, we build a "Cartesian Theater" to present those representations for conscious experience (Dennett 1991b). However, an influential cadre of philosophers has attacked this "picture of the mind which has become so ingrained in our philosophical tradition that it is almost impossible to escape its influence even when its faults are recognized and repudiated" (Davidson 2001a, p. 34). The model's weakness centers on the postulate that some "inner viewer" adjudicates the representations, which introduces a regress that has no end point. Argument has been made that representations themselves can only serve in late (or higher-level) cognitive processes, and instead of regarding cognition from a computational or connectionist perspective that employs representations as the métier of mental functions, a dynamic system of "embedded cognition" better models robotics and other experimental investigations of perception (Shapiro 2011). A two-tier mind model attempts to address

both a dynamic embedded nonrepresentational model of cognition with one that allows for "representation-hungry" scenarios (Clark and Toribio 1994, p. 419). Accordingly, the cognitive system is posited as composed of (1) a basic nonconscious, nonlinguistic mind and (2) a "super-mind" in which language and consciousness lodge. The latter serves as the site of the representational thinking characteristic of folk models of cognition and thereby accounts for behavior and reasoning characteristic of higher-order functions (Frankish 2004). However, higher-level processes need not necessarily deal in representations either if subvocalized thoughts are "merely *output* arising from deeper processes, [which] . . . play no further role in the production of behavior or significant cognitive operations that underlie our various psychological capacities" (Ramsey 2007, p. 231). Simply, on the "subvocalization hypothesis," conscious thoughts are the effects of more central psychological operations, which are nonrepresentational but which we experience as representational as constitutive to the way consciousness functions. Following Quine (1995), this position essentially considers private language as an artifact of the monitoring perspective consciousness offers.

14. "One of the most misleading representational techniques in our language is the use of the word 'I,' particularly when it is used in representing immediate experience, as in 'I can see a red patch.' It would be instructive to replace this way of speaking by another in which immediate experience would be represented without using the personal pronoun; for then we would be able to see that the previous representation wasn't essential to the facts. . . . [The 'error' arises because] all forms of speech are taken from ordinary, physical language and cannot be used in epistemology and phenomenology without casting a distorting light on their objects. The very expression, 'I can perceive *x*' is itself taken from the idiom of physics, and *x* ought to be a physical object. . . . Things have already gone wrong if this expression is used in phenomenology, where *x* must refer to datum. For then 'I' and 'perceive' cannot have their previous senses" (Wittgenstein 1975, p. 88; see Murdoch 1993, pp. 269–88).

15. The parallels between the thought of Heidegger and Wittgenstein are striking (albeit, following radically different strategies) in regard to their closely aligned antimetaphysical stances that stretched from an antifoundationalism to the rejection of predicate thinking. That posture

informed their respective deconstruction of the ego, the tacit understanding that informs prereflective acting and speaking, the discarding of representational models of the mind, an epistemological holism from which a dynamic conception of meaning emerges, the contextual character of speech and knowledge, and their efforts to reconfigure traditional philosophy to an altogether different kind of activity following a new form of "argument" directed toward nontraditional philosophical problems (see Braver 2012).

16. And of course, this extends even more to social communication: "In the everyday language of communication, there is no a priori privileged position of sign over meaning or meaning over sign; the act of interpretation will always again have to establish this relation for the case at hand. The interpretation of everyday language is a Sisyphean task, a task without end and without progress, for the other is always free to make what he wants differ from what he says he wants. [This state constitutes] a built-in discrepancy within the inter-subjective relationship" (de Man 1993, p. 12).

17. For example, Coleridge formulates the Imagination into two tiers, primary and secondary. The primary closely relates to "the will" that represents the unmediated expression of subjectivity, whereas the secondary imagination, which he demotes as a mere "echo" of the primary, is charged with the translation of the primary imagination's vitality into language and thereby "dissolves, diffuses, dissipates, in order to re-create; or where this process is rendered impossible, yet still at all events it struggles to idealize and to unify" (1983, 1:304). "If then I know myself only through myself, it is contradictory to require any other predicate of self, but that self-consciousness. Only in the self-consciousness of a spirit is there the required identity of object and of representation; for herein consists the essence of a spirit, that it is self-representative. If therefore this be the one and only truth, in the certainty of which the reality of our collective knowledge is grounded, it must follow that the spirit in all the objects which it views, views only itself. If this could be proved, the immediate reality of intuitive knowledge would be assured. It has been shown, that a spirit is that, which is its own object, yet not originally an object, but an absolute subject for which all, itself included, may become an object. It must therefore be an ACT; for every object is, as an *object*,

dead, fixed, incapable in itself of any action, and necessarily finite. Again, the spirit (the identity of object and subject) must in some sense dissolve this identity, in order to be conscious of it. . . . But this implies an act, and it follows therefore that intelligence or self-consciousness is impossible, except by and in a will. The self-conscious spirit therefore is a will; and freedom must be assumed as a ground of philosophy, and can never be deduced from it" (ibid., pp. 278–80).

18. In the Hegelian tradition, the relational other largely defines the self (Tauber 2006)—e.g., husband, carpenter, father—whereas in the Kantian tradition, personal autonomy maintains an insular, if not sacrosanct, inner core of personhood to serve as the ballast against an encroaching outer world and to assert the agency of moral responsibility (Tauber 2001, 2005). So in stark contrast to Kant's conception of the self-constituting character of human consciousness, Hegel argued that human consciousness was mediated by the sociohistorical conditions of specific individuals (Fagan 2005).

19. "The grammars of the self, of the 'I,' of consciousness, do not behave, on inspection, at all like the way we expected under the influence of misleading analogies, bewitching language, and conceptual pictures, and indeed we will be enabled to see those grammars as exhibited in usage clearly, nonprismatically, *only* if we therapeutically free ourselves of their domination" (Hagberg 2004, p. 232).

20. And to fix what is seemingly broken, a scientific (specifically, a medical) solution was sought. Biomedicine emerged as a daughter of the life sciences just as Freud invented psychoanalysis, and as such, psychiatry (including his own version) sought to ground its own methods, theories, and practices in line with the natural sciences. That complex endeavor borrowed from many sources, ranging from attempts to establish the links between neurological processes and the psychiatric, to more subtle rhetorical practices and social organization (Sadoff 1998).

Conclusion

1. For instance, biology has also informed the construction of personal identity from the early modern period into our own era (Tauber 1994). Mirroring the appearance of the independent citizen, the notion of the autonomous individual agent framed a biology that was organized around

the study of living entities. Anatomical, physiological, and developmental criteria were conceived solely in terms of individuals, and even Darwin regarded aggregates of individuals, the species, as identifiable units in competition with one another. With the understanding that living cells composed complex organisms, a new orientation slowly developed concerning the integration of physiological processes and anatomic units, but still within the confines of a singular organism that would maintain its autonomy. Only with the emergence of ecology in the second half of the nineteenth century did organic systems—composed of individuals in cooperative and competitive relationships—complement the individual-based conceptions of the life sciences. This ecological perspective has gained ascendency, and we now appreciate that all organisms live in a complex dialectical exchange with the environment and others (Tauber 2008). The notion of individuality offers an important means to conceptualize the units of complex systems, but such formulations also impose a constructive order that determines how that larger system is understood. Simply, a subject-object modality of organization inherently restricts a fuller understanding of the organism in its dialectical interchanges with the world. Furthermore, the discovery of widespread symbiosis throughout the animal kingdom (Gilbert and Epel 2009; Douglas 2010) is an important contribution to this new understanding, which supplants the notion of insular individuality of organisms with a conception of interactive relationships. Indeed, symbiosis has become a core principle of contemporary biology, having replaced an essentialist conception of individuality with a conception fitting within the larger systems approach now pushing the life sciences in diverse directions (Gilbert, Sapp, and Tauber 2012). And these biological precepts apply to our understanding of the social world in which humans create their interactive cultural environment.

2. According to Freud, psychoanalysis is a way to break the causal chain of instinctual drives by rational understanding and free choice and to empower the ego with tools of rational control. Later formulations would substitute "integration and dialogue" between ego and id for "rational control" and thereby permit the analysand to achieve psychic integration, growth, and development. Some form of dialogue between the conscious and unconscious components of the psyche has been postulated since the

1920s (Groddeck 1976), yet how such a dialogue ensues and on what basis a conversation is even possible between these psychic elements that speak different languages and are governed by different logics remain critical unresolved theoretical issues. From rational interpretation, coupled to emotional insight, a metaphorical, internal dialogue may develop, but to achieve that, rational discernment and comprehension must begin the process, and from that enlightened platform, integration may then be sought.

3. The indispensability of the ego for ethics and a trenchant refutation of the post-Cartesian positions described here has been argued, among others, by Murdoch (1993) and Frank (1989, 1995).

4. Given contemporary studies of reason's own unconscious processes, Freud would likely have argued that the notion of free will had been further humbled. Accordingly, agents have the capacity to navigate the world through reasoned stratagems and choices, but the exercise of such rationality operates under unconscious constraints that are determinative. To the extent that the self as a monitoring system feels "free" only characterizes its epistemological location and function as an observer of deeper mental functions (Wegner 2002). In some sense, the self-conscious self must experience freedom in order to fulfill its functional judgment role. Or, as Kant maintained—with an entirely different basis—Reason must judge itself.

References

Adams, F. R., and Dietrich, L. A. 2004. Swampman's revenge: Squabbles among the representationalists. *Philosophical Psychology* 17:323–40.

Adorno, T. W. 1973a. *The Jargon of Authenticity.* Evanston, IL: Northwestern University Press.

———. 1973b. *Negative Dialectics.* New York: Seabury Press.

———. 1997. *Aesthetic Theory.* Trans. R. Hullot-Kentor. Minneapolis: University of Minnesota Press.

———. 2005. *Minima Moralia. Reflections from a Damaged Life.* Trans. E. F. N. Jephcott, London: Verso, 2006. Available at http://www.efn.org/~dredmond/MinimaMoralia.html. Trans. D. Redmond.

———. 2007. *Philosophy of Modern Music.* New York: Continuum.

Adorno, T., Benjamin, W., Bloch, E., Brecht, B., and Lukács, G. 1977. *Aesthetics and Politics.* London: Verso.

Adorno, T., and Horkheimer, M. 2011. *Towards a New Manifesto.* Trans. R. Livingston. London: Verso.

Alford, F. 1988. *Narcissism. Socrates, the Frankfurt School and Psychoanalytic Theory.* New Haven, CT: Yale University Press.

Allison, H. 2004. *Kant's Transcendental Idealism. An Interpretation and Defense.* New Haven, CT: Yale University Press.

Althusser, L. 1996. *Writings on Psychoanalysis: Freud and Lacan.* Ed. O. Corpet and F. Matheron. Trans. J. Mehlman. New York: Columbia University Press.

Anderson, R. L. 2005. Neo-Kantianism and the roots of anti-psychologism. *British Journal for the History of Philosophy* 13:287–323.

Askay, R., and Farquhar, J. 2006. *Apprehending the Inaccessible: Freudian Psychoanalysis and Existential Phenomenology*. Evanston, IL: Northwestern University Press.

Auxier, R. E., and Hahn, L. E. (eds.). 2010. *The Philosophy of Richard Rorty*. Chicago: Open Court.

Baker, G. 2004. *Wittgenstein's Method. Neglected Aspects*. Ed. K. A. Morris. Malden, MA: Blackwell.

Bambach, C. R. 1995. *Heidegger, Dilthey, and the Crisis of Historicism*. Ithaca, NY: Cornell University Press.

Barthes, R. 1978. *A Lover's Discourse. Fragments*. Trans. R. Howard. New York: Hill and Wang.

Bechtel, W. 2008. *Mental Mechanisms. Philosophical Perspectives on Cognitive Neuroscience*. New York: Routledge.

Benjamin, J. 1988. *The Bonds of Love: Psychoanalysis, Feminism, and the Problem of Domination*. London: Virago.

———. 1998. *Shadow of the Other*. New York: Routledge.

Ben-Ze'ev, A. 1993. *The Perceptual System. A Philosophical and Psychological Perspective*. New York: Peter Lang.

———. 2000. *The Subtlety of Emotions*. Cambridge, MA: MIT Press.

Bergo, B. 2004. Psychoanalytic models: Freud's debt to philosophy and his Copernican revolution. In *The Philosophy of Psychiatry: A Companion*, ed. J. Radden, pp. 338–50. New York: Oxford University Press.

Berman, E. 2000. The utopian fantasy of a new person and the danger of a false analytic self. *Psychoanalytic Psychology* 17:38–60.

Berman, M. 1982. *All That Is Solid Melts into Air. The Experience of Modernity*. New York: Penguin.

Bernheimer, C., and Kahane, C. (eds.). 1990. *In Dora's Case: Freud—Hysteria—Feminism*. 2nd ed. New York: Columbia University Press.

Bernstein, J. M. 1997. Why rescue semblance? Metaphysical experience and the possibility of ethics. In *The Semblance of Subjectivity: Essays in Adorno's Aesthetic Theory*, ed. T. Huhn and L. Zuidervaat, pp. 177–212. Cambridge, MA: MIT Press.

Bernstein, R. J. 2006. An allegory of modernity/postmodernity: Habermas and Derrida. In *The Derrida-Habermas Reader*, ed. L. Thomassen, pp. 71–97. Chicago: University of Chicago Press.

Best, S., and Kellner, D. 1991. *Postmodern Theory. Critical Interrogations*. New York: Guilford Press.

Bettelheim, B. 1982. *Freud and Man's Soul*. London: Penguin.

Binswanger, L. 1957. *Sigmund Freud: Reminiscences of a Friendship*. Trans. N. Guterman. New York: Grune and Stratton.

———. 1967. *Being-in-the-World. Selected Papers of Ludwig Binswanger*. Trans. J. Needleman. New York: Harper Torchbooks.

Boothby, R. 2001. *Freud as Philosopher. Metapsychology after Lacan*. New York: Routledge.

Borch-Jacobsen, M. 1991. *Lacan. The Absolute Master*. Trans. D. Brick. Stanford: Stanford University Press.

Boss, M. 1963. *Psychoanalysis and Daseinsanalysis*. New York: Basic Books.

———. 1979. Martin Heidegger's Zollikon seminars. *Review of Existential Psychology and Psychiatry* 16:7–20.

Bouveresse, J. 1995. *Wittgenstein Reads Freud. The Myth of the Unconscious*. Trans. C. Cosman. Princeton: Princeton University Press.

Bouwsma, O. K. 1986. *Wittgenstein Conversations, 1949–1951*. Ed. J. L. Craft and R. E. Hustwit. Indianapolis, IN: Hackett.

Brandom, R. B. (ed.). 2000. *Rorty and His Critics*. Malden, MA: Blackwell.

Braver, L. 2012. *Groundless Grounds. A Study of Wittgenstein and Heidegger*. Cambridge, MA: MIT Press.

Brook, A. 2003. Kant and Freud. In *Psychoanalytic Knowledge and the Nature of Mind*, ed. M. C. Chung and C. Feltman, pp. 20–39. New York: Palgrave Macmillan.

Brown, N. O. 1959. *Life against Death. The Psychological Meaning of History*. Middletown, CT: Wesleyan University Press.

Brueckner, A., and Ebbs, G. 2012. *Debating Self-Knowledge*. Cambridge: Cambridge University Press.

Buck-Morss, S. 1977. *The Origin of Negative Dialectics. Theodor W. Adorno, Walter Benjamin, and the Frankfurt Institute*. New York: Free Press.

Buller, D. J. 2006. *Adapting Minds: Evolutionary Psychology and the Persistent Quest for Human Nature*. Cambridge, MA: MIT Press.

Burckhardt, J. 1995. *The Civilization of the Renaissance in Italy*. London: Phaidon.

Carruthers, P. 2011. *The Opacity of Mind. An Integrative Theory of Self-Knowledge*. New York: Oxford University Press.

Cassirer, E. 1953. *The Philosophy of Symbolic Forms. Volume 1: Language*. Trans. R. Manheim. New Haven, CT: Yale University Press.

———. 1955. *The Philosophy of Symbolic Forms. Volume 2: Mythical Thought*. Trans. R. Manheim. New Haven, CT: Yale University Press.

———. 1957. *The Philosophy of Symbolic Forms. Volume 3: The Phenomenology of Knowledge*. Trans. R. Manheim. New Haven, CT: Yale University Press.

Cavell, M. 1993. *The Psychoanalytic Mind. From Freud to Philosophy*. Cambridge, MA: Harvard University Press.

———. 2006. *Becoming a Subject. Reflections in Philosophy and Psychoanalysis*. Oxford: Clarendon Press.

Cavell, S. 1962. The availability of Wittgenstein's later philosophy. *Philosophical Review* 71:67–93. Reprinted in *Must We Mean What We Say?*, pp. 44–72. Cambridge: Cambridge University Press.

———. 1979. *The Claim of Reason. Wittgenstein, Skepticism, Morality, and Tragedy*. Oxford: Oxford University Press.

————. 1990. *Conditions Handsome and Unhandsome: The Constitution of Emersonian Perfectionism*. Chicago: University of Chicago Press.

Caygill, H. 1995. *A Kant Dictionary*. Malden, MA: Blackwell.

Cerbone, D. R. 2000. How to do things with wood: Wittgenstein, Frege and the problem of illogical thought. In *The New Wittgenstein*, ed. A. Crary and R. Read, pp. 293–314. London: Routledge.

Chase, J., and Reynolds, J. 2010. *Analytical versus Continental. Arguments on the Methods and Value of Philosophy*. Montreal: McGill-Queen's University Press.

Cherniak, C. 1986. *Minimal Rationality*. Cambridge, MA: MIT Press.

Chessick, R. D. 2007. *The Future of Psychoanalysis*. Albany: State University of New York Press.

Chiesa, L. 2007. *Subjectivity and Otherness. A Philosophical Reading of Lacan*. Cambridge, MA: MIT Press.

Cioffi, F. 1998. *Wittgenstein on Freud and Frazer*. Cambridge: Cambridge University Press.

Clapin, H. (ed.). 2002. *Philosophy of Mental Representation*. New York: Oxford University Press.

Clark, A., and Toribio, J. 1994. Doing without representing? *Synthese* 101:401–31.

Clark, T. J. 1999. *Farewell to an Idea. Episodes from a History of Modernism*. New Haven, CT: Yale University Press.

Clore, G. 1992. Cognitive phenomenology: Feelings and the construction of judgment. In *The Construction of Social Judgments*, ed. L. L. Martin, pp. 133–63. Hillsdale, NJ: Erlbaum.

Coffa, A. 1991. *The Semantic Tradition from Kant to Carnap*. Cambridge: Cambridge University Press.

Colebrook, C. 2005. *Philosophy and Post-structuralist Theory. From Kant to Deleuze*. Edinburgh: Edinburgh University Press.

Coleridge, S. T. 1983. *Biographica Literaria or Biographical Sketches of My Literary Life and Opinions*. Ed. J. Engell and W. J. Bate. Princeton: Princeton University Press.

Conant, J. 1991. Throwing away the top of the ladder. *Yale Review* 79:328–64.

———. 2000. Elucidation and nonsense in Frege and early Wittgenstein. In *The New Wittgenstein*, ed. A. Crary and R. Read, pp. 174–217. London: Routledge.

Cook, D. 2004. *Adorno, Habermas and the Search for a Rational Society*. New York: Routledge.

Cousins, M. 2005. Introduction. In *Sigmund Freud the Unconscious*, trans. G. Frankland, pp. vii–xx. London: Penguin.

Crary, A. 2000. Introduction. In *The New Wittgenstein*, ed. A. Crary and R. Read, pp. 1–18. London: Routledge.

Crary, A., and Read, R. (eds.). 2000. *The New Wittgenstein*. London: Routledge.

Cusset, F. 2008. *French Theory. How Foucault, Derrida, Deleuze, & Co. Transformed the Intellectual Life of the United States*. Minneapolis: University of Minnesota Press.

Dahlstrom, D. O. 2001. *Heidegger's Concept of Truth*. Cambridge: Cambridge University Press.

Dallmayr, F. 1989. Adorno and Heidegger. *Diacritics* 19:82–100.

———. 1993. Heidegger and Freud. *Political Psychology* 14:235–53.

Dalton, S. 1999. Bodies of experience and bodies of thought. Freud and Kant on excessively intense ideas. *Angelaki: Journal of the Theoretical Humanities* 4:93–101.

Damasio, A. R. 1994. *Descartes' Error. Emotion, Reason, and the Human Brain*. New York: Putnam.

Davidson, D. 1980a. Actions, reasons, and causes. In *Essays on Actions and Events*, pp. 3–19. Oxford: Clarendon Press.

———. 1980b. Psychology as philosophy. In *Essays on Actions and Events*, pp. 229–39. Oxford: Clarendon Press.

———. 2001a. Knowing one's own mind. In *Subjective, Intersubjective, Objective*, pp. 15–38. Oxford: Oxford University Press.

———. 2001b. The irreducibility of the concept of the self. In *Subjective, Intersubjective, Objective*, pp. 85–91. Oxford: Oxford University Press.

Deigh, J. 2010. Concepts of emotions in modern philosophy and psychology. In *The Oxford Handbook of the Emotions*, ed. P. Goldie, pp. 17–40. Oxford: Oxford University Press.

De Kesel, M. 2009. *Eros and Ethics. Reading Lacan's Seminar VII.* Trans. S. Jöttkandt. Albany: State University of New York Press.

Deleuze, G. 1983. *Nietzsche and Philosophy.* Trans. H. Tomlinson. New York: Columbia University Press.

———. 1988. *Bergsonism.* Trans. H. Tomlinson and B. Habberjam. New York: Zone Books.

———. 1990. *The Logic of Sense.* Ed. C. V. Boundas. Trans. M. Lester. New York: Columbia University Press.

———. 1994. *Difference and Repetition.* Trans. P. Patton. New York: Columbia University Press.

Deleuze, G., and Guattari, F. 1977. *Anti-Oedipus. Capitalism and Schizophrenia, vol. 1.* Trans. R. Hurley, M. Seem, and H. R. Lane. New York: Penguin.

———. 1987. *A Thousand Plateaus. Capitalism and Schizophrenia, vol. 2.* Trans. B. Massumi. Minneapolis: University of Minnesota Press.

De Man, P. 1993. The Gauss seminar of 1967. In *Romanticism and Contemporary Criticism, the Gauss Seminar and Other Papers*, ed. E. S. Burt, K. Newmark, and A. Warminski, pp. 3–122. Baltimore: Johns Hopkins University Press.

De Mey, M. 1992. *The Cognitive Paradigm. An Integrated Understanding of Scientific Development.* Chicago: University of Chicago Press.

Dennett, D. 1981. *The Intentional Stance.* Cambridge, MA: MIT Press.

———. 1991a. *Consciousness Explained.* Boston: Little, Brown.

———. 1991b. Two contrasts: Folk craft vs. folk science, and belief vs. opinion. In *The Future of Folk Psychology: Intentionality and Cognitive Science*, ed. J. Greenwood, pp. 135–48. Cambridge: Cambridge University Press.

d'Entrèves, M. P. 1997. Introduction. In *Habermas and the Unfinished Project of Modernity. Critical Essays on "The Philosophical*

Discourse of Modernity," ed. M. P. d'Entrèves and S. Benhabib, pp. 1–37. Cambridge, MA: MIT Press.

d'Entrèves, M. P., and Benhabib, S. (eds.) 1997. *Habermas and the Unfinished Project of Modernity. Critical Essays on "The Philosophical Discourse of Modernity."* Cambridge, MA: MIT Press.

Derrida, J. 1978. *Writing and Difference.* Trans. A. Bass. Chicago: University of Chicago Press.

Dewey, J. 1927. The role of philosophy in the history of the civilian. *The Philosophical Review* 36:1–9.

———. 1980. *Art as Experience.* New York: Berkeley Publishing Group.

Dews, P. 1987. *Logics of Disintegration. Post-structuralist Thought and the Claims of Critical Theory.* London: Verso.

———. 1995. *The Limits of Disenchantment. Essays on Contemporary European Philosophy.* London: Verso.

Diamond, C. 1991. *The Realistic Spirit. Wittgenstein, Philosophy and the Mind.* Cambridge, MA: MIT Press.

———. 2000. Does Bismarck have a beetle in his box? The private language argument in the *Tractatus.* In *The New Wittgenstein,* ed. A. Crary and R. Read, pp. 262–92. London: Routledge.

Dienstag, J. F. 2006. *Pessimism: Philosophy, Ethic, Spirit.* Princeton: Princeton University Press.

Dijksterhuis, A., and Nordgren, L. F. 2006. A theory of unconscious thought. *Perspectives on Psychological Science* 1:95–109.

Douglas, A. E. 2010. *The Symbiotic Habit.* Princeton: Princeton University Press.

Drassinower, A. 2003. *Freud's Theory of Culture. Eros, Loss, and Politics.* Lanham, MD: Rowman and Littlefield.

Dretske, F. 1988. *Explaining Behavior.* Cambridge, MA: MIT Press.

Dummett, M. 1981. *Frege. Philosophy of Language.* Cambridge, MA: Harvard University Press.

Eagleton, T. 1990. *The Ideology of the Aesthetic.* London: Basil Blackwell.

Eckstein, R., and Caruth, E. 1965. From Eden to utopia. *American Imago* 22:128–41.

Edwards, J. C. 1982. *Ethics without Philosophy. Wittgenstein and the Moral Life.* Tampa: University Presses of Florida.

———. 2004. From myth to metaphysics: Freud and Wittgenstein as philosophical thinkers. In *Psychoanalysis at the Limit. Epistemology, Mind, and the Question of Science*, ed. J. Mills, pp. 117–37. Albany: State University of New York Press.

Egginton, W. 2007. *The Philosopher's Desire. Psychoanalysis, Interpretation, and Truth.* Stanford: Stanford University Press.

Ellenberger, H. F. 1970. *The Discovery of the Unconscious. The History and Evolution of Dynamic Psychiatry.* New York: Basic Books.

Elliott, A., and Spezzano, C. (eds.). 2000. *Psychoanalysis at Its Limits. Navigating the Postmodern Turn.* London: Free Association Books.

Eriksson, J. 2010. Freud and philosophy. *Scandinavian Psychoanalytic Review* 33:142–48.

———. 2012. Freud's metapsychology—the formal a priori of psychoanalytic experience. *Scandinavian Psychoanalytic Review* 35:16–29.

Evans, D. 1996. *An Introductory Dictionary of Lacanian Psychoanalysis.* New York: Routledge.

Fagan, A. 2005. Theodor Adorno (1903–1969). *Internet Encyclopedia of Philosophy.* Available at http://www.iep.utm.edu/adorno/.

Faye, E. 2012. Being, history, technology, and extermination in the work of Heidegger. *Journal of the History of Philosophy* 50:111–30.

Ferry, L., and Renaut, A. 1990. *French Philosophy of the Sixties. An Essay on Antihumanism.* Trans. M. S. Cattani. Amherst: University of Massachusetts Press.

——— (eds.). 1997. *Why We Are Not Nietzscheans.* Trans. R. Loaiza. Chicago: University of Chicago Press.

Fink, B. 1995. *The Lacanian Subject: Between Language and Jouissance.* Princeton: Princeton University Press.

———. 1997. *A Clinical Introduction to Lacanian Psychoanalysis. Theory and Practice.* Cambridge, MA: Harvard University Press.

Fisch, M., and Benbaji, Y. 2011. *The View from Within. Normativity and the Limits of Self-Criticism.* Notre Dame, IN: University of Notre Dame Press.

Fodor, J. A. 1987. *Psychosemantics.* Cambridge, MA: MIT Press.

Fogelin, R. 2003. *Walking the Tightrope of Reason: The Precarious Life of a Rational Animal.* New York: Oxford University Press.

Foucault, M. 1970. *The Order of Things. An Archaeology of the Human Sciences.* New York: Random House.

———. 1986. *The Care of the Self. Vol. 3: History of Sexuality.* Trans. R. Hurley. New York: Pantheon.

———. 2001. *Power. The Essential Works of Foucault, 1954–1984, Vol. 3.* New York: New Press.

———. 2003. *Abnormal. Lectures at the Collège de France. 1974–1975.* Trans. G. Burchell. New York: Picador.

———. 2006. *History of Madness.* Trans. J. Murphy and J. Khalfa. London: Routledge.

Frank, M. 1989. *What Is Neostructuralism?* Trans. S. Wilke and R. Gray. Minneapolis: Minnesota University Press.

———. 1995. The subject v. language: Mental familiarity and epistemic self-ascription. Trans. L. K. Schmidt and B. Allen. *Common Knowledge* 4:30–50.

———. 1997. Subjectivity and individuality: Survey of a problem. In *Figuring the Self. Subject, Absolute, and Others in Classical German Philosophy*, ed. D. E. Klemm and G. Zöller, pp. 1–30. Albany: State University of New York Press.

Frankfurt, H. 2005. *On Bullshit.* Princeton: Princeton University Press.

Frankish, K. 2004. *Mind and Supermind.* Cambridge: Cambridge University Press.

Frege, G. 1977. *Logical Investigations.* Trans. P. T. Geach and R. H. Stoothoff. New Haven, CT: Yale University Press.

————. 1980. *Foundations of Arithmetic.* 2nd rev. ed. Trans. J. L. Austin. Evanston, IL: Northwestern University Press.

Freud, S. (1891) 1953. *On Aphasia. A Critical Study.* New York: International Universities Press.

————. (1895) 1953–74. Project for a scientific psychology. In *The Standard Edition of the Complete Psychological Works of Sigmund Freud*, ed. and trans. J. Strachey in collaboration with A. Freud, assisted by A. Strachey and A. Tyson, 1:295–397. London: Hogarth Press and The Institute of Psycho-analysis.

————. 1898. Sexuality in the aetiology of the neuroses. In *Standard Edition*, 3:261–85.

————. 1900. *Interpretation of Dreams.* In *Standard Edition*, vols. 4–5.

————. 1905. *Three Essays on Sexuality.* In *Standard Edition*, 7:130–243.

————. 1908. "Civilized" sexual morality and modern nervous illness. In *Standard Edition*, 9:179–204.

————. 1909. Analysis of a phobia in a five-year-old boy. In *Standard Edition*, 10:5–149.

————. 1910a. *Five Lectures on Psycho-Analysis.* In *Standard Edition*, 11:3–55.

————. 1910b. The future prospects of psycho-analytic therapy. In *Standard Edition*, 11:141–51.

————. 1912. Recommendations to physicians practicing psycho-analysis. In *Standard Edition*, 12:111–20.

————. 1913. *Totem and Taboo.* In *Standard Edition*, 13:1–162.

————. 1914a. On narcissism: An introduction. In *Standard Edition*, 14:73–102.

————. 1914b. On the history of the psycho-analytic movement. In *Standard Edition*, 14:7–66.

————. 1915a. Repression. In *Standard Edition*, 14:141–58.

————. 1915b. The unconscious. In *Standard Edition*, 14:166–215.

————. 1916. *Introductory Lectures on Psycho-analysis.* In *Standard Edition*, vols. 15, 16.

———. 1919. Preface to Reik's *Ritual: Psycho-Analytic Studies*. In *Standard Edition*, 17:259–63.

———. 1920. *Beyond the Pleasure Principle*. In *Standard Edition*, 18:7–64.

———. 1921. *Group Psychology and the Analysis of the Ego*. In *Standard Edition*, 18:69–143.

———. 1923a. *The Ego and the Id*. In *Standard Edition*, 19:12–66.

———. 1923b. Two encyclopedia articles. In *Standard Edition*, 18:235–59.

———. 1925. An autobiographical study. In *Standard Edition*, 20:7–74.

———. 1926a. *The Question of Lay Analysis*. In *Standard Edition*, 20:183–250.

———. 1926b. Psychoanalysis, Freudian School. In *Standard Edition*, 20:263–70.

———. 1927. *The Future of an Illusion*. In *Standard Edition*, 20:5–56.

———. 1930. *Civilization and Its Discontents*. In *Standard Edition*, 21:64–145.

———. 1932. Why war? In *Standard Edition*, 21:203–15.

———. 1933. *New Introductory Lectures*. In *Standard Edition*, 22:5–182.

———. 1937a. Analysis, terminable and interminable. In *Standard Edition*, 23:216–53.

———. 1937b. Constructions in analysis. In *Standard Edition*, 23:255–70.

———. 1940. *An Outline of Psycho-analysis*. In *Standard Edition*, 23:144–207.

———. 1990. *The Letters of Sigmund Freud to Eduard Silberstein, 1871–1881*. Ed W. Boehlich. Trans. A. J. Pomerans. Cambridge, MA: Harvard University Press.

Freud, S., and Breuer, J. 1895. *Studies on Hysteria*. In *Standard Edition*, 2:1–305.

Friedman, M. 2000. *A Parting of the Ways. Carnap, Cassirer, and Heidegger*. Chicago: Open Court.

Fromm, E. 1955. *The Sane Society.* New York: Holt.

———. 1969. *Escape from Freedom.* New York: Holt.

———. 1973. *The Anatomy of Human Destructiveness.* New York: Holt.

Früchtl, J. 2008. The struggle of the self against itself: Adorno and Heidegger on modernity. In *Adorno and Heidegger. Philosophical Questions,* ed. I. Macdonald and K. Ziarek, pp. 138–54. Stanford: Stanford University Press.

Fulgencio, L. 2005. Freud's metapsychological speculations. *International Journal of Psycho-analysis* 86:99–123.

Gay, V. P. 1992. *Freud on Sublimation. Reconsiderations.* Albany: State University of New York Press.

Gilbert, S. F., and Epel, D. 2009. *Ecological Developmental Biology.* Sunderland, MA: Sinauer Associates.

Gilbert, S. F., Sapp, J., and Tauber, A. I. 2012. A symbiotic view of life: We have never been individuals. *Quarterly Review of Biology* 87 (4): 325–41.

Glock, H-J. 1996. *A Wittgenstein Dictionary.* Oxford: Blackwell.

Godfrey-Smith, P. 2004. On folk psychology and mental representation. In *Representation in Mind: New Approaches to Mental Representation,* ed. H. Clapin, P. Staines, and P. Slezak, pp. 147–62. Amsterdam: Elsevier Science.

Goldberg, S. E. 1988. *Two Patterns of Rationality in Freud's Writings.* Tuscaloosa: University of Alabama Press.

Gordon, P. E. 2010. *Continental Divide. Heidegger, Cassirer, Davos.* Cambridge, MA: Harvard University Press.

Greenberg, V. D. 1997. *Freud and His Aphasia Book. Language and the Sources of Psychoanalysis.* Ithaca, NY: Cornell University Press.

Groddeck, G. 1976. *The Book of the It.* New York: International Universities Press.

Grünbaum, A. 1984. *The Foundations of Psychoanalysis: A Philosophical Critique.* Berkeley: University of California Press.

Guerlac, S. 2006. *Thinking in Time. An Introduction to Henri Bergson.* Ithaca, NY: Cornell University Press.

Guignon, C. 1993. Authenticity, moral values, and psychotherapy. In *The Cambridge Companion to Heidegger*, ed. C. Guignon, pp. 215–39. Cambridge: Cambridge University Press.

Guttman, S. A. 1984. *The Concordance to the "Standard Edition of the Complete Psychological Works of Sigmund Freud."* New York: International Universities Press.

Guyer, P. 1987. *Kant and the Claims of Knowledge*. New York: Cambridge University Press.

Habermas, J. 1971. *Knowledge and Human Interests*. Trans. J. J. Shapiro. Boston: Beacon Press.

———. 1984. *The Theory of Communicative Action. Vol. 1: Reason and the Rationalization of Society*. Trans. T. McCarthy. Boston: Beacon Press.

———. 1987. *The Philosophical Discourse of Modernity. Twelve Lectures*. Trans. F. Lawrence. Cambridge, MA: MIT Press.

———. 1990. *Moral Consciousness and Communicative Action*. Trans. C. Lenhardt and S. W. Nicholson. Cambridge, MA: MIT Press.

———1992. *Postmetaphysical Thinking: Philosophical Essays*. Trans. W. M. Hohengarten. Cambridge, MA: MIT Press.

———. 2003. *Truth and Justification*. Trans. B. Fultner. Cambridge, MA: MIT Press.

Hacker, P. M. S. 2000. Was he trying to whistle it? In *The New Wittgenstein*, ed. A. Crary and R. Read, pp. 353–88. London: Routledge.

Hagberg, G. L. 2004. Autobiographical consciousness: Wittgenstein, private experience, and the "inner picture." In *The Literary Wittgenstein*, ed. J. Gibson and W. Huemer, pp. 228–50. London: Routledge.

———. 2008. *Describing Ourselves. Wittgenstein and Autobiographical Consciousness*. Oxford: Clarendon Press.

Hall, D. L. 1994. *Richard Rorty. Prophet and Poet of the New Pragmatism*. Albany: State University of New York Press.

Halliwell, M. 1999. *Romantic Science and the Experience of the Self. Transatlantic Crosscurrents from William James to Oliver Sacks.* Aldershot, UK: Ashgate.

Halpern, J. 2001. *From Detached Concern to Empathy.* New York: Oxford University Press.

Hanly, C. 1992. *The Problem of Truth in Applied Psychoanalysis.* New York: Guilford Press.

Hanna, R. 2001. *Kant and the Foundations of Analytic Philosophy.* Oxford: Clarendon Press.

———. 2006. *Rationality and Logic.* Cambridge, MA: MIT Press.

Hart, H. L. A., and Honré, A. M. 1959. *Causation in the Law.* London: Oxford University Press.

Harvey, D. 1990. *The Condition of Postmodernity. An Enquiry into the Origin of Cultural Change.* Cambridge, MA: Blackwell.

Hayles, N. K. 1999. *How We Became Posthuman: Virtual Bodies in Cybernetics, Literature, and Informatics.* Chicago: University of Chicago Press.

Hegel, G. W. F. 2001. *Philosophy of Right.* Trans. S. W. Dyde. Kitchener, Ontario [Canada]: Batoche Books. Reprint 1896, translation of 1821 text. Also available at http://www.marxists.org/reference/archive/hegel/.

Heidegger, M. 1962. *Being and Time.* Trans. J. Macquarrie and E. Robinson. New York: Harper and Row.

———. 1976. *What Is Called Thinking?* Trans. J. Glenn Gray. New York: Harper Perennial.

———. 1977a. The age of the world picture. In *The Question concerning Technology and Other Essays,* trans. W. Lovitt, pp. 115–54. New York: Harper Torchbooks.

———. 1977b. Science and reflection. In Lovitt, *The Question concerning Technology and Other Essays,* pp. 155–82.

———. 1977c. The word of Nietzsche. In Lovitt, *The Question concerning Technology and Other Essays,* pp. 53–122.

————. 1979. *Nietzsche*. Vol. 1. Ed. D. F. Kressl. Trans. F. A. Capuzzi. San Francisco: Harper.

————. 1982. *Nietzsche*. Vol. 4. Ed. D. F. Kressl. Trans. F. A. Capuzzi. San Francisco: Harper.

————1991. *The Principle of Reason*. Trans. R. Lilly. Bloomington: Indiana University Press.

————. 1993a. Letter on humanism. In *Martin Heidegger. Basic Writings*, ed. D. F. Krell, pp. 213–65. New York: HarperCollins.

————. 1993b. On the essence of truth. In Krell, *Martin Heidegger. Basic Writings*, pp. 115–38.

————. 1993c. What is metaphysics? In Krell, *Martin Heidegger. Basic Writings*, pp. 93–110.

————. 1997. *Kant and the Problem of Metaphysics*. 5th ed. Trans. R. Taft. Bloomingdale: Indiana University Press.

————. 2001. *Zollikon Seminars. Protocols—Conversations—Letters*. Ed. M. Boss. Trans. F. Mayr and R. Askay. Evanston, IL: Northwestern University Press.

Helfer, M. B. 1996. *The Retreat of Representation. The Concept of* Darstellung *in German Critical Discourse*. Albany: State University of New York Press.

Henry, M. 1993. *The Genealogy of Psychoanalysis*. Trans. D. Brick. Stanford: Stanford University Press.

Herzog, P. 1988. The myth of Freud as anti-philosopher. In *Freud: Appraisals and Re-appraisals: Contributions to Freud Studies,* vol. 2, ed. P. E. Stepansky, pp. 163–89. New York: Analytic Press. First published 1972.

Horkheimer, M. 2004. *The Eclipse of Reason*. London: Continuum. First published 1947.

Horkheimer, M., and Adorno, T. W. 1993. *Dialectic of Enlightenment*. New York: Continuum.

Huhn, T. 1999. Kant, Adorno and the social opacity of the aesthetic. In *The Semblance of Subjectivity: Essays in Adorno's Aesthetic Theory*, ed. T. Huhn and L. Zuidervaart, pp. 237–58. Cambridge, MA: MIT Press.

Husserl, E. 1970. The Vienna lecture. In *The Crisis of European Sciences and Transcendental Phenomenology*, trans. D. Carr, pp. 269–99. Evanston, IL: Northwestern University Press.

Ingram, D. 2010. *Habermas. Introduction and Analysis.* Ithaca, NY: Cornell University Press.

Jackson, F. 2003. *From Metaphysics to Ethics. A Defense of Conceptual Analysis.* Oxford: Oxford University Press.

Jacoby, R. 2007. *Picture Imperfect.* New York: Columbia University Press.

James, W. 1983. *The Principles of Psychology.* Cambridge, MA: Harvard University Press.

Johnston, P. 1993. *Wittgenstein: Rethinking the Inner.* London: Routledge.

Jolley, K. D. 2010. Psychologism and *Philosophical Investigations.* In *Wittgenstein, Key Concepts*, ed. K. D. Jolley, pp. 109–15. Durham, UK: Acumen.

Kahneman, D., and Tversky, A. (eds.). 2000. *Choices, Values, and Frames.* Cambridge: Cambridge University Press.

Kant, I. 1987. *Critique of Judgment.* Trans. W. S. Pluhar. Indianapolis, IN: Hackett Publishing.

———. 1996. An answer to the question: What is enlightenment? In *What Is Enlightenment? Eighteenth-Century Answers and Twentieth-Century Questions*, ed. J. Schmidt, pp. 58–64. Berkeley: University of California Press.

———. 1998. *Critique of Pure Reason.* Trans. P. Guyer and A. W. Wood. Cambridge: Cambridge University Press.

———. 2002. Prolegomena to any future metaphysics that will be able to come forward as science. Trans. G. Hatfield. In *Theoretical Philosophy after 1781*, ed. H. Allison and P. Heath, pp. 29–169. Cambridge: Cambridge University Press.

Kaufman, R. 2004. Adorno's social lyric and literary criticism today: Poetics, aesthetics, modernity. In *The Cambridge Companion to Adorno*, ed. T. Huhn, pp. 254–75. Cambridge: Cambridge University Press.

Keller, P. 1998. *Kant and the Demands of Self-Consciousness.* Cambridge: Cambridge University Press.

Kernberg, O. 1980. *Internal World and External Reality. Object Relations Theory Applied.* New York: Jason Aronson.

Kitcher, P. 1992. *Freud's Dream. A Complete Interdisciplinary Science of the Mind.* Cambridge, MA: MIT Press.

Kockelmans, J. J. 1979. Daseinsanalysis and Freud's unconscious. *Review of Existential Psychology and Psychiatry* 16:21–42.

Koelb, C. (ed.). 1990. *Nietzsche as Postmodernist. Essays Pro and Con.* Albany: State University of New York Press.

Könke, K. C. 1991. *The Rise of Neo-Kantianism. German Academic Philosophy between Idealism and Positivism.* Trans. R. J. Hollingdale. Cambridge: Cambridge University Press.

Krakauer, E. L. 1998. *The Disposition of the Subject. Reading Adorno's Dialectic of Technology.* Evanston, IL: Northwestern University Press.

Kristeva, J. 1987. *Tales of Love.* Trans. L. S. Roudiez. New York: Columbia University Press.

Kusch, M. 2011. Psychologism. In *The Stanford Encyclopedia of Philosophy* (Winter 2009 ed.), ed. E. N. Zalta. Available at http://plato.stanford.edu/entries/psychologism/.

Kuusela, O. 2011. The dialectic of interpretations. Reading Wittgenstein's *Tractatus.* In *Beyond the Tractatus Wars. The New Wittgenstein Debate,* ed. R. Read and M. A. Lavery, pp. 121–48. New York: Routledge.

Lacan, J. 1978. *The Four Fundamental Concepts of Psychoanalysis. The Seminar of Jacques Lacan Book XI.* Ed. J-A Miller. Trans. A. Sheridan. New York: W. W. Norton.

———. 1988. *Freud's Papers on Technique, 1953–1954. The Seminar of Jacques Lacan Book I.* Trans. J. Forrester. New York: W. W. Norton.

———. 1991. *The Ego in Freud's Theory and in the Technique of Psychoanalysis, 1954–1955. The Seminar of Jacques Lacan Book II.* Ed. J-A Miller. Trans. S. Tomaselli. New York: W. W. Norton.

———. 1992. *The Ethics of Psychoanalysis, 1959–1960. The Seminar of Jacques Lacan Book VII*. Ed. J-A Miller. Trans. D. Porter. New York: W. W. Norton.

———. 1993. *The Psychoses, 1955–1956. The Seminar of Jacques Lacan Book III*. Ed. J-A Miller. Trans. R. New York: W. W. Norton.

———. 2001. *Écrits. A Selection*. Trans. A. Sheridan. London: Routledge.

———. 2006. *Écrits. The First Complete Edition in English*. Trans. B. Fink. New York: W. W. Norton.

Lacey, A. R. 1989. *Bergson*. New York: Routledge.

Laing, R. D. 1967. *The Politics of Experience: The Bird of Paradise*. London: Penguin.

Lanier, J. 2010. *You Are Not a Gadget. A Manifesto*. New York: Knopf.

Laplanche, J., and Pontalis, J. B. 1973. *The Language of Psycho-analysis*. Trans. D. Nicholson-Smith. New York: W. W. Norton.

Latour, B. 1993. *We Have Never Been Modern*. Trans. C. Porter. Cambridge, MA: Harvard University Press.

Lear, J. 1990. *Love and Its Place in Nature. A Philosophical Interpretation of Freudian Psychoanalysis*. New York: Farrar, Straus and Giroux.

Lee, J. S. 1990. *Jacques Lacan*. Amherst: University of Massachusetts Press.

Lipton, P. 1991. *Inference to the Best Explanation*. 2nd ed. London: Routledge.

Ludlow, P. 1997. *Readings in the Philosophy of Language*. Cambridge, MA: MIT Press.

Lyotard, J-F. 1974. Adorno as the devil. Trans. R. Hurley. *Telos* 19:128–37.

———. 1984a. *The Postmodern Condition: A Report on Knowledge*. Trans. G. Bennington and B. Massumi. Minneapolis: University of Minnesota Press.

————. 1984b. Answering the question: What is postmodernism? Trans. R. Durand. In Bennington and Massumi, *The Postmodern Condition: A Report on Knowledge*, pp. 71–82.

————. 1988. *The Differend: Phrases in Dispute.* Trans. G. V. D. Abbeele. Minneapolis: University of Minnesota Press.

————. 1993. *Libidinal Economy.* Trans. I. H. Grant. Indianapolis: Indiana University Press.

————. 2011. *Discourse, Figure.* Trans. A. Hudek and M. Lydon. Minneapolis: University of Minnesota Press.

Macdonald, I., and Ziarek, K. (eds.). 2008a. *Adorno and Heidegger. Philosophical Questions.* Stanford: Stanford University Press.

————. 2008b. Introduction. In Macdonald and Ziarek, *Adorno and Heidegger. Philosophical Questions*, pp. 1–5.

MacIntyre, A. C. 1958. *The Unconscious.* Bristol, UK: Thoemmes Press.

Macmillan, M. 1997. *Freud Evaluated: The Completed Arc.* Cambridge, MA: MIT Press.

Maddy , P. 2007. *Second Philosophy. A Naturalistic Perspective.* New York: Oxford University Press.

Makari, G. 1994. In the eye of the beholder: Helmholtzian perception and the origins of Freud's 1900 theory of transference. *Journal of the American Psychoanalytic Association* 42:549–80.

Malachowski, A. 2002. *Richard Rorty.* Princeton: Princeton University Press.

Malcolm, N. 1954. Wittgenstein's *Philosophical Investigations. Philosophical Review* 63:530–59.

Marbach, E. 1993. *Mental Representationalism and Consciousness.* Dordrecht, Netherlands: Kluwer Academic Publishers.

Marcuse, H. 1955. *Eros and Civilization. A Philosophical Inquiry into Freud.* Boston: Beacon Press.

Marx, K. 1997. Letter to Arnold Ruge (1843). In *Karl Marx: Writings of the Young Marx on Philosophy and Society*, ed. D. Easton and K. H. Guddat, p. 213. Indianapolis: Hackett Publishing.

Available at http://www.marxists.org/archive/marx/works/1843/letters/43_09.htm.

McDowell, J. 1981. Non-cognitivism and rule following. In *Wittgenstein: To Follow a Rule*, ed. S. H. Holtzman and C. M. Leich, pp. 141–62. London: Routledge and Kegan Paul.

McGuiness, B. 1982. Freud and Wittgenstein. In *Wittgenstein and His Times*, ed. B. McGuiness, pp. 27–43. Oxford: Blackwell.

Meissner, W. W. 2003. *The Ethical Dimension of Psychotherapy. A Dialogue*. Albany: State University of New York Press.

Menand, L. 2001. *The Metaphysical Club. A Story of Ideas in America*. New York: Farrar, Straus and Giroux.

Metzinger, T. 2003. *Being No One. The Self-Model Theory of Subjectivity*. Cambridge, MA: MIT Press.

———. 2009. *The Ego Tunnel. The Science of the Mind and the Myth of the Self*. New York: Basic Books.

Mohanty, J. 1999. Heidegger on logic. In *Logic, Truth and the Modalities: From a Phenomenological Point of View*, by J. Mohanty, pp. 79–109. Dordrecht, Netherlands: Kluwer Academic Publishers.

Moore, G. E. 1993. Wittgenstein's lectures in 1930–1933. In *Ludwig Wittgenstein. Philosophical Occasions, 1912–1951*, ed. J. C. Klagge and A. Nordmann. Indianapolis, IN: Hackett.

Moss, D. 2005. On the utopian politics of love the sin: Commentary on *Love the Sin: Sexual Regulation and the Limits of Religious Tolerance* by J. R. Jakobsen and A. Pelligrini. *Studies in Gender and Sexuality* 6:377–85.

Mullarkey, J. 2000. *Bergson and Philosophy*. Notre Dame, IN: Notre Dame University Press.

Murdoch, I. 1993. *Metaphysics as a Guide to Morals*. London: Penguin.

Musgrave, A. 1972. George Boole and psychologism. *Scientia* 107:593–608.

Natsoulas, T. 1984. Freud and consciousness. I. Intrinsic consciousness. *Psychoanalysis and Contemporary Thought* 7:195–232.

————. 1985. Freud and consciousness. II. Derived consciousness. *Psychoanalysis and Contemporary Thought* 8:183–220.

————. 2001. The Freudian unconscious. *Consciousness and Emotion* 2:1–28.

Needleman, J. 1967. Introduction. In *Being-in-the-World. Selected Papers of Ludwig Binswanger*, trans. J. Needleman, pp. 1–144. New York: Harper Torchbooks.

Neill, C. 2011. *Lacanian Ethics and the Assumption of Subjectivity.* Houndmills, UK: Palgrave Macmillan.

Neiman, S. 1994. *The Unity of Reason. Rereading Kant.* New York: Oxford University Press.

Nietzsche, F. 1967. *Ecce Homo.* In *On the Genealogy of Morals and Ecce Homo*, trans. W. Kaufmann, pp. 217–335. New York: Random House.

————. 1999. *The Birth of Tragedy and Other Writings.* Trans. R. Speirs. Cambridge: Cambridge University Press.

————. 2003. *Nietzsche. Writings from the Late Notebooks.* Ed. R. Bittner. Trans. K. Sturge. Cambridge: Cambridge University Press.

————. 2008. *Beyond Good and Evil. Prelude to a Philosophy of the Future.* Trans. M. Faber. New York: Oxford University Press.

Nisbett, R. E. 2003. *The Geography of Thought. How Asians and Westerners Think Differently.* New York: Free Press.

Nussbaum, M. 2001. *Upheavals of Thought: The Intelligence of Emotions.* Cambridge: Cambridge University Press.

O'Neill, O. 1989. *Constructions of Reason. Explorations of Kant's Practical Philosophy.* Cambridge: Cambridge University Press.

Perlow, M. 1995. *Understanding Mental Objects.* London: Routledge.

Peter, F., and Schmid, H. B. (eds.). 2007. *Rationality and Commitment.* Oxford: Oxford University Press.

Peterman, J. F. 1992. *Philosophy as Therapy. An Interpretation and Defense of Wittgenstein's Later Philosophical Project.* Albany: State University of New York Press.

Piaget, J. 1929. *The Child's Conception of the World*. Trans. J. Tomlinson and A. Tomlinson. London: Routledge and Kegan Paul.

Pinker, S. 2003. *The Blank Slate. The Denial of Human Nature*. New York: Penguin.

Putnam, H. 1994. Rethinking mathematical necessity. In *Words and Life*, ed. J. Conant, pp. 245–63. Cambridge, MA: Harvard University Press.

———. 2004. *Ethics without Ontology*. Cambridge, MA: Harvard University Press.

Quine, W. V. O. 1990. Three indeterminacies. In *Perspectives on Quine*, ed. R. B. Barrett and R. F. Gibson, pp. 1–16. London: Blackwell.

———. 1995. *From Stimulus to Science*. Cambridge, MA: Harvard University Press.

Ramsey, W. A. 2007. *Representation Reconsidered*. Cambridge: Cambridge University Press.

Rawls, J. 1971. *A Theory of Justice*. Cambridge, MA: Harvard University Press.

Read, R., and Lavery, M. A. (eds.). 2011. *Beyond the "Tractatus" Wars. The New Wittgenstein Debate*. New York: Routledge.

Reck, E. 1997. Frege's influence on Wittgenstein: Reversing metaphysics via the context principle. In *Early Analytic Philosophy. Frege, Russell, Wittgenstein*, ed. W. W. Tait, pp. 183–85. Chicago: Open Court.

Reeder, J. 2002. *Reflecting Psychoanalysis. Narrative and Resolve in the Psychoanalytic Experience*. London: Karnac.

———. 2012. The empty core. Metapsychological reflections upon the lost object, an ethical order, and the inevitable void at the center of our existence. *Scandinavian Psychoanalytic Review* 35:35–44.

Reid, L. 1998. Wittgenstein's ladder: The *Tractatus* and nonsense. *Philosophical Investigations* 21:97–151.

Renaut, A. 1997. *The Era of the Individual. A Contribution to a History of Subjectivity*. Trans. M. B. De Bevoise and F. Philip. Chicago: University of Chicago Press.

Rey, G. 1997. *Contemporary Philosophy of Mind: A Contentiously Classical Approach*. Malden, MA: Blackwell.

Rhees, R. 1966. Conversations on Freud. In *Wittgenstein, Lectures and Conversations on Aesthetics, Psychology, and Religious Belief*, ed. C. Barrett, pp. 41–52. Los Angeles: University of California Press.

———. 1981. *Ludwig Wittgenstein. Personal Recollections*. Totowa, NJ: Rowman and Littlefield.

Richardson, W. J. 1979. The mirror inside: The problem of the self. *Review of Existential Psychology and Psychiatry* 16:95–112.

Ricketts, T. 1996. Pictures, logic, and the limits of sense in Wittgenstein's *Tractatus*. In *The Cambridge Companion to Wittgenstein*, ed. H. Sluga and D. G. Stern, pp. 59–99. Cambridge: Cambridge University Press.

Rieff, P. 1959. *Freud, Mind of the Moralist*. New York: Viking.

Rockmore, T. 1995. *Heidegger and French Philosophy. Humanism, Antihumanism, and Being*. London: Routledge.

———. 2006. *In Kant's Wake. Philosophy in the Twentieth Century*. Malden, MA: Blackwell.

Rogozinski, J. 2010. *The Ego and the Flesh. An Introduction to Egoanalysis*. Trans. R. Vallier. Stanford: Stanford University Press.

Rorty, R. 1979. *Philosophy and the Mirror of Nature*. Princeton: Princeton University Press.

———. 1989a. The contingency of language. In *Contingency, Irony, and Solidarity*, pp. 3–22. Cambridge: Cambridge University Press.

———. 1989b. The contingency of selfhood. In *Contingency, Irony, and Solidarity*, pp. 23–43. Cambridge: Cambridge University Press.

———. 1991a. Freud and moral reflection. In *Essays on Heidegger and Others. Philosophical Papers*, 2:143–63. Cambridge: Cambridge University Press.

———. 1991b. Science as solidarity. In *Objectivity, Relativism, and Truth. Philosophical Papers*, 1:35–45. Cambridge: Cambridge University Press.

———. 1991c. Solidarity or objectivity. In *Objectivity, Relativism, and Truth. Philosophical Papers*, 1:21–34. Cambridge: Cambridge University Press.

———. 1991d. Wittgenstein, Heidegger, and the reification of language. In *Essays on Heidegger and Others. Philosophical Papers*, 2:50–65. Cambridge: Cambridge University Press.

———. 1999. *Philosophy and Social Hope*. London: Penguin Books.

———. 2001. Wittgenstein and the linguistic turn. In *Philosophy as Cultural Politics. Philosophical Papers*, 4:160–75. Cambridge: Cambridge University Press.

———. 2006. Habermas, Derrida and the functions of philosophy. In *The Derrida-Habermas Reader*, ed. L. Thomassen, pp. 46–65. Chicago: University of Chicago Press.

Rose, M. A. 1991. *The Post-modern and the Post-industrial. A Critical Analysis*. Cambridge: Cambridge University Press.

Rothenberg, M. A. 2010. *The Excessive Subject. A New Theory of Social Change*. Cambridge, UK: Polity.

Roudinesco, E. 2003. The mirror-stage: An obliterated archive. In *The Cambridge Companion to Lacan*, ed. J-M. Rabaté, trans. B. Bray, pp. 25–35. Cambridge: Cambridge University Press.

Roustang, F. 1993. A philosophy for psychoanalysis. In *The Genealogy of Psychoanalysis*, by M. Henry, pp. ix–xxiii. Stanford: Stanford University Press.

Rubovits-Seitz, P. F. D. 1998. *Depth-Psychological Understanding. The Methodologic Grounding of Clinical Interpretations*. Hillsdale, NJ: Analytic Press.

Ryle, M., and Soper, K. 2002. *To Relish the Sublime? Culture and Self-Realization in Postmodern Times*. London: Verso.

Sadoff, D. F. 1998. *Sciences of the Flesh. Representing Body and Subject in Psychoanalysis*. Stanford: Stanford University Press.

Sandler, J., Holder, A., Dare, C., and Dreher, A. U. 1997. *Freud's Models of the Mind. An Introduction.* London: Karnac.

Sartre, J-P. 1956. *Being and Nothingness. An Essay on Phenomenological Ontology.* Trans. H. E. Barnes. New York: Philosophical Library.

Sarup, M. 1993. *An Introductory Guide to Post-structuralism and Postmodernism.* 2nd ed. Athens: University of Georgia Press.

Schafer, R. 1983. *The Analytic Stance.* New York: Basic Books.

Scheck, R. 1988. Did the children's crusade of 1212 really consist of children? Problems of writing childhood history. *Journal of Psychohistory* 16:176–82. Available at http://www.geocities.ws/kidhistory/didthe.htm.

Scheler, M. 1958. *Philosophical Perspectives.* Boston: Beacon Press.

Schmidt, J. 1998. Language, mythology, and enlightenment: Historical notes of Horkheimer and Adorno's *Dialectic of Enlightenment. Social Research* 65:807–38.

Schopenhauer, A. 1969. *The World as Will and Representation.* 2 vols. Trans. E. F. J. Payne. New York: Dover.

Schwab, G. 2007. Introduction: Derrida, Deleuze, psychoanalysis, and the psychoanalysis to come. In *Derrida, Deleuze, Psychoanalysis*, ed. G. Schwab, pp. 1–34. New York: Columbia University Press.

Searle, J. 1992. *The Rediscovery of the Mind.* Cambridge, MA: MIT Press.

Seigel, J. 2005. *The Idea of the Self. Thought and Experience in Western Europe since the Seventeenth Century.* Cambridge: Cambridge University Press.

Shanon, B. 1993. *The Representational and the Presentational. An Essay on Cognition and the Study of Mind.* London: Harvester Wheatsheaf.

Shapiro, L. 2011. *Embodied Cognition.* London: Routledge.

Shepherdson, J. 2003. Lacan and philosophy. In *The Cambridge Companion to Lacan*, ed. J-M. Rabaté, pp. 116–52. Cambridge: Cambridge University Press.

Sherratt, Y. 2002. *Adorno's Positive Dialectic*. Cambridge: Cambridge University Press.

Sherwood, M. 1969. *The Logic of Explanation in Psychoanalysis*. New York: Academic Press.

Shoemaker, S. 1984. Personal identity: A materialist account. In *Personal Identity*, by S. Shoemaker and R. Swinburne, pp. 67–132. Oxford: Basil Blackwell.

Sio, U. N., and Ormerod, T. C. 2009. Does incubation enhance problem solving? A meta-analytic review. *Psychological Bulletin* 135: 94–120.

Skorupski, J. 2010. *The Domain of Reasons*. Oxford: Oxford University Press.

Sloterdijk, P. 1988. *Critique of Cynical Reason*. Minneapolis: University of Minnesota Press.

Smith, D. L. 1999a. *Freud's Philosophy of the Unconscious*. Dordrecht, Netherlands: Kluwer Academic Publishers.

———. 1999b. Sigmund Freud's programme for a science of consciousness. *British Journal of Psychotherapy* 15:412–24.

———. 2004. Freud and Searle on the ontology of the unconscious. In *Psychoanalysis at the Limit: Epistemology, Mind, and the Question of Science*, ed. J. Mills, pp. 73–90. Albany: State University of New York Press.

Smith, G. B. 1996. *Nietzsche, Heidegger and the Transition to Postmodernity*. Chicago: University of Chicago Press.

Soames, S. 2003. *Philosophical Analysis in the Twentieth Century*. 2 vols. Princeton: Princeton University Press.

Stavrakakis, Y. 1999. *Lacan and the Political*. New York: Routledge.

Steiner, G. 1978. *Martin Heidegger*. Chicago: University of Chicago Press.

Stepansky, P. E. 1999. *Freud, Surgery, and the Surgeons*. Hillsdale, NJ: Analytic Press.

Steuerman, E. 2000. *The Bounds of Reason. Habermas, Lyotard and Melanie Klein on Rationality*. London: Routledge.

Stich, S. P., and Warfield, T. A. (eds.). 1994. *Mental Representation: A Reader*. Cambridge: Blackwell.

Strawson, P. F. 1959. *Individuals. An Essay in Descriptive Metaphysics*. London: Methuen.

Strenger, C. 1989. The classic and the romantic vision in psychoanalysis. *International Journal of Psycho-Analysis* 70:593–610.

———. 1997. Further remarks on the classic and the romantic visions in psychoanalysis: Klein, Winnicott, and Ethics. *Psychoanalysis and Contemporary Thought* 20:207–43.

Szasz, T. S. 1961. *The Myth of Mental Illness: Foundations of a Theory of Personal Conduct*. New York: Dell.

Tauber, A. I. 1994. *The Immune Self: Theory or Metaphor?* Cambridge: Cambridge University Press.

———. 2001. *Henry David Thoreau and the Moral Agency of Knowing*. Berkeley: University of California Press.

———. 2005. *Patient Autonomy and the Ethics of Responsibility*. Cambridge, MA: MIT Press.

———. 2006. The reflexive project: Reconstructing the moral agent. *History of the Human Sciences* 18:49–75.

———. 2008. The immune system and its ecology. *Philosophy of Science* 75:224–45.

———. 2009a. Freud's dreams of reason: The Kantian structure of psychoanalysis. *History of the Human Sciences* 22:1–29.

———. 2009b. Freud's philosophical path: From a science of the mind to a philosophy of human being. *Scandinavian Psychoanalytic Review* 32:32–43.

———. 2009c. *Science and the Quest for Meaning*. Waco, TX: Baylor University Press.

———. 2010. *Freud, the Reluctant Philosopher*. Princeton: Princeton University Press.

———. 2012a. Freud's social theory: Modernist and postmodernist revisions. *History of the Human Sciences* 25:41–70.

———. 2012b. Review of *The View from Within: Normativity and the Limits of Self-Criticism*, by M. Fisch and Y. Benbaji. *Philosophy in Review* 32 (2011): 266–69.

———. 2012c. Thoreau's moral-epistemology and its contemporary relevance. In *Thoreau's Importance for Philosophy*, ed. R. A. Furtak, J. Ellsworth, and J. D. Reid, pp. 127–42. New York: Fordham University Press.

———. 2013. Freud without Oedipus. The cognitive unconscious. *Philosophy, Psychiatry & Psychology*, in press.

Taylor, C. 1989. *The Sources of the Self.* Cambridge, MA: Harvard University Press.

Thomas-Fogiel, I. 2011. *The Death of Philosophy. Reference and Self-Reference in Contemporary Thought.* Trans. R. A. Lynch. New York: Columbia University Press.

Thomassen, L. (ed.). 2006. *The Derrida-Habermas Reader.* Chicago: University of Chicago Press.

Thompson, A. E. 1991. Freud's pessimism, the death instinct, and the theme of disintegration in "Analysis Terminable and Interminable." *International Journal of Psycho-Analysis* 18:165–79.

Tugendhat, E. 1982. *Traditional and Analytical Philosophy. Lectures on the Philosophy of Language.* Trans. P. A. Gorner. Cambridge: Cambridge University Press.

———. 1986. *Self-Consciousness and Self-Determination.* Trans. P. Stern. Cambridge, MA: MIT Press.

Turkle, S. 1978. *Psychoanalytic Politics. Jacques Lacan and Freud's French Revolution.* New York: Basic Books.

Varela, F., Thompson, E. T., and Rosch, E. 1991. *The Embodied Mind: Cognitive Science and Human Experience.* Cambridge, MA: MIT Press.

Vogel, S. 1996. *Against Nature. The Concept of Nature in Critical Theory.* Albany: State University of New York Press.

Wallon, H. 1983. *Les origines du caractère chez l'enfant.* Paris: Presses Universitaires de France.

Watkins, E. 2005. *Kant and the Metaphysics of Causality.* Cambridge: Cambridge University Press.

Webster, R. 1995. *Why Freud Was Wrong: Sin, Science, and Psychoanalysis.* New York: Basic Books.

Wegner, D. 2002. *The Illusion of Conscious Will*. Cambridge, MA: MIT Press.

Wellmer, A. 1985. Truth, semblance and reconciliation: Adorno's aesthetic redemption of modernity. *Telos* 62:89–116.

Werbart, A. 2007. Utopic ideas of cure and joint exploration in psychoanalytic supervision. *International Journal of Psycho-Analysis* 88:1391–1408.

Whitebook, J. 1988. Perversion and utopia: A study in psychoanalysis and social theory. *Psychoanalysis in Contemporary Thought* 11:415–46.

———. 1995. *Perversion and Utopia. A Study in Psychoanalysis and Critical Theory*. Cambridge, MA: MIT Press.

———. 2004. Weighty objects. On Adorno's Kant-Freud interpretation. In *The Cambridge Companion to Adorno*, ed. T. Huhn, pp. 51–78. Cambridge: Cambridge University Press.

Whyte, L. L. 1978. *The Unconscious before Freud*. London: Julian Friedman Publishers.

Willey, T. E. 1978. *Back to Kant. The Revival of Kantianism in German Social and Historical Thought, 1860–1914*. Detroit, MI: Wayne State University Press.

Williams, M. 1999. *Wittgenstein, Mind and Meaning. Towards a Social Conception of Mind*. London: Routledge.

Wilson, E. O. 1999. *Consilience. The Unity of Knowledge*. New York: Vintage.

———. 2004. *On Human Nature*. Rev. ed. Cambridge, MA: Harvard University Press.

Wilson, T. D. 2002. *Strangers to Ourselves. Discovering the Adaptive Unconscious*. Cambridge, MA: Harvard University Press.

Windelband, W. 1921. *An Introduction to Philosophy*. Trans. J. McCabe. New York: Henry Holt.

Winquist, C. E. 1998. Lacan and theology. In *Post-secular Philosophy. Between Philosophy and Theology*, ed. P. Blond, pp. 305–17. London: Routledge.

Wispe, L. 1986. The distinction between sympathy and empathy: To call forth a concept, a word is needed. *Journal of Personality and Social Psychology* 50:314–21.

Wittgenstein, L. 1958. *The Blue and Brown Books.* New York: Harper and Row.

———. 1968. *Philosophical Investigations.* 3rd ed. Trans. G. E. M. Anscombe. New York: Macmillan.

———. 1975. *Philosophical Remarks.* Ed. R. Rhees. Trans. R. Hargreaves and R. White. Chicago: University of Chicago Press.

———. 1979. *Notebooks, 1914–1916.* 2nd ed. Trans. G. E. M. Anscombe. Chicago: University of Chicago Press.

———. 1980a. *Culture and Value.* Ed. G. H. von Wright. Chicago: University of Chicago Press.

———. 1980b. *Remarks on the Philosophy of Psychology, Vol. 1.* Ed. G. E. M. Anscombe and G. H. von Wright. Chicago: University of Chicago Press.

———. 1980c. *Remarks on the Philosophy of Psychology, Vol. 2.* Ed. G. H. von Wright and H. Nyman. Chicago: University of Chicago Press.

———. 1981. *Tractatus-Philosophicus.* Trans. C. K. Ogden. London: Routledge.

———. 1990. *Last Writings on the Philosophy of Psychology. Vol. 1: Preliminary Studies for Part II of Philosophical Investigations.* Ed. G. H. von Wright and H. Nyman. Trans. C. J. Luckhardt and M. A. E. Aue. Chicago: University of Chicago Press.

———. 1992. *Last Writings on the Philosophy of Psychology. Vol. 2: The Inner and the Outer.* Ed. G. H. von Wright and H. Nyman. Oxford: Blackwell.

———. 1993. Notes for the "Philosophical Lecture." In *Philosophical Occasions: 1912–1951,* ed. J. Klagge and A. Nordmann. Indianapolis, IN: Hackett.

Wolfe, C. 2010. *What Is Posthumanism?* Minneapolis: University of Minnesota Press.

Wollheim, R. 1971. *Sigmund Freud*. Cambridge: Cambridge University Press.

Woolgar S. (ed.). 1988a. *Knowledge and Reflexivity: New Frontiers in the Sociology of Knowledge*. London: Sage Publications.

———. 1988b. *Science: The Very Idea*. Chichester, UK: Ellis Harwood; London: Tavistock Publications.

Zuidervaart, L. 1991. *Adorno's Aesthetic Theory. The Redemption of Illusion*. Cambridge, MA: MIT Press.

———. 2008. Truth and authentication: Heidegger and Adorno in reverse. In *Adorno and Heidegger. Philosophical Questions*, ed. I. Macdonald and K. Ziarek, pp. 22–46. Stanford: Stanford University Press.

Index